D1611783

DEFINING MOMENTS
THE SEPTEMBER 11 TERRORIST ATTACKS

DEFINING MOMENTS

THE SEPTEMBER 11 TERRORIST ATTACKS

Kevin Hillstrom

155 W. Congress, Suite 200
Detroit, MI 48226

Omnigraphics, Inc.

Kevin Hillstrom, *Series Editor*
Cherie D. Abbey, *Managing Editor*

Peter E. Ruffner, *Publisher*
Matthew P. Barbour, *Senior Vice President*

Elizabeth Collins, *Research and Permissions Coordinator*
Kevin M. Hayes, *Operations Manager*

Allison A. Beckett and Mary Butler, *Research Staff*
Cherry Edwards, *Permissions Assistant*
Shirley Amore, Martha Johns, and Kirk Kauffmann, *Administrative Staff*

Library of Congress Cataloging-in-Publication Data

Hillstrom, Kevin, 1963-
  The September 11 terrorist attacks / by Kevin Hillstrom.
      p. cm. – (Defining moments)
  Includes bibliographical references and index.
  Summary: "Provides a comprehensive account of the origins of Islamic radicalism; the development of Osama bin Laden and al-Qaeda into a deadly force; the horrible events of September 11; the post-9/11 investigations; and the legacy of the 9/11 attacks. Includes a narrative overview, biographies, primary sources, chronology, glossary, bibliography, and index" — Provided by publisher.
  ISBN 978-0-7808-1240-6 (hardcover : alk. paper) 1. September 11 Terrorist Attacks, 2001. 2. Terrorism — United States. 3. Qaida (Organization) I. Title.
  HV6432.7.H534 2012
  973.931--dc23   2011050673

TABLE OF CONTENTS

NARRATIVE OVERVIEW

BIOGRAPHIES

PRIMARY SOURCES

PREFACE

Throughout the course of America's existence, its people, culture, and institutions have been periodically challenged—and in many cases transformed—by profound historical events. Some of these momentous events, such as women's suffrage, the civil rights movement, and U.S. involvement in World War II, invigorated the nation and strengthened American confidence and capabilities. Others, such as the Great Depression, the Vietnam War, and Watergate, have prompted troubled assessments and heated debates about the country's core beliefs and character.

Some of these defining moments in American history were years or even decades in the making. The Harlem Renaissance and the New Deal, for example, unfurled over the span of several years, while the American labor movement and the Cold War evolved over the course of decades. Other defining moments, such as the Cuban missile crisis and the Japanese attack on Pearl Harbor, transpired over a matter of days or weeks.

But although significant differences exist among these events in terms of their duration and their place in the timeline of American history, all share the same basic characteristic: they transformed the United States' political, cultural, and social landscape for future generations of Americans.

Taking heed of this fundamental reality, American citizens, schools, and other institutions are increasingly emphasizing the importance of understanding our nation's history. Omnigraphics' *Defining Moments* series was created for the express purpose of meeting this growing appetite for authoritative, useful historical resources. This series will be of enduring value to anyone interested in learning more about America's past—and in understanding how those historical events continue to reverberate in the twenty-first century.

Each individual volume of *Defining Moments* provides a valuable resource for readers interested in learning about the most profound events in our nation's history. Each volume is organized into three distinct sections—Narrative Overview, Biographies, and Primary Sources.

- The **Narrative Overview** provides readers with a detailed, factual account of the origins and progression of the "defining moment" being examined. It also explores the event's lasting impact on America's political and cultural landscape.

- The **Biographies** section provides valuable biographical background on leading figures associated with the event in question. Each biography concludes with a list of sources for further information on the profiled individual.

- The **Primary Sources** section collects a wide variety of pertinent primary source materials from the era under discussion, including official documents, papers and resolutions, letters, oral histories, memoirs, editorials, and other important works.

Individually, each of these sections is a rich resource for users. Together, they comprise an authoritative, balanced, and absorbing examination of some of the most significant events in U.S. history.

Other notable features contained within each volume in the series include a glossary of important individuals, places, and terms; a detailed chronology featuring page references to relevant sections of the narrative; an annotated bibliography of sources for further study; an extensive general bibliography that reflects the wide range of historical sources consulted by the author; and a subject index.

New Feature—Research Topics for Student Reports

Each volume in the *Defining Moments* series now includes a list of potential research topics for students. Students working on historical research and writing assignments will find this feature especially useful in assessing their options.

Information on the highlighted research topics can be found throughout the different sections of the book—and especially in the narrative overview, biography, and primary sources sections. This wide coverage gives readers the flexibility to study the topic through multiple entry points.

Acknowledgements

This series was developed in consultation with a distinguished Advisory Board composed of public librarians, school librarians, and educators. They evaluated the series as it developed, and their comments and suggestions were invaluable throughout the production process. Any errors in this and other volumes in the series are ours alone. Following is a list of board members who contributed to the *Defining Moments* series:

Gail Beaver, M.A., M.A.L.S.
Adjunct Lecturer, University of Michigan
Ann Arbor, MI

Melissa C. Bergin, L.M.S., NBCT
Library Media Specialist
Niskayuna High School
Niskayuna, NY

Rose Davenport, M.S.L.S., Ed.Specialist
Library Media Specialist
Pershing High School Library
Detroit, MI

Karen Imarisio, A.M.L.S.
Assistant Head of Adult Services
Bloomfield Twp. Public Library
Bloomfield Hills, MI

Nancy Larsen, M.L.S., M.S. Ed.
Library Media Specialist
Clarkston High School
Clarkston, MI

Marilyn Mast, M.I.L.S.
Kingswood Campus Librarian
Cranbrook Kingswood Upper School
Bloomfield Hills, MI

Rosemary Orlando, M.L.I.S.
Library Director
St. Clair Shores Public Library
St. Clair Shores, MI

Comments and Suggestions

We welcome your comments on *Defining Moments: The September 11 Terrorist Attacks* and suggestions for other events in U.S. history that warrant treatment in the *Defining Moments* series. Correspondence should be addressed to:

Editor, *Defining Moments*
Omnigraphics, Inc.
155 West Congress, Suite 200
Detroit, MI 48226
E-mail: editorial@omnigraphics.com

HOW TO USE THIS BOOK

Defining Moments: The September 11 Terrorist Attacks provides users with a detailed and authoritative overview of this pivotal episode in U.S. history. The preparation and arrangement of this volume—and all other books in the *Defining Moments* series—reflect an emphasis on providing a thorough and objective account of events that shaped our nation, presented in an easy-to-use reference work.

The September 11 Terrorist Attacks is divided into three primary sections. The first of these sections, Narrative Overview, provides a comprehensive account of the origins of Islamic radicalism in the Arab world; explains how Osama bin Laden and his al-Qaeda terrorist organization metastasized into such a deadly force; details the horrible events of September 11; explains how post-9/11 investigations into the attacks unfolded; and examines the ways in which the 9/11 attacks have changed America and its world outlook.

The second section, Biographies, provides valuable biographical background on leading figures associated with the events of September 11. Biographies are provided for terrorist figures who had important roles in planning or executing the attack, including bin Laden, hijacker Mohammed Atta, and 9/11 mastermind Khaled Sheikh Mohammed. In addition, this section provides biographies for important American politicians and officials, including President George W. Bush, National Security Advisor Condoleezza Rice, counterterrorism czar Richard Clarke, and CIA Director George Tenet.

The third section, Primary Sources, collects essential and illuminating documents on the September 11 terrorist attacks. These documents include such historic primary sources as Osama bin Laden's 1998 statement of jihad against "Jews and Crusaders," President Bush's statement to the American people on the night of September 11, and Richard Clarke's testimony before the 9/11 Commission, as well as personal accounts from civilians, firefighters, and police officers who survived the attacks on the World Trade Center and the Pentagon.

Other valuable features in *The September 11 Terrorist Attacks* include the following:

- A list of Research Topics that provide students with starting points for research.
- Attribution and referencing of primary sources and other quoted material to help guide users to other valuable historical research resources.
- Glossary of Important People, Places, and Terms.
- Detailed Chronology of events with a *see reference* feature. Under this arrangement, events listed in the chronology include a reference to page numbers within the Narrative Overview wherein users can find additional information on the event in question.
- Photographs of the leading figures and major events associated with 9/11.
- Sources for Further Study, an annotated list of noteworthy works about al-Qaeda, the September 11 attacks, and America's evolving response to the threat of terrorism.
- Extensive bibliography of works consulted in the creation of this book, including books, periodicals, Internet sites, and videotape materials.
- A Subject Index.

Note: Many of the names of Arabic people and organizations discussed in this volume are spelled in a variety of ways in U.S. media and government reports. In the interest of consistency, the authors selected common spellings of these names and groups and used them throughout. The only exception to this rule can be found in the Primary Sources section; the authors kept the original spelling in the documents featured here.

RESEARCH TOPICS FOR
DEFINING MOMENTS: THE SEPTEMBER 11 TERRORIST ATTACKS

When students receive an assignment to produce a research paper on a historical event or topic, the first step in that process—settling on a subject for the paper—can also be one of the most difficult. In recognition of that reality, each book in the *Defining Moments* series now highlights research areas that receive extensive coverage within that particular volume.

Potential research topics for students using *Defining Moments: The September 11 Terrorist Attacks* include the following:

- Ways in which Israel's relationship with its Arab neighbors contributed to the rise of radical Islamic movements in the Middle East.

- Social and political factors that enabled Osama bin Laden to build his al-Qaeda terrorist network into an organization with cells operating around the world.

- The importance of Ayman al-Zawahiri and other Islamic radicals in pushing terrorist activities that directly contradicted teachings of the Koran.

- Key points in the development of the September 11 terrorist plot.

- Counterterrorism policies of the Clinton and Bush administrations.

- Reasons why the United States failed to uncover and derail the plot before it could be carried out, with special emphasis on failures within the FBI and CIA.

- Challenges that the 9/11 Commission confronted in its investigation of the September 11 attacks and America's failure to stop them.

- Ways in which America's clashes with Iraqi dictator Saddam Hussein in 1991 and 2003 have influenced the trajectory of U.S. counterterrorism efforts.

- Impact of 9/11 on Americans' attitudes about their country and the wider world.

NARRATIVE OVERVIEW

PROLOGUE

When the sun crept over the horizon on the morning of Tuesday, September 11, 2001, it appeared that New York City residents and workers were going to be treated to a beautiful early autumn day. The sky was blue and cloudless, temperatures were mild, and the crowded streets of downtown Manhattan—the heart of America's financial industry—teemed with men and women who took an extra moment to enjoy the day before entering the huge skyscrapers where they worked. "It was the sort of late summer day," wrote *New York Times* journalist Wilborn Hampton, "that makes you think of baseball more than football, of picnics more than hayrides, of ice cream more than apple pie. It was a day that made you glad just to be alive."[1]

At 8:45 A.M., however, the picture-perfect day started to go horribly wrong. That was the moment that a U.S. commercial jet filled with passengers plowed into the northernmost of the "Twin Towers"—the World Trade Center skyscrapers that dominated the city's skyline. Over the next few hours, Americans would learn that this awful event was only the first in a series of deadly attacks by Islamic terrorists on the American people and their way of life.

New York City police officer Steven Bienkowski had a bird's-eye view of this unfolding horror. As a veteran member of the city's scuba team, he was accustomed to taking helicopter rides to accident scenes where a water rescue or body retrieval operation might be necessary. But his years of roaming the city's skies did not prepare him for what he saw on the morning of September 11:

> We got a call that a plane had hit the tower. Probably like so many other people, we were thinking it was a small private aircraft. But as we lifted up and came across Brooklyn, we saw

---

Indented quotation from *Never Forget: An Oral History of September 11, 2001* by Mitchell Fink and Lois Mathias. Copyright © 2002 by Mitchell Fink and Lois Mathias. Reprinted by permission.

that it was no small aircraft. There was a gaping hole in the North Tower and black smoke was pouring out.

It was pretty clear that people were trapped. There was nobody on the roof. About 80 percent of the roof was engulfed in black smoke. People were hanging out of the building, gasping for air. Some were jumping and others were accidentally being pushed by people behind them who were just trying to get out of the smoke and get to the air. Everything I've seen in my seventeen years as a police officer became miniscule. The past became insignificant. It was just so much more horrible than anything your mind could have ever conjured up.

People saw the helicopter and I'm sure many of them were thinking that we were going to be able to save them. In fact, we weren't able to do anything. We were as close as you could possibly be, and still we were helpless, totally helpless. There was no way of getting near anybody in a window. And then you're watching these people plunge to their death. We were so close.

Then we came around to the South Tower. We were still at the point of impact on the first building, seeing these poor people taking their plunge to certain death. I happened to be sitting in the back left side of the ship. There were two pilots, two crew chiefs, my partner, and I. We were on the southwest side of the South Tower, and I glanced over my shoulder and there came a United Airlines aircraft right at us, a little bit underneath where we were. And I do mean a little underneath us. It probably missed us by about three hundred feet, and it proceeded to fly right through the building, right in front of us. I must have gone numb. I don't remember hearing an explosion, although it must have been extremely loud. I don't remember the helicopter moving. I think it was all I could handle just to watch that happen.

When that second plane went into the building, it just looked like an evil magician's trick. It looked nothing like what I would have imagined a plane crashing into a building would look like. The plane just completely disappeared and turned into a giant fireball. Being there was surreal. I guess the brain tries to protect you in times like that. You have some kind of defense mechanism in there that shuts down some of your senses. It just doesn't allow you to believe.

And for me, the realization still hadn't set in that this was a terrorist attack. But the reality was becoming all too apparent. There was really no place to put the ship down in Manhattan because people were running like roaches. So we went and landed over on Governor's Island, just to regroup and refuel.

Coming back across Brooklyn again you could see that the South Tower was already down. The entire lower Manhattan was covered in a giant white dust cloud. And as you came around to the North Tower again, you could still see the people falling and jumping, except it didn't look so violent anymore because you weren't watching them hit the ground. It was almost peaceful because they were falling into a white cloud.

As we're coming around to the North Tower, I said, "Oh, my God, it looks like it's tilting." It came down a couple of minutes afterward, completely straight down, like a deck of cards.

The entire thickness of the cloud of dust was like nothing you've ever seen, and we watched the boats come in from everywhere. Our guys were down there, the scuba launch, the harbor launches, tugboats, and fishing boats were coming in. Boats from everywhere evacuated people over the sea wall. And after that we just went back to Floyd Bennett Field in total disbelief, trying to absorb the reality of it all.

Even though it's unreasonable and I know, rationally, that there was nothing we could do, it doesn't matter. The fact is, I was right there and I watched all those people die, and there wasn't a damn thing I could do about it. You sit there and you're powerless. It's like being forced to watch something with your hands tied. It was torture, total torture.[2]

Notes

[1] Hampton, Wilborn. *September 11, 2001: Attack on New York City.* Cambridge, MA: Candlewick Press, 2003, p. ix.

[2] Quoted in *Never Forget: An Oral History of September 11.* Edited by Mitchell Fink and Lois Mathias. New York: Regan, 2002, pp. 15-17.

Chapter One

RAGE AND DESPAIR
IN THE ARAB WORLD

The white man in Europe or America is our number-one enemy.... The white man crushes us underfoot while we teach our children about his civilization, his universal principles and noble objectives.... Let us instead plant the seeds of hatred, disgust, and revenge in the souls of these children. Let us teach [our] children from the time their nails are soft that the white man is the enemy of humanity, and that they should destroy him at the first opportunity.

—Sayyid Qutb, after returning to Egypt from the
United States in 1950

During the early twentieth century, religious and political life in the Middle East began to undergo radical and wrenching changes. Arab natives of the region, which stretches from southwest Asia into northeast Africa, expressed deep frustration with the impact of "the West"—the cultural, economic, and political traditions of the United States and Western Europe—on their families and communities. This influence stemmed from the fact that large swaths of the Middle East had come into the possession of Great Britain and France. These colonial empires added Arab lands to their territorial holdings after World War I, when the Ottoman Empire—an Islamic kingdom that had controlled sections of the Middle East since the sixteenth century—collapsed.

In Middle Eastern countries like Egypt and Iraq (ruled by British authorities) and Syria (colonized by France), laws and policies were instituted that placed significant curbs on the political rights and economic opportunities of

The Middle East

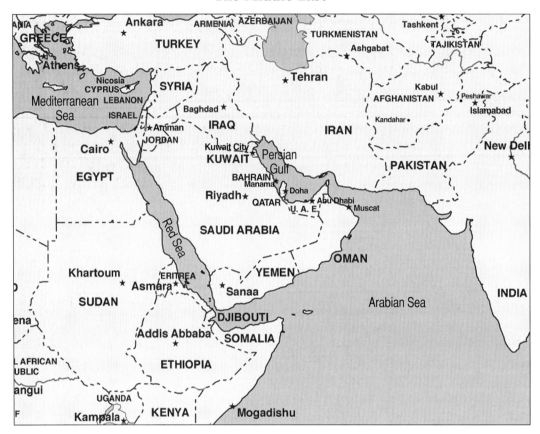

the native populations. Officials in London and Paris controlled the lives of millions of Arab people, many of whom began to agitate for independence. The Europeans reluctantly heeded these calls and bestowed independence on various Arab states. But "the West" still exerted a tremendous amount of influence over the political and economic affairs of their former colonies.

The Fight for Palestine

Political and social unrest further intensified across the Arab world after World War II, even as the last remnants of European colonialism faded away. One significant source of turmoil was a 1947 proposal by the United Nations (UN) to divide Palestine, a region in the heart of the Middle East, into two distinct nations. One would belong to the Palestinians, an Arab people that had lived on the eastern shores of the Mediterranean Sea for centuries. Like most other Arabs, the Palestinians were Muslims, the term used to denote believers in the religious faith of Islam.

According to the UN proposal, the other section of Palestine would become a Jewish state for the hundreds of thousands of Jews who had settled in the region during the first half of the twentieth century. This great migration of Jewish settlers to Palestine was partly attributable to a 1917 declaration by the British government that the region, which was regarded by Jews as their ancestral birthplace, was the best place to establish a "national home for the Jewish people." But the migration picked up even greater momentum during the 1930s and early 1940s, when Jewish families fled rising levels of anti-Semitism in Germany and many other European nations. This tide of anti-Jewish hatred eventually culminated in the Holocaust—the systematic extermination of an estimated six million Jews across Europe by German dictator Adolf Hitler and his Nazi war machine.

The Jewish population of Palestine accepted the United Nations proposal to partition Palestine, but Palestinian Arabs—and much of the rest of the Arab world—rejected it as an unfair land grab. The proposal also fed anti-Semitic feelings that had been building in Arab communities since the early 1930s, when hateful Nazi propaganda about Jews had begun seeping into the region. The Arab rejection of the partition proposal sparked repeated bouts of bloody violence between Jews and Palestinians.

The escalating clashes reflected the desperation of both the Jewish and Palestinian people. "On the one hand," wrote journalist David Margolick, "the Jews were fighting for a safe haven three years after six million of them had been murdered…. And then there were the Palestinians, who had watched in horror over the past 75 years as these aliens first trickled, then poured, into their homeland."[1] Jewish forces soon gained the advantage. Thousands of Palestinian Arabs were uprooted from their homes and forced to find refuge in other parts of the Middle East.

Arab Outrage over the Creation of Israel

On May 14, 1948, Jewish leaders in Palestine announced that they were creating an independent state, called Israel, in accordance with the territorial boundaries that had been drawn by the United Nations. One day later, the armies of four Arab nations—Egypt, Jordan, Iraq, and Syria—and smaller

An Israeli soldier stands guard outside of a mosque in the Palestinian town of Ramlah, which was seized by Israeli forces on July 12, 1948.

groups of fighters from Lebanon, Saudi Arabia, and other Arab countries joined together to attack Israel. The Arab army was the larger of the two, but the Israelis had better training and leadership. By the end of the year, Israeli military forces had won a resounding victory and firmly established Israel as the world's newest state.

The people of Israel described this triumph as the "War of Independence." To Palestinian Arabs, though, the event was *Al Nakba*—"the Catastrophe." Indeed, the 1948 Arab-Israeli War, as it came to be known to the rest of the world, had long-lasting implications for the Middle East region and for Arab-Jewish relations. An estimated 700,000 Palestinians left Israel during the war—some voluntarily, but others because of the widespread violence and destruction. Meanwhile, the defeated Arab nations lashed out against the Jews in their own homelands, forcing them into exile in Israel, the United States, and other non-Arab parts of the world.

Many Arabs felt so humiliated by the military defeat that they vowed not to rest until Israel had been destroyed and Palestine returned to Arab hands. Israeli leaders such as David Ben-Gurion, who was the nation's first prime minister, responded to these threats by investing heavily in Israel's military defenses. Even Ben-Gurion, though, understood the reasons for the rage being directed at Israel. "We [the Jews] come from Israel, it's true, but two thousand years ago, and what is that to them?" Ben-Gurion said in 1956. "If I was an Arab leader I would never make [peace] terms with Israel.... They only see one thing: we have come here and stolen their country. Why should they accept that?"[2]

Dethroning a King in Egypt

The 1948 war added to the tensions in Egypt, the most populous country in the Arab world. Egypt was already simmering with political unrest because of widespread public discontent with King Farouk, who had taken leadership of the country in 1936. Farouk and his royal family had become notorious for their corruption, greed, and luxurious lifestyles—the king alone owned dozens of palaces and hundreds of automobiles—at a time when average Egyptian men and women struggled mightily to provide their families with food, clothing, and shelter. Egyptians also grumbled that although England had officially granted Egypt its independence in 1922, the British continued to exercise enormous influence over the country's political, military, cultural, and economic affairs.

Unhappiness with Farouk's regime showed itself in a variety of ways. During the 1930s and 1940s, for example, the membership of a political opposition group known as the Muslim Brotherhood (formally known as the Society of Muslim Brothers) experienced tremendous growth. This group, which had been formed by an Islamic scholar named Hassan al-Banna in 1928, was dedicated to transforming Egypt into a state governed explicitly by Islamic teachings. Members argued that "secular" governments—ones that were not guided or otherwise influenced by religion—were at the root of the Arab world's problems. They asserted that if Arab populations rose up and converted their nations into Islamic states, God would restore the Arab world to its ancient glory. This message of revolution appealed to some Egyptian Muslims, but an even bigger factor in the Brotherhood's growth was that it helped families negotiate the challenges of everyday life. By providing people with hospitals, schools, employment opportunities, and other forms of assistance, the Muslim Brotherhood was able to attract more than one million members by 1949, when al-Banna was assassinated (most historians think his killer was an agent of the Egyptian government).

In the end, though, King Farouk's reign was not brought down by the Muslim Brotherhood. Instead, he was toppled on July 23, 1952, in a nonviolent coup by a group of army officers led by Lieutenant Colonel Gamal Abdel Nasser and General Muhammad Naguib. This so-called Free Officers Movement had arisen partly in response to the continued British influence over Egyptian affairs. But it also stemmed from evidence that the Egyptian Army's performance in the 1948 Arab-Israeli War had been hampered by government corruption.

The Free Officers Movement formally dissolved the monarchy and established a republic, with Naguib serving as Egypt's first president. By late 1953, though, political tensions between Naguib and Nasser became too great for either man to ignore. Nasser won the ensuing power struggle, and from 1954 until his death in 1970, he was Egypt's head of state.

Nasser emerged during these years as the most influential political leader of the Arab world. His reputation was greatly enhanced in 1956-1957, when he wrested control of the strategically vital Suez Canal from Western interests. Nasser also adopted Socialist policies that relieved some of the worst poverty in Egypt, although his decision to take major privately owned industries (including European-owned corporations) and make them the property of the Egyptian government was heavily criticized in the West. He also pushed through major social reforms designed to modernize Egypt, from expansions of women's rights to huge new investments in education. Perhaps most importantly, however, Nasser relentlessly hammered home a message of Arab unity and pride. This rhetoric made him a hero to Arabs of many different nationalities.

Sayyid Qutb and the Call for *Sharia*

Nasser's policies were not popular with all Egyptians, however. Nasser believed that religion had no place in government, and so he crafted and maintained agencies and policies that were secular in orientation. This attitude dismayed leaders of the Muslim Brotherhood and other Islamic radicals. They believed that restoration of Arabia's ancient glory could only be

Egyptian president Gamal Abdel Nasser, seen here at a diplomatic conference in Ethiopia, became the most prominent leader of the Arab world in the 1960s.

accomplished by rejecting the "white man's" concepts of modern life and establishing a government dedicated to *Sharia*—Islamic legal codes drawn from the Koran and the words of the Prophet Mohammed, who founded the Islamic religion.

On October 26, 1954, a member of the Muslim Brotherhood tried to assassinate Nasser while he was giving a speech in Alexandria, Egypt. The assassin failed, but the plot convinced Nasser to order a fierce crackdown on the organization. Six Egyptian conspirators were hanged, and thousands of Islamic radicals across Egypt were imprisoned. One of the men caught up in the massive wave of arrests was Sayyid Qutb.

To outward appearances, Qutb was a quiet and mild-mannered scholar. But his writings about the decadence of the West and the need for Arabs to embrace *Sharia* law became quite influential among Islamic radicals in the

13

early 1950s. Qutb told his Arab readers that materialism, social interaction between the sexes, democracy, and other modern "values" of the United States and Europe threatened to poison their culture forever. Qutb insisted that "only by restoring Islam to the center of their lives, their laws, and their government could Muslims hope to recapture their rightful place as the dominant culture in the world," wrote scholar Lawrence Wright. "That was their duty, not only to themselves but also to God."[3]

> *"No middle ground exist[ed] in what [Sayyid] Qutb conceived as a struggle between God and Satan," stated the 9/11 Commission. "Any Muslim who rejects his ideas is just one more nonbeliever worthy of destruction."*

The trials of the alleged anti-government conspirators were overseen by a panel of judges who were clearly interested in handing down convictions. One of these judges was Anwar al-Sadat, who succeeded Nasser as president of Egypt after he suffered a fatal heart attack in late 1970. Prosecutors relied on confessions—many of them obtained through torture—to send hundreds of Brotherhood members to prison.[4] Qutb was one of those convicted. He initially received a life sentence, but it was later reduced to fifteen years because of health problems and requests for leniency from other Arab states.

During his imprisonment Qutb penned his most important and famous work, which he called *Milestones* [*Ma'alim fi al-Tariq*]. Individual chapters of the book were smuggled out of the prison by Qutb and his followers, and in 1964 *Milestones* was published in its entirety. Like previous works by Qutb, the pages of *Milestones* burned with hatred for America and the West. But *Milestones* also included ominous new instructions in the campaign to bring Sharia—governance by Islamic law—to Egypt.

For years, the radical quest to impose Sharia had been complicated by the fact that the Koran explicitly prohibits Muslims from taking the life of a fellow Muslim, except as punishment for murder. Qutb, though, constructed a loophole that in effect gave radical Muslims the religious cover they needed to kill fellow members of their faith. Qutb seized on a famous teaching of Mohammed, who stipulated that Muslims could only be killed if they committed murder, cheated on their spouse, or abandoned Islam. In *Milestones*, Qutb asserted that any Muslims who did not support Sharia were *takfir*—guilty of abandoning Islam. Since Nasser had rejected Sharia in favor of a secular government, Qutb was in effect saying that it was the duty of devout

Muslims to kill him and his supporters.[5] "No middle ground exist[ed] in what Qutb conceived as a struggle between God and Satan," explained the 9/11 Commission, a special U.S. commission that was established to investigate the September 11, 2001, attacks on the United States. "Any Muslim who rejects his ideas is just one more nonbeliever worthy of destruction."[6]

Many Islamic clergy condemned this corruption of the faith's generally peaceful teachings. In addition, Egyptian authorities expressed outrage at *Milestones* and promptly outlawed publication, sale, or possession of the book. By this time, however, copies of the book (and pamphlets featuring excerpts) had been widely distributed within the radical Islamic community of Egypt and several other Arab countries.

Qutb was finally released from prison in late 1964, after authorities received assurances that he would behave himself. Instead, he became involved in new plots to overthrow Nasser and assassinate other Egyptian government officials. He was arrested once again in August 1965 and charged with treason. At his trial, which began in April 1966, prosecutors repeatedly quoted incriminating passages from *Milestones* to support their case. But instead of distancing himself from the work, Qutb defiantly defended his fanatical ideas. He was found guilty of plotting to overthrow the government and executed by hanging on August 29, 1966.

The Six-Day War

Less than one year later, the Middle East was rocked by another momentous clash between Israel and the Arab nations that surrounded it. Ever since Israel had been created in 1948, Arab states had refused to acknowledge its right to exist. To the contrary, they called for Israel to be destroyed and its lands returned to the Palestinians (many Palestinians continued to live in Israel, but the majority had resettled in other parts of the Middle East). By the mid-1960s, attacks on Israeli cities and military posts by Palestinian rebels and Syrian and Egyptian guns had become commonplace.

In May 1967 Nasser increased the military pressure on Israel by erecting a blockade of the Straits of Tiran, Israel's primary marine passageway to and from the Indian Ocean. The blockade made it impossible for Eilat, Israel's main southern port city, to receive or send out commercial transport ships. At the same time that Egypt imposed the blockade—widely viewed as an act of war—it began massing troops near the borders of Israel. On June 5 Israel

The Six-Day War created a huge refugee population in the Middle East. These Arab refugees are crossing into Jordan from the Israeli-occupied West Bank region.

responded by launching a devastating air and ground attack that virtually obliterated Egypt's air force within a matter of a few hours. Jordan, Syria, and Iraq then joined the fray against Israel, only to be battered into submission by Israeli jets and tanks over the next few days. By the close of June 10, the sixth and last day of fighting, Israeli military forces had captured the city of Jerusalem (a holy city to Jews, Muslims, and Christians) as well as the Sinai Peninsula, the West Bank, and the Golan Heights—a total of roughly 42,000 square miles that only a week earlier had been Arab territory.[7]

The Six-Day War was a complete and utter disaster for the Arab states that had taken up arms against Israel. For every Israeli casualty in the conflict, twenty-five Arab soldiers were injured or killed. The armed forces of Egypt, Syria, and the other states lay in ruins as well. Their territorial losses, meanwhile, pushed Arab forces out of firing range of Israel's major population centers. Conversely, Israel's gains made it possible for its army to train its fearsome guns on Cairo, Damascus, and Amman—the capital cities of Egypt, Syria, and Jordan, respectively.[8] The event, wrote Wright, "was a psychological turning point in the history of the modern Middle East. The speed and decisiveness of the Israeli victory in the Six-Day War humiliated many Muslims who had believed until then that God favored their cause. They had lost not only their armies and their territories but also faith in their leaders, in their countries, and in themselves."[9]

Saudi Arabian Oil and the Rise of Wahhabism

The Six-Day War unfolded at the same time that the Arab world was struggling with the economic and cultural forces that had been unleashed by the region's "oil boom." Large oil deposits had been discovered across the Middle East during the first half of the twentieth century. Exploration and drilling had proceeded slowly at first, in large part because there seemed to be plenty of petroleum in the United States, the world's leading consumer of oil. But as automobiles, airplanes, and other modes of gasoline-dependent transportation became more popular, concerns about the capacity of America's reserves to meet demand intensified. By the 1950s, Western energy companies were collaborating with Arab governments all across the Middle East on vast industrial operations that pulled millions of gallons of oil from beneath the region's sandy surface on a daily basis.

Arab nations such as Iran, Iraq, and Kuwait were transformed by the oil boom. They vaulted into the ranks of the world's wealthiest nations in a matter of a few short years, and thus became objects of intense interest to energy companies and governments that had once ignored them. But perhaps no country was changed as much by the oil boom as the desert kingdom of Saudi

Terror at the Summer Olympics

After Israel became a nation in 1948, some Palestinians turned to terrorism to punish the "invaders." They justified their murderous actions against Jewish military personnel and civilians as retribution for the loss of their homeland, and they hoped that bloodshed would shake Israel's control over Palestine.

The most infamous example of Palestinian terrorism against Israel came on September 15, 1972, in Munich, West Germany, during the Summer Olympic Games. Early that morning, eight members of a shadowy Palestinian group known as Black September invaded the quarters of the Israeli team in Munich's Olympic Village. The terrorists, who wielded automatic rifles and wore dark ski masks, murdered two team members and took nine other athletes and coaches hostage. As news of the brazen attack raced around the world, the terrorists demanded the release of more than 200 Palestinian rebels from Israel's prisons, as well as the release of two imprisoned German radicals.

West German military and police tried to rescue the hostages by offering the terrorists huge sums of money. But when the kidnappers refused to budge from their initial demands, West German officials hur-

Arabia, which held the largest petroleum reserves of all—about 20 percent of the world's oil, by most estimates.

Until the 1950s, the people of Saudi Arabia lived a nomadic existence, caring for livestock and small farming plots in much the same manner as their ancestors. But when the oil companies of the West moved in to tap Saudi Arabia's great lakes of oil, they were swamped by a massive wave of economic and cultural changes, from glitzy nightclubs and sprawling universities to highways and oil refineries. "Their country—and their lives—became alien to them," wrote one historian. "Unimaginable wealth had fallen on these austere desert nomads—a gift from God because of their piety, they genuinely believed. Paradoxically, this gift was undermining every facet of their identity."[10]

These feelings of disorientation were heavily laced with emotions of anger and resentment, for many Saudis did not share in the wealth that was

riedly cobbled together a rescue plan. Using helicopters to transport the terrorists and hostages, the West Germans managed to move the action out of Olympic Village and to the Munich Airport. The Black September commandos went willingly, for they had been told—falsely—that a jet was being prepared to take them to Egypt.

When the negotiations settled into another stalemate, German authorities approved a rescue plan using snipers. But the plan was poorly executed, and the Black September terrorists killed all the Israeli hostages. Five Palestinians were killed in the assault, but the remaining three terrorists were captured by German forces. In October 1972 the surviving Black September members were released by Germany when other Palestinian terrorists hijacked a German commercial airliner. Israeli agents reportedly tracked down the terrorists, however, and killed them.

Despite the horrors endured by the Israeli team, organizers of the 1972 Summer Games decided to continue with the Olympics. Several events went on as scheduled during the hostage drama itself, and although the competition was temporarily suspended for a memorial service, all of the events were eventually held. This decision to go on with the Games even after the tragedy was extremely controversial, but it was supported by Israeli authorities.

being generated by the oil. Some managed to find jobs in the oil fields and ports, where oil tankers came and went at all hours of the day and night. But the House of Al Saud, which was the royal monarchy that ruled Saudi Arabia, hoarded most of the treasure to itself. Exhibiting a truly gargantuan appetite for power and money, King Saud and members of his extended family directed much of the country's oil profits into their own private coffers. In 1964 Saud was overthrown by his younger brother, Faisal, who ended some of the more outrageous practices of Al Saud and invested more heavily in infrastructure projects that benefited all Saudis. But unemployment rates remained high, and few Saudis had access to a good education.

Many Saudis, angry and bewildered by the changes swirling around them, decided that the nation should return to a simpler time. They yearned for a time when people's daily lives were guided not by the quest for money, but by the tenets of Islam. And in many parts of Saudi Arabia, people practiced a particularly severe and rigid form of Islam called Wahhabism. According to practitioners, known as Wahhabis, every message and guideline in the Koran had to be followed to the letter. Christians, Jews, atheists, and Muslims who had other interpretations of the Koran's teachings were seen as heathens and enemies.

Many followers of Islam in other parts of the Middle East and the world viewed Wahhabism as a strange and dangerous form of religious extremism. In the 1970s, however, public discontent with the Saudi regime fed explosive growth in Wahhabi mosques and schools, known as *madrassas*. Political radicalism flourished as well, fueled by Wahhabi clerics who called for the overthrow of the Saudi monarchy and the installation of a theocracy (a government controlled by religious authorities) that would impose Sharia law.

> *"Government-subsidized religious vigilantes became an overwhelming presence in the [Saudi] Kingdom, roaming through the shopping malls and restaurants, chasing men into the mosques at prayer time and ensuring that women were properly cloaked—even a strand of hair poking out from under a hijab could rate a flogging with the swagger sticks these men carried."*

On November 20, 1979, this tense environment exploded in a great spasm of violence at the Grand Mosque of Mecca, Saudi Arabia's greatest Islamic shrine. That day, hundreds of rifle-wielding religious fanatics led by Juhaiman al-Oteibi seized control of the mosque, which contained tens of thousands of pilgrims who had traveled to Mecca to honor their God, known as Allah. A tense standoff ensued for the next two weeks, until Saudi military forces reclaimed the mosque in a bloody gun battle. The clash claimed the lives of hundreds of soldiers, worshippers, and radicals (most scholars believe that the Saudi government underestimated the death toll when it released its official casualty figures).

Oteibi and 62 of his followers were beheaded in public ceremonies in four different Saudi cities on January 9, 1980. This spectacle was clearly intended to show the citizenry that the monarchy remained in firm control. In reality, though, King Khalid Al-Saud (who led the country from 1975 until his death in 1982) and his administration were greatly alarmed by the revolutionary fever that gripped many parts of the kingdom. Rather than confront the Wahhabi radicals, however, the government decided to bribe them. As journalist Seymour Hersh wrote, the corrupt regime had become "so weakened and frightened that it …

brokered its future by channeling hundreds of millions of dollars in what amounts to protection money to fundamentalist groups that wish[ed] to overthrow it."[11]

The regime bankrolled the construction of new Wahhabi schools and mosques all across the country—and then around the world. The royal family also agreed to censor or stamp out music, art, and literature that aroused the disapproval of the Islamic fundamentalists. Finally, the government provided financial support to the *mattawa*, a type of religious police that developed a fearsome reputation in the 1980s and 1990s for enforcing their strict vision of Islam in Saudi Arabian villages and cities. These "government-subsidized religious vigilantes," according to Wright, "became an overwhelming presence in the Kingdom, roaming through the shopping malls and restaurants, chasing men into the mosques at prayer time and ensuring that women were properly cloaked—even a strand of hair poking out from under a hijab [a headscarf worn by Muslim women] could rate a flogging with the swagger sticks these men carried. In their quest to stamp out sinfulness and heresy, they even broke into private homes and businesses."[12]

Revolution in Iran—and a Historic Treaty

The shocking bloodshed at the Grand Mosque in Mecca in 1979 was not the only event of that year to have lasting repercussions in the Middle East. In early 1979 Islamic fundamentalists in Iran overthrew that country's monarchy and imposed a religious state headed by Ayatollah Ruhollah Khomeini. This revolution, which marked the first time that Islamic radicals actually succeeded in taking control of a national government, triggered great anxiety in the West and among moderate Arabs. But the 1979 revolution in Iran was a source of immense pride and inspiration to fundamentalists across the Middle East.

A few months later, Egyptian President Anwar el Sadat and Israeli Prime Minister Menachem Begin signed a landmark peace treaty. This treaty was based on a 1978 agreement, known as the Camp David Accords, that had been painstakingly shepherded into being by U.S. President Jimmy Carter.

The formal signing of the treaty in Washington, D.C., on March 26, 1979, was historic for several reasons. It ended the state of war that had officially existed between the two countries since the 1948 Arab-Israeli War. It also resulted in the departure of Israeli forces from the Sinai Peninsula, which Israel had captured in 1967. Treaty provisions also guaranteed Israel's ship-

U.S. President Jimmy Carter congratulates Egyptian President Anwar Sadat and Israeli Prime Minister Menachem Begin at the signing of the 1979 Egyptian-Israeli Peace Treaty.

ping rights in Egyptian-controlled waters, including the Suez Canal. The agreement also included U.S. military and economic aid to Egypt, which was still recovering from the disastrous Six-Day War. Most importantly of all, however, the treaty included a formal admission from Egypt that Israel was a legitimate nation that had a right to exist. The agreement, in other words, made Sadat the first Arab leader to officially recognize Israel.

The signing of the 1979 Egypt-Israel Peace Treaty elicited a wide range of responses in the Arab world. Many Arabs, including devout Muslims, expressed happiness about the event. They hoped that the accord marked the beginning of a new era of peace and prosperity across the region. But Islamic radicals raged against the treaty, which they viewed as a betrayal, and they vowed to carry on their quest to bring Sharia law to the entire Middle East.

Notes

[1] Margolick, David. "Endless War," *New York Times Book Review,* May 4, 2008.
[2] Quoted in Morris, Benny. *1948: A History of the First Arab-Israeli War.* New Haven, CT: Yale University Press, 2008, p. 393.

[3] Wright, Lawrence. *The Looming Tower: Al-Qaeda and the Road to 9/11.* New York: Vintage Books, 2006, p. 208.

[4] Wright, pp. 33-34.

[5] Wright, pp. 36-37.

[6] National Commission on Terrorist Attacks Upon the United States [The 9/11 Commission]. *The 9/11 Commission Report.* New York: Norton, 2004, p. 51.

[7] Oren, Michael B. *Six Days of War: June 1967 and the Making of the Modern Middle East.* New York: Oxford University Press, 2002, p. 307.

[8] Oren, p. 305.

[9] Wright, p. 45.

[10] Wright, p. 99.

[11] Hersh, Seymour. "King's Ransom," *New Yorker,* October 16, 2001.

[12] Wright, p. 167.

Chapter Two

JIHAD IN AFGHANISTAN AND THE BIRTH OF AL-QAEDA

These filthy, infidel Crusaders must not be allowed to remain in the Holy Land.

—Osama bin Laden, 1995

The fundamentalist Islamists who condemned the 1979 Egypt-Israel Peace Treaty focused much of their anger on Egyptian ruler Anwar al Sadat. After succeeding Gamal Nasser as president of Egypt in 1970, Sadat followed the same secular model of government as his predecessor. He made efforts to get along with Islamic radicals—in 1976, for example, he lifted a law that prohibited the publication of two Muslim Brotherhood periodicals. But Sadat also approved a new law that granted women the right to divorce, a step that infuriated conservative Islamists. He also acted to limit the civil liberties of religious scholars and clerics who spoke out against his policies.

By the early 1970s, a number of new radical Islamic groups had sprouted up in opposition to the governments of Nasser and Sadat. One of the most important of these new movements was al-Jihad (also known as Egyptian Islamic Jihad). Its leaders included a physician named Ayman al-Zawahiri, who had been plotting against Egypt's secular rulers since his mid-teens. Another influential radical organization of this period was the Islamic Group, which was led by a blind, charismatic cleric named Sheikh Omar Abdel Rahman.

The Assassination of Sadat

Sadat's refusal to support Sharia—laws based on strict Islamic codes—made Egypt a political powder keg before the peace treaty with the hated Jewish "Zionists" had even been signed. Zawahiri, Rahman, and other anti-Sadat revolutionaries told their followers that the president was a heretic—a nonbeliever—to the Islamic faith. This was a dangerous accusation. Radicals operating in Egypt understood that according to the teachings of leaders like Sayyid Qutb, faithful Islamists had a duty to kill those who betrayed the faith. Rahman further encouraged talk of revolution when he issued a *fatwa* (a formal ruling by an Islamic religious authority) approving the taking of Sadat's life.

The Egyptian government understood that they faced a growing threat from the religious fanatics within the country. Sadat ordered a major crackdown on political activity in the nation's universities, newspapers, and especially its mosques, where most of his critics were based. Thousands of Egyptians were arrested in the sweep, which took place in September 1981. During this same time Sadat reiterated his belief in the superiority of secular government, adopting the slogan of "no politics in religion and no religion in politics."[1]

One month later, on October 6, 1981, Sadat's presidency came to a sudden and bloody close. A small group or "cell" of al-Jihad radicals killed him in a hail of gunfire at a military parade in Cairo. The outburst of violence stunned friendly governments in the West but sparked celebrations in many Arabic communities across the Middle East. A typical reaction came from a spokesman for the Palestinian Liberation Organization (PLO), the main political representative of the Palestinian people (and a group that was becoming increasingly controversial for its own links to terrorism). The PLO official declared that "we were expecting this end of President Sadat because we are sure he was against the interests of his people, the Arab nations, and the Palestinian people."[2] Sadat's funeral was attended by political leaders from the United States and around the world, but most Arab countries declined to send any official representatives to the service.

Sadat was succeeded by his vice president, Hosni Mubarak. A former commander in the Egyptian Air Force, Mubarak displayed a ruthless determination to squash the Islamic radicals. Following his orders, Egyptian security forces swept through Cairo and other major cities across the country, arresting hundreds of men. Rahman and Zawahiri were among the radicals caught in the dragnet. A lieutenant colonel in the Egyptian Army named Khalid Islambouli was also captured. Islambouli had been the leader and prime executor of the Sadat assassination scheme. He was convicted and executed on April 15, 1982, as were three other conspirators.

On October 6, 1981, armed assassins shot and killed Egyptian President Anwar Sadat as he sat in a reviewing stand during a military parade. This photograph shows the killers firing into the president's reviewing area.

Many of the men who had been detained after Sadat's death, however, were only convicted of lesser charges. Zawahiri, for example, was only found guilty of illegal weapons possession, and he gained his release from prison in 1984. Rahman spent nearly three years in prison before he went to trial. He was acquitted of any involvement in the assassination plot, but he was nonetheless expelled from Egypt upon his release. According to Rahman, Zawahiri, and many other sources, the two radical leaders and many of their followers were subjected to brutal torture and other sadistic forms of punishment throughout their incarceration.

When they finally walked free, both men burned with an all-consuming desire for revenge against the Egyptian authorities. Zawahiri settled in the city of Peshawar, Pakistan, where he began the process of rebuilding al-Jihad. Rahman, meanwhile, landed in neighboring Afghanistan, which was in the midst of a desperate and brutal civil war against the military might of the Soviet Union.

27

The Jihad in Afghanistan

The shattering of Afghanistan had begun in December 1979, when the Soviet Union launched a massive military invasion of the country. The Soviets claimed that the invasion amounted to military "assistance" to the pro-Communist central government, which was struggling to put down rebellions from radical Islamic factions scattered throughout the country. The United States saw the move, however, as a clear attempt by the Soviets to increase their presence in the oil- and trade-rich region.

Within months of its arrival, the Soviet military had reconstructed the central government to its liking and imposed a series of so-called reforms that sent rates of hunger, disease, and political repression soaring. The Soviet occupation enraged much of the Afghan population and greatly boosted enlistment in native armies of resistance, many of which were organized in accordance with tribal affiliations. These Islamic fighters, known as *mujahedeen*, vowed to push the invaders out, and before long they were carrying out punishing guerrilla strikes on Soviet troops and military posts.

The mujahedeen were greatly aided in these efforts by several foreign governments. The United States supplied huge quantities of money and military weaponry to the Afghan "freedom fighters." The Americans did so partly because they wanted to keep the Soviets, their long-time Cold War foe, out of the region. But they also saw that a long and costly war had the potential to drain the Soviet treasury—and thus make it more difficult for the Soviets to keep pace with the United States in the nuclear arms race. Saudi Arabia also contributed funding for the resistance. The Saudis were motivated primarily by a sense of kinship to the mostly Islamic Afghan population. Pakistan's intelligence service established a secret network capable of delivering all of these funds and weapons from the Americans and Saudis to the mujahedeen. By the mid-1980s this aid had enabled the mujahedeen to transform the rugged mountains and plains of Afghanistan into deadly killing grounds.

The mujahedeen cause was also aided by individual Arabs who saw the Soviet invasion primarily as an attack on fellow believers in Islam. In late 1984 a prominent Palestinian cleric named Abdullah Azzam issued a fatwa calling all able-bodied Muslims to come to the aid of their Afghan brothers. According to Azzam, all Islamic people needed to see the conflict in Afghanistan as a *jihad*—a holy war—against loathsome nonbelievers.

This May 1988 photograph shows Afghan Muslim guerrillas inspecting the wreckage of a Soviet-built helicopter gunship they claim to have shot down.

Azzam's fatwa drew considerable attention in Arab nations, but most of the young men who wanted to answer his call did not have the financial resources to get to Afghanistan. This problem was solved by another Arab—a religiously devout and immensely wealthy Saudi Arabian businessman named Osama bin Laden.

Osama bin Laden and the Anti-Soviet Jihad

Born in 1957 in the Saudi Arabian city of Jiddah, bin Laden was the seventeenth of fifty-seven children fathered by Mohammed bin Laden. Bin Laden's father had been born in Yemen, but he built a fabulous construction empire in Saudi Arabia, which he adopted as his home. By the time Mohammed died in a helicopter crash in 1967, his business dealings had made him a close friend to the royal family and one of the most famous people in the entire country.

Osama bin Laden inherited an estimated $80 million upon his father's death, and his wider family remained extremely wealthy as well. Bin Laden thus continued to live a life of luxury and privilege. In the late 1970s, though, he began to explore the ideas of radical voices like Sayyid Qutb and the Muslim Brotherhood, both of which called for remaking the Middle East in accordance with the laws of the Koran. Bin Laden also expressed bitterness about events that he perceived as insulting or damaging to Muslims, such as the Egypt-Israel Peace Treaty and the Soviet invasion of Afghanistan.

In mid-1987 bin Laden and his Arab Afghans defeated Soviet troops in a fierce firefight that came to be known as the Battle of the Lion's Den. For the rest of his life the Saudi millionaire carried a trophy from the battle—an AK-47 assault rifle taken from a fallen Soviet commander—wherever he went.

By the mid-1980s bin Laden had decided to use his wealth to help finance the jihad against the Soviets. Operating from Peshawar, a Pakistani city located a few miles from the Afghan border, bin Laden put out the word that he would supply any Arab willing to come to Afghanistan with an airplane ticket, a place to live, and a monthly allowance. He even offered to cover the travel and living expenses of the volunteers' wives and children. Before long, bin Laden and Azzam had established a fundraising and recruitment network that specialized in targeting bored and disillusioned young Arab men seeking some sort of direction in their lives.

Peshawar was also where bin Laden met Zawahiri, who arrived in the city in 1986 after his release from Egypt's prison system. The two men quickly built a close business relationship. "Each man filled a need in the other," wrote journalist Lawrence Wright. "Zawahiri wanted money and contacts, which bin Laden had in abundance. Bin Laden, an idealist given to causes, sought direction.... Until he met Zawahiri, he had never voiced opposition to his own government or other repressive Arab regimes. His main interest was in expelling the infidel invader from a Muslim land, but he also nursed an ill-formed longing to punish America and the West for what he believed were crimes against Islam. The dynamic of the two men's relationship made Zawahiri and bin Laden into people they never would have been individually."[3]

Estimates of the number of Arabs who answered the call to war in Afghanistan vary considerably. Some scholars place the number at no more than 3,000 or so, but others believe that 30,000 or more took part in the conflict at one time or another.[4] Bin Laden himself spent large stretches of time in the mountains of Afghanistan with a band of followers. Much of his focus was on outfitting and supervising military training camps for new arrivals. With one exception, he participated in only a few minor skirmishes against Soviet forces. But the exception was a big one. In mid-1987 bin Laden and a group of so-called Arab Afghans—Middle Eastern Arabs who went to Afghanistan to push out Moscow's occupying army—defeated Soviet troops in a fierce firefight that came to be known as the Battle of the Lion's Den. The event gave bin Laden's reputation a huge lift. For the rest of his life the Saudi millionaire carried a trophy from the battle—an AK-47 assault rifle taken from a fallen Soviet commander—wherever he went.[5]

In April 1988 the Soviet Union announced that it intended to pull its forces out of Afghanistan within the next nine months. The announcement was in effect an admission that the vaunted Soviet war machine could not defeat its mujahedeen enemy. In mid-February 1989 the last Soviet troops departed the war-torn country. The total Soviet death toll for the war was 15,000, and its army also suffered an additional 30,000 casualties. The bloodshed was far greater for the Afghans, however. At least one million Afghans—most of them civilians—perished in the fighting, and another five million Afghans fled the country for refugee camps in Iran and Pakistan during the decade-long war.

The Birth of al-Qaeda

As the Soviets carried out their retreat, various radical Islamic leaders who had flocked to Afghanistan and Pakistan for the holy war began to ask themselves what they should do next. At an August 11, 1988, meeting with Azzam and several other Arab leaders, bin Laden decided that the spirit of jihad should be kept alive. He discussed plans to use his mujahedeen training camps as the foundation for a new organization, which he began calling al-Qaeda ("The Camp" or "The Base"). Over the next weeks and months, bin Laden, Azzam, Zawahiri, and other Islamists hailing from Egypt, Libya, and other hotbeds of radicalism met repeatedly to make plans for the new entity. They crafted a formal constitution and set up individual committees devoted to politics, security, surveillance, recruitment, and other issues. They even crafted loyalty oaths, salary guidelines, and health care benefits for members. All of these features, bankrolled by bin Laden, were meant to frame al-Qaeda as a career opportunity for young Arab men.[6]

Initially, though, the ranks of al-Qaeda were filled primarily by Arab veterans of the Afghanistan war. "The Arab Afghans were often unwanted renegades in their own countries, and they found that the door closed behind them as soon as they left," noted Wright. "Other young Muslims, prompted by their own governments to join the jihad, were stigmatized as fanatics when they did so. It would be difficult for many of them ever to return home. These abandoned idealists were naturally looking for a leader. They had little to cling to except their cause and each other."[7]

In the fall of 1989 bin Laden returned to his hometown of Jeddah in Saudi Arabia. He arrived as a celebrity of sorts, praised by his followers and ordinary Saudi Arabians alike as a war hero and a model Muslim. As bin Laden basked in the adulation, he began to turn his attention to the United States for the first time. He expressed frustration with America's steadfast political and military support for Israel. He also complained that America's popular culture (television, music, films) and its "modern" ideas about sexuality, religion, and gender roles were eroding the traditional foundations of the Muslim world.

Still, bin Laden's primary focus remained on the Middle Eastern takfir governments that, to his way of thinking, had turned their backs on Islam (see "An al-Qaeda Manual Urges the Overthrow of 'Apostate' Arab Rulers," p. 192). Zawahiri played a major role in keeping bin Laden's attention on the Arab world during these months. The founder of al-Jihad had become bin Laden's chief counselor (as well as his private physician) by this time, and Zawahiri was desperate to exact revenge on Mubarak's regime in Egypt for the torture that he had endured back in the early 1980s.

American Troops in Islam's Holy Land

In 1990-1991, however, a flurry of events in the Middle East placed the United States squarely in the crosshairs of bin Laden and al-Qaeda. In August 1990 Saddam Hussein, who had ruled the Middle Eastern nation of Iraq with an iron fist since 1979, ordered an invasion of neighboring Kuwait. Hussein coveted Kuwait's wealth of oil, and his military forces quickly seized control of the tiny country. Iraq's aggression was condemned by the United States and many other nations that feared that Hussein's actions would result in steep increases in world oil prices. These same countries—including many in the Arab world—also expressed concern that Iraq's conquest might cause political instability in the Middle East and other parts of the world. "If we let [the

President George H.W. Bush enjoying a conversation with Saudi Arabian King Fahd (right) during a 1992 tour of the Middle East.

invasion] succeed no small country can ever feel safe again," declared British Prime Minister Margaret Thatcher. "The law of the jungle takes over."[8]

Over the next several weeks U.S. President George H.W. Bush and his administration coordinated the creation of an international military coalition to pressure Iraq to release Kuwait. This multi-nation coalition was organized under the banner of the United Nations, but the United States contributed the bulk of the troops and firepower. Coalition forces poured into various military bases all around the Persian Gulf, but the main destination was Saudi Arabia. The Saud royal family believed that Hussein might next try to seize their country's oil fields, so they welcomed the American military presence with open arms.

Hussein responded to these unwelcome developments with a furious campaign to rally Muslim support for his cause. He called on Arabs across the region to carry out a jihad against the American "invaders." His angry words resonated with some Islamic radicals, but they failed to spark rebellions against the U.S.-led military presence in Saudi Arabia and elsewhere. On January 17, 1991, Bush announced on national television that the U.S.-led coalition had launched a full-scale offensive against Iraqi forces in Kuwait. This operation, dubbed Operation Desert Storm, was a resounding success. Led by America's fearsome military superiority, the UN armies trounced Iraq's forces. Kuwait was liberated, and American-led troops chased the battered remnants of the Iraqi army deep into Iraq itself before Bush declared victory and ordered a cease-fire.

Saudi Arabia's King Fahd had promised the people of Saudi Arabia and the wider Arab world that American military forces would leave the country as soon as the war was over. U.S. troops did not leave, however. Instead, they took up residence in Saudi military bases in several parts of the country. Fahd and Bush explained that the troops were staying put in order to ensure that Iraq did not get any ideas about resuming its belligerent ways. But many Muslims—including millions who did not subscribe to the fanatical beliefs of the Islamic radicals—expressed dismay over this development. They disliked having soldiers from America—widely seen as a Christian nation—permanently encamped in a country that housed Mecca, the holiest site in the entire Muslim world. The arrangement also prompted widespread complaints that many Arab regimes were little more than colonial outposts of the all-powerful West.

The reaction was even more explosive among bin Laden, Zawahiri, and their cohorts. They believed that they were witnessing a permanent American occupation of Saudi Arabia. From this point forward, bin Laden and al-Qaeda saw the United States as an evil force on earth. They also came to see America as the primary obstacle to their coalescing dream of establishing a world governed by their radical vision of Islam. "Their view was that the West had been corrupted by greed, sin, and selfishness," wrote the editors of *Der Spiegel*. "And that the Islamic world was an oasis of faith and culture—but an oasis threatened and humiliated by the West, and by the United States in particular. They misunderstood the West as they misunderstood Islam; in one they saw only destruction, in the other only decline."[9]

Bin Laden in Sudan

In 1992 bin Laden moved to the country of Sudan in northeast Africa with his entire family, which by this time included four wives and seventeen children.

Sudan was an ideal location for bin Laden in many ways. Back in 1989 Islamic radicals had overthrown the secular government and set about establishing Sudan as a global center for jihad. The primary architect of this scheme was an Islamic scholar named Hasan al-Turabi, who recognized that bin Laden's riches could be a big asset to the country. Al-Turabi repeatedly invited bin Laden to join him in Sudan, and the al-Qaeda leader finally took him up on the offer.

Bin Laden spent the next four years in Sudan, where he divided his time between major construction projects and building up the al-Qaeda organization. His political and religious views continued to darken during this period, in large part because of the influence of Zawahiri and Mamdouh Mahmud Salim, a Sudanese cleric who had participated in the founding meeting of al-Qaeda in 1988. Salim relentlessly trumpeted his belief that al-Qaeda should be attacking America—and that terrorist attacks on civilians were perfectly acceptable. According to Salim's warped views, any devout Muslims who lost their lives in such attacks would be rewarded with eternal life in Paradise, while all other victims (including children) deserved to die for being nonbelievers. This perspective echoed Sayyid Qutb's mid-century writings in support of the principle of takfir. Before long, Salim's ruthless perspective on the taking of innocent lives came to be shared by bin Laden as well, even though it was completely at odds with the teachings of the Koran.

Islamist radicals ignored the Prophet Mohammed's explicit condemnation of suicide and told themselves that the suicide bomber was a "heroic martyr whose selfless sacrifice [would] gain him an extraordinary reward in Paradise."

Zawahiri, meanwhile, was responsible for another frightening evolution in the ongoing construction of al-Qaeda. In August 1993 he approved an al-Jihad assassination attempt on an Egyptian government official. In this attack, a motorcyclist carrying explosives pulled up next to the official's automobile and detonated the bomb strapped to his body. With this action, observed Wright, "Zawahiri introduced the use of suicide bombers, which became the signature of al-Jihad assassinations and later of al-Qaeda 'matyrdom operations.' The strategy broke a powerful religious taboo against suicide." From this point forward, Wright added, Islamist radicals simply ignored the Prophet Mohammed's explicit condemnation of suicide and told themselves that the suicide bomber was a "heroic martyr whose selfless sacrifice [would] gain him an extraordinary reward in Paradise."[10]

A New York City police officer leads a woman to safety following the February 26, 1993, terrorist attack on the World Trade Center.

The 1993 World Trade Center Attack

In early 1993 the hatred that Islamic radicals had come to feel for the United States became more evident than ever before. On February 26, 1993, a religious fanatic named Ramzi Yousef drove a rented van packed with high-powered explosives into a basement parking garage under New York City's World Trade Center. The World Trade Center—which consisted of a complex of seven buildings dominated by two towers that ranked among the tallest buildings in the world—was a prominent symbol of American high finance and power. Yousef fled the garage, then watched from a distance as the bomb detonated, blowing through six stories of the North Tower.

Yousef hoped that the explosion would trigger a collapse of the towers and claim the lives of as many as 250,000 people.[11] The buildings proved stronger than Yousef anticipated, however, and they continued to stand. The

36

blast did claim the lives of six people, however, and it injured 1,042 more. In the ensuing investigation, U.S. officials determined that Yousef was a dedicated follower of Sheikh Omar Abdel Rahman, who had become the leader of a mosque in Brooklyn. They also learned that Rahman, who came to be known in U.S. media as "the Blind Sheikh," was filling his religious services with demands that Muslims rise up and fight their American tormentors. Investigators also learned that Yousef had attended an al-Qaeda camp in Afghanistan in the late 1980s. It has never been decisively determined, however, what direct role—if any—bin Laden and his emerging al-Qaeda organization played in the 1993 World Trade Center bombing plot.

Yousef avoided capture until 1995, when he was caught hiding out in Pakistan. Agents of the Federal Bureau of Investigation (FBI) learned around this time that Yousef and his uncle, another Islamist extremist named Khaled Sheikh Mohammed, were crafting a plan to plant tiny bombs packed with nitroglycerine on a dozen American airliners and blow them up simultaneously as they flew over the Pacific Ocean. In addition to this diabolical scheme, which came to be known as the Bojinka Plot, investigators learned that Yousef had also been concocting plans to assassinate Pope John Paul II and U.S. President Bill Clinton.[12]

The Saudis Cast bin Laden into Exile

By late 1993 bin Laden and his inner circle were bursting with confidence. Their calls for a mass Islamic uprising against corrupt Arab regimes and decadent Western values were being heard in Wahhabi mosques and schools across the Middle East and around the world. They also were coming to feel that the United States, despite its great power, was essentially a weak-willed foe. This view was further strengthened in October 1993, when Clinton withdrew all American peacekeeping forces from the war-torn African nation of Somalia after eighteen U.S. troops were killed in a gun battle with rebel mercenaries.

In the spring of 1994, however, bin Laden was blindsided by a decision by Saudi Arabia's King Fahd to revoke his Saudi citizenship. Fahd took this step in response to intense pressure from Egyptian authorities. President Hosni Mubarak recognized that even from their headquarters in Sudan, bin Laden and Zawahiri were stirring up unrest and violence in Egypt and other parts of the Middle East. Shortly after Fahd revoked bin Laden's citizenship, members of bin Laden's family living in Saudi Arabia publicly disowned the al-Qaeda leader. This condemnation from his own family was a major emotional and financial blow to bin Laden, who channeled his anger and embarrassment into new plans to strike against his many enemies.

On June 26, 1995, members of al-Qaeda and the Islamic Group nearly succeeded in assassinating Mubarak in Ethiopia. Investigators subsequently learned that the terrorists had been aided by members of Sudan's radical Islamic government. Acting on this evidence, the United Nations imposed crippling economic sanctions on Sudan, which it described as a state sponsor of terrorism. Five months later, Zawahiri's al-Jihad group carried out a suicide bombing attack on the Egyptian embassy in Islamabad, Pakistan. The truck bombing obliterated the embassy compound, claimed sixteen lives, and wounded another sixty people.

> *Bin Laden fumed that "it is unconscionable to let the country become an American colony with American soldiers—their filthy feet roaming everywhere—for no reason other than protecting your throne and protecting oil sources for their own use."*

Mubarak responded to these attacks by ordering a massive crackdown on political dissenters. The crackdown tore such a great hole in the ranks of al-Jihad that Zawahiri had no choice but to let the remnants of his organization be absorbed into al-Qaeda. The merger of the two organizations was not officially completed until June 2001, but during the late 1990s al-Jihad came to behave more like a division of al-Qaeda than an independent entity.

Some Arabs speculated that the rupture between bin Laden and the Saudi government might heal someday, provided bin Laden quieted down, publicly renounced violence, and ended his financial support for radical Islamic institutions and groups. In August 1995, though, the al-Qaeda leader destroyed any hopes for a reconciliation. Bin Laden issued a public letter to King Fahd himself, denouncing him as a corrupt, deceitful, and oppressive ruler who had turned his back on Islam. The proof of Fahd's faithlessness, said bin Laden, could be seen by the continued presence of U.S. troops in Saudi Arabia. "The truth is that a foreign power is [in the Kingdom] to protect your throne from the inevitable and growing threat of Islam," charged bin Laden. "It is unconscionable to let the country become an American colony with American soldiers—their filthy feet roaming everywhere—for no reason other than protecting your throne and protecting oil sources for their own use."[13]

Bin Laden's letter shocked and scandalized the Kingdom. But his defiance drew the attention and admiration of many disaffected Arab youths and young men who were beginning to regard him as a heroic champion of Islam. In addition, bin Laden's identification of the United States as the chief reason for Saudi Arabia's subservient position in the world struck a chord with many Arabs who were looking for a non-Arab villain to blame for the political oppression and economic deprivation that shadowed the Middle East. To many disillusioned and frustrated Muslims, the evil Americans who stalked through bin Laden's speeches and statements seemed like the most obvious candidates for that role.

Notes

1 Abdo, Geneive. *No God but God: Egypt and the Triumph of Islam.* New York: Oxford University Press, 2002, p. 54.
2 "1981: Egypt's President Sadat Assassinated," *BBC: On This Day: 1950-2005 (October 6).* Retrieved from http://news.bbc.co.uk/onthisday/hi/dates/stories/october/6/newsid_2515000/2515841.stm.
3 Wright, Lawrence. *The Looming Tower: Al-Qaeda and the Road to 9/11.* New York: Vintage Books, 2006, p. 146.
4 Rashid, Ahmed. *Taliban: Militant Islam, Oil, and Fundamentalism in Central Asia.* New Haven, CT: Yale University Press, 2000, p. 130; Wright, p. 121.
5 Wright, p. 138.
6 Wright, pp. 161-62.
7 Wright, p. 121.
8 Thatcher, Margaret. *The Downing Street Years.* New York: HarperCollins, 1993, p. 820.
9 *Der Spiegel* Writers and Editors. *Inside 9-11: What Really Happened.* New York: St. Martin's Press, 2002, p. xi.
10 Wright, p. 211, 249.
11 National Commission on Terrorist Attacks Upon the United States [The 9/11 Commission]. *The 9/11 Commission Report.* New York: Norton, 2004, p. 72.
12 Reeve, Simon. *The New Jackals: Ramzi Yousef, Osama bin Laden, and the Future of Terrorism.* Boston: Northeastern University Press, 1999, pp. 74-81.
13 Quoted in *Jihad: Bin Laden in His Own Words: Declarations, Interviews, and Speeches.* Brad K. Berner, ed. New Delhi, India: Peacock, 2007, p. 25.

Chapter Three

AL-QAEDA EMERGES
AS A GLOBAL THREAT

⊸══╍╏╮╍══⊷

The call to wage war against America was made because America has spearheaded the crusade against the Islamic nation, sending tens of thousands of its troops to the land of the two Holy Mosques.... Any effort directed against America and the Jews yields positive and direct results—Allah willing. It is far better for anyone to kill a single American soldier than to squander his efforts on other activities.

—Osama bin Laden, May 1998 interview with ABC News

At the same time that Osama bin Laden was severing his last links with his Saudi homeland, his Sudanese hosts felt extreme pressure to expel him from their own country. The United Nations sanctions that had been imposed on Sudan for its sponsorship of terrorism were taking a heavy toll. Sudanese officials recognized that removing the welcome mat for bin Laden was one of the first steps the country would have to take if it wanted to see those sanctions lifted.

In early 1996 Sudan informed bin Laden that he would have to go. In one respect this news may have come as something of a relief to the terrorist financier. Bin Laden endured at least one attempt on his life during his time in Sudan (probably from agents of Egypt or Saudi Arabia), and he may have been open to the idea of finding a safer harbor. The expulsion had a severe impact on his personal finances, however. He was forced to sell off his many business interests to the Sudanese government at a small fraction of their value. This setback, combined with the loss of financial assistance from his family in Saudi Arabia, greatly reduced his capacity to bankroll terrorist operations.

Bin Laden and the Taliban

Bin Laden also faced the problem of figuring out where to go. Already regarded as an enemy of the state in Egypt and Saudi Arabia, he knew that he would not be welcomed in most other Arab states, either. In the end, bin Laden decided to return to the country where he had made his reputation in the first place. He left Sudan on May 18, 1996, and headed for Afghanistan, where Islamic religious fanaticism had established a deadly stranglehold over the population since his departure seven years earlier.

The Afghanistan to which bin Laden returned was ruled by a fundamentalist group called the Taliban. The Taliban had been created during the Soviet occupation of Afghanistan in the 1980s by Afghan mujahedeen—"holy" warriors fighting under the flag of Islam—and fundamentalist tribesmen from neighboring Pakistan. In 1994 the group seized control of Kandahar, a city in southern Afghanistan with deep religious significance to the nation's Muslim population. By 1996 the group, which was led by a mysterious one-eyed cleric named Mullah Mohammed Omar, had taken control of the national government and consolidated its control over most Afghan territory. The only resistance to their cruel reign came from a handful of tribal warlords. The most formidable of these commanders was Ahmed Shah Massoud, who led a rebel army known to the West as the Northern Alliance (the official name was the United Islamic Front).

Members of the Taliban subscribed to Wahhabism, a rigid variation of Islam that had first gained prominence in Saudi Arabia. They rejected music, television, and most other forms of entertainment as unholy, and they insisted on strict codes of conduct that were particularly damaging and demeaning to women. The Taliban demanded, for example, that all women cover themselves from head to toe in veiled garments when in public. They also opposed educating girls or allowing women to hold jobs. Men or women who resisted the Taliban's nightmarish interpretations of the Koran were frequently beaten, whipped, or executed in gruesome ways.

The Taliban did not initially welcome bin Laden with open arms. On the contrary, they were wary of the Saudi exile. Mullah Omar and his advisors were well aware that Sudan's experience providing sanctuary to the al-Qaeda leader had ended badly. They did not want bin Laden, who settled in Kandahar, to give them a slate of new problems at a time when they were focused on establishing Islamic rule across the country. Their anxiety was further height-

Osama bin Laden speaking to reporters in Khost, Afghanistan, in 1998.

ened when Zawahiri and other important al-Qaeda operatives joined bin Laden in Kandahar.

Bin Laden responded to this skepticism by actively courting Omar's favor. "He arrived in the desert warmth of Kandahar that winter with praise for Omar's wisdom and grand ideas about construction projects that could transform [the city]," wrote journalist Steve Coll, "filling it with enduring symbols of Taliban faith and power."[1] Bin Laden also swore an oath of personal loyalty to the Taliban leader. All of these efforts paid off, as Omar gradually came to see bin Laden as both a friend and a fellow champion of the true Islamic faith. According to some reports, Omar even took bin Laden's oldest daughter as a wife in the late 1990s. Perhaps the most notable symbol of their relationship came on September 9, 2001, a mere two days before the infamous terrorist attacks on America. On that day, al-Qaeda suicide bombers assassinated rebel leader Massoud, Omar's most formidable foe in Afghanistan.

The Face of Terrorism

As bin Laden's position in Afghanistan became more secure, the al-Qaeda leader returned his attention to the United States and Israel, the Jewish state that was America's closest ally in the Middle East. On August 23, 1996, he issued a fatwa, a type of Islamic religious degree, that was entitled "Declaration of War against the Americans Occupying the Land of the Two Holy Places." Bin Laden charged that it was "no longer possible [for him] to be quiet" in the face of "the aggression, iniquity, and injustice imposed on [the people of Islam] by the Zionist-Crusaders alliance and their collaborators." He called on his Muslim brothers to join him in "destroying, fighting, and killing the enemy until, by the Grace of Allah, it is completely defeated." Bin Laden's fatwa alarmed some Taliban leaders who worried that it would cause trouble for Afghanistan, but his relationship with Omar protected him from any reprisals.

Emboldened, bin Laden launched a public relations campaign to gather new warriors to his cause. He issued a series of statements and interviews in which he condemned America for its interference in Middle Eastern affairs and Israel for its continued occupation of lands that rightly belonged to the Palestinians. This rhetoric, coupled with his 1996 fatwa, attracted the attention of U.S. analysts and intelligence officials in a way that his earlier activities in Sudan and Saudi Arabia had failed to do. "In recent videotaped messages, Osama bin Laden has increasingly referred to the Palestinian cause as the basis for his campaign," wrote defense analyst Brian M. Jenkins. "He sees it as an issue that is likely to win broad support in the Arab world. These public messages and shifts in explanation show a politician seeking a constituency. Terrorism is not his end, and religious belief, however sincere, is not his sole motive for violence. His is the politics of mass mobilization. Without constituents, terrorist violence becomes meaningless."[2]

Bin Laden's campaign gathered considerable attention in the cities and villages of the Arab world. "Publicity was the currency bin Laden was spending, replacing his wealth with fame, and it repaid him with recruits and donations," wrote journalist Lawrence Wright.[3] Angry, disillusioned, and easily manipulated young Arabs began to flock to al-Qaeda training camps that bin Laden set up in Tora Bora, a mountainous region near the Pakistan border. "The Taliban seemed to open the doors to all who wanted to come to Afghanistan to train in the camps," reported the 9/11 Commission. "The alliance with the Taliban provided al-Qaeda a sanctuary in which to train and indoctrinate fighters and terrorists, import weapons, forge ties with other jihad groups and leaders, and plot and staff terrorist schemes."[4] According to U.S. intelligence estimates, between 10,000 and 20,000 jihadists went through these camps from 1996 through 2001.

The alliance with the Taliban also gave the al-Qaeda leader the freedom to provide financial and logistical support to radical Islamic cells that were taking root in Germany, the United States, and other parts of the globe. Many of these cells became populated with "graduates" of the Tora Bora camps. Bin Laden thus created a new type of terrorist organization. Al-Qaeda, summarized counterterrorism expert David Long, "is more like a gathering place for diverse subgroups to obtain financing, support, and military training. It's a chameleon, an amoeba that constantly changes form and color but has only one leader: Osama bin Laden."[5]

By the late 1990s the camps of Tora Bora, where bin Laden came to spend most of his time, had emerged as the central hub of an Islamic terrorist movement that was spreading its tentacles across the planet. Bin Laden welcomed a wide assortment of prominent terrorist figures during this time. These men came in search of funding for terrorist plots, to bask in the glow of

"The Taliban seemed to open the doors to all who wanted to come to Afghanistan to train in the camps," reported the 9/11 Commission. "The alliance with the Taliban provided al-Qaeda a sanctuary in which to train and indoctrinate fighters and terrorists, import weapons, forge ties with other jihad groups and leaders, and plot and staff terrorist schemes."

bin Laden's presence, or—in the case of Khaled Sheikh Mohammed—to suggest various schemes for attacking al-Qaeda's enemies. Mohammed reportedly told bin Laden all about the failed plot devised by his nephew, World Trade Center bomber Ramzi Yousef, to explode a dozen U.S. airliners over the Pacific. He also discussed the possibility of crashing airplanes into the Pentagon, the central headquarters of the U.S. Department of Defense, and other buildings of strategic significance. Many analysts and historians believe that the seeds for the September 11, 2001, terrorist attacks were first planted at this meeting, which took place sometime in 1996.

A Rising Tide of Terrorist Attacks

As al-Qaeda gathered strength in the late 1990s, a series of deadly terrorist attacks made headlines around the world. The organization proudly claimed a hand in virtually all of these attacks, and indeed, some of them were traced directly to bin Laden's organization. Al-Qaeda's involvement in several of the attacks, however, remained wrapped in a haze of rumors and circumstantial evidence. Intelligence officials also warned that bin Laden had been known to claim responsibility for attacks in which he had no role, such as the deadly 1993 ambush of U.S. troops in Somalia.

The new wave of terrorist assaults began on June 25, 1996, with a bombing at Khobar Towers in Dhahran, Saudi Arabia. This sprawling military barracks provided housing for American soldiers, who were clearly the main target of the attack. Nineteen members of the U.S. Air Force lost their lives in the attack, which also caused hundreds of injuries to military personnel and civilians. The FBI launched an investigation of the attack, but they were obstructed at every turn by Saudi officials who feared that the investigation would reveal widespread Saudi hate for the central government.

Nonetheless, the FBI persevered, and agents acquired significant evidence that pointed to a radical Saudi group known as Hezbollah Al-Hejaz. In addition, some investigators and terrorism experts have also claimed that agents of Iran's radical Islamic government and/or al-Qaeda might have been involved. Saudi investigators have asserted that foreign parties had no role in the attack, but American officials and agents voiced open skepticism about the trustworthiness of the Saudis.

The next major terrorist attack occurred seventeen months later in Egypt, and it was a truly horrific event. On November 17, 1997, a small

Coffins containing the bodies of thirty-six Swiss victims of the Luxor Massacre sit in a Zurich airport hangar after arriving from Egypt.

group of gunmen from a radical anti-government organization known as the Islamic Group seized the Temple of Hatshepsut, a popular tourism destination on the west bank of the Nile River outside of Luxor. The terrorists spent forty-five minutes murdering and mutilating the bodies of tourists, including women, young children, and honeymooners. A total of fifty-eight foreign tourists (including thirty-six from Switzerland) and twelve Egyptian temple workers were killed in the bloodshed. The murderers then fled to a nearby cave and committed suicide before the authorities could catch them.

Investigators later linked both bin Laden and Zawahiri to the so-called Luxor Massacre. The al-Qaeda leader provided financing for the operation, while his chief deputy helped develop the plot. But the terrorists badly miscalculated the public reaction to the massacre. They thought that by striking a terrible blow against Egypt's vitally important tourism industry, they might weaken Mubarak's regime to the point that it could be toppled. Instead, Egypt's mainstream Islamic community expressed almost universal outrage and sadness about the killings. "The sense of mourning went deeper than economic concerns," wrote British journalist Barbara Plett. "Egyptians pride themselves on giving foreigners a warm welcome, and were appalled at this gross violation of their hospitality. Again and again people said to me: how could this happen to our guests? We are so horrified that this terrible attack took place in our country. Five hundred kilometers north of Luxor in Cairo the sense of shame and anger was just as strong."[6] The popular backlash in Egypt was so great that Zawahiri and other Islamic terrorists frantically started blaming Israel or Egyptian security forces for the carnage.

Bin Laden Issues a Second Fatwa

On February 23, 1998, bin Laden issued a second fatwa in a London-based Arabic newspaper (see "Osama bin Laden and the World Islamic Front Call for a 'Holy War' Against Jews and Crusaders," p. 189). This call to Islamic holy war was co-signed by Zawahiri (who actually wrote much of its contents) and several other prominent terrorist leaders around the Middle East and Asia. It once again called on all devout Muslims around the world to wage war against the United States and Israel for various crimes against the Islamic faith. "The ruling to kill the Americans and their allies—civilians and military—is an individual duty for every Muslim who can do it in any country in which it is possible to do it," stated the decree. "We—with God's help—call on every Muslim who believes in God and wishes to be rewarded to comply with God's order to kill the Americans and plunder their money wherever and whenever they find it. We also call on Muslim ulema [scholars], leaders, youths, and soldiers to launch the raid on Satan's U.S. troops and the devil's supporters allying with them."[7]

The 1998 fatwa brought new waves of recruits to Tora Bora and inspired a fresh batch of terrorist plots around the world. Many young men enthusiastically signed on for the holy war in the full knowledge that they might be asked to sacrifice their lives to the cause. Their willingness to die reflected not only their limited life opportunities, but also their desperate desire to attach meaning and significance to their lives. "Radicalism usually prospers in the gap between rising expectations and declining opportunities," wrote Wright.

> This is especially true where the population is young, idle and bored; where the art is impoverished; where entertainment—movies, theater, music—is policed or absent altogether; and where young men are set apart from the consoling and social-

This August 1999 rally in Pakistan was organized by Islamic religious leaders who condemned the United States and praised Osama bin Laden for standing up to America and Israel.

izing presence of women. Adult illiteracy remained the norm in many Arab countries. Unemployment was among the highest in the developing world. Anger, resentment, and humiliation spurred young Arabs to search for dramatic remedies. Martyrdom promised such young men an ideal alternative to a life that was so sparing in its rewards.[8]

Six months later al-Qaeda carried out, for the first time, a terrorist strike that did not rely on any outside groups or terrorists. On August 7, 1998, al-Qaeda suicide drivers drove massive truck bombs into the American embassies in two major African cities—Nairobi in Kenya and Dar es Salaam in Tanzania. The attacks took an appalling human toll. In Kenya, 213 people lost their lives (including 12 Americans) and another 4,500 people were injured. In Tanzania, the tally was 11 dead and 85 wounded—all of them Africans. When bin Laden and other radical Islamists heard about the devas-

President Clinton Addresses the Nation on Operation Infinite Reach

Thirteen days after al-Qaeda terrorists destroyed two American embassies in eastern Africa, the United States carried out cruise missile attacks against al-Qaeda camps in Afghanistan and a factory in Sudan that was thought to be a potential source of chemical weapons. These strikes, which were carried out on August 20, 1988, were the centerpiece of a military operation known as Operation Infinite Reach. On the afternoon of August 20, President Bill Clinton explained the goals of this operation in a nationally televised address (excerpted here).

> Our mission was clear—to strike at the network of radical groups affiliated with and funded by Osama bin Laden, perhaps the preeminent organizer and financier of international terrorism in the world today.
>
> The groups associated with him come from diverse places, but share a hatred for democracy, a fanatical glorification of violence, and a horrible distortion of their religion to justify the murder of innocents.
>
> They have made the United States their adversary precisely because of what we stand for and what we stand against.
>
> A few months ago, and again this week, bin Laden publicly vowed to wage a terrorist war against America, saying—and I quote—"We do not differentiate between those dressed in military uniforms and civilians. They are all targets."

tation, they reacted with dark glee. The rest of the Muslim world received the news of the attacks with horror.

America Hits al-Qaeda with Operation Infinite Reach

In the United States, the initial response to the embassy bombings was shock and fury, combined with a recognition that a deadly new threat to American lives was stalking the world. Most Americans heard the names "bin

Their mission is murder. And their history is bloody....

I want you to understand, I want the world to understand that our actions today were not aimed against Islam, the faith of hundreds of millions of good, peace-loving people all around the world, including the United States. No religion condones the murder of innocent men, women and children. But our actions were aimed at fanatics and killers who wrap murder in the cloak of righteousness, and in so doing, profane the great religion in whose name they claim to act.

My fellow Americans, our battle against terrorism did not begin with the bombing of our embassies in Africa, nor will it end with today's strike....

We must be prepared to do all that we can for as long as we must. America is and will remain a target of terrorists precisely because we are leaders; because we act to advance peace, democracy and basic human values; because we're the most open society on earth; and because, as we have shown yet again, we take an uncompromising stand against terrorism....

Source

Clinton, Bill. Remarks in Martha's Vineyard, Massachusetts, on Military Action against Terrorist Sites in Afghanistan and Sudan, August 20, 1988. *Public Papers of the Presidents: William J. Clinton—1998*. Vol. 2. Washington, DC: U.S. Government Printing Office, 1999, p. 1460.

Laden" and "al-Qaeda" for the first time in the days following the embassy attacks. They followed the news as federal authorities launched an investigation and manhunt for the perpetrators, and as the FBI placed bin Laden on its famed "Ten Most Wanted" list.

A number of the surviving terrorists who planned the embassy attacks were captured or killed by U.S. military strikes over the next several years. On May 29, 2001, four men were convicted in the bombings of the American embassies in a New York courtroom. Other leaders of the plot that have been captured, including Walid bin Attash (taken into custody in Pakistan in 2003), have not been put on trial. Instead, they remain in custody at Guantanamo Bay, Cuba, where the United States maintains a maximum-security military prison. But other men believed to have been involved in the plot, including Zawahiri, have remained at large.

President Bill Clinton and his administration also responded to the terrorist attacks in Nairobi and Dar es Salaam with a military strike called Operation Infinite Reach. On August 20, 1988, Tomahawk cruise missiles blasted al-Qaeda terrorist training camps in Afghanistan. They also destroyed a warehouse in Sudan that was allegedly manufacturing chemical weapons for terrorist use (the factory was later determined to have been an ordinary producer of medicine). The U.S. strikes on Tora Bora reportedly killed a few dozen terrorist trainers and recruits, but they failed to knock out bin Laden, Zawahiri, or any other major al-Qaeda figures.

According to many analysts, bin Laden's survival further burnished his reputation in the Arab world. "We have survived the American attack," Zawahiri proclaimed in a telephone call that he placed to a British journalist about twenty-four hours after the bombing. "Tell the Americans that we aren't afraid of bombardment, threats, and acts of aggression. We suffered and survived the Soviet bombings for ten years in Afghanistan, and we are ready for more sacrifices. The war has only just begun; the Americans should now await the answer."[9]

In December 1999 investigators in the Middle Eastern country of Jordan uncovered a terrorist plot to blow up hotels and other tourist sites in the country that were popular with Americans and other Westerners. The Jordanian authorities captured sixteen men suspected of being involved in the operation, but one of the leaders—a Jordanian militant named Abu Musab al-Zarqawi, who would go on to become one of al-Qaeda's leading figures—escaped the country.

Al-Qaeda Strikes the USS *Cole*

One month later an al-Qaeda plan to attack the U.S. warship *The Sullivans* while it rested in the harbor in Aden, Yemen, fell apart due to poor planning. But the idea of taking down one of America's mightiest fighting vessels remained irresistible to bin Laden and his minions. On October 12, 2000,

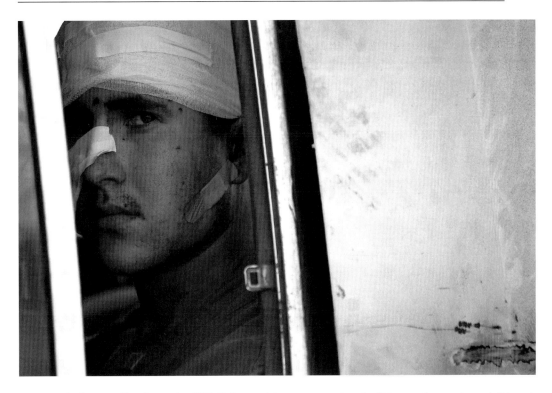

A wounded U.S. sailor from the USS *Cole* awaiting transport out of Yemen to receive additional medical treatment at a U.S. base in Germany.

another American destroyer, the USS *Cole*, was refueling in Aden's harbor when a small fiberglass fishing boat carrying two passengers pulled up alongside the boat's hull. As sailors peered down from the deck, the two men smiled and waved, then stood at attention before detonating the explosive charge that was packed inside their boat. The resulting fireball blew a huge hole in the side of the warship, killing seventeen American sailors, wounding another thirty-nine (many of whom suffered severe burns), and nearly sinking the *Cole*.

The terrorist attack on the *Cole* dominated headlines across the Middle East. The coverage attracted still more recruits to al-Qaeda and inspired wealthy Islamic radicals to bestow financial gifts on bin Laden to help him carry out his "holy" work. In the United States, President Clinton vowed to bring all of the terrorists responsible for the attack to justice. Over the next few years many of the *Cole* conspirators were identified by U.S. investigators and either killed by military action, arrested by Yemen, or taken prisoner by

CIA agents. Abd al-Rahim al-Nashiri, a Saudi terrorist who has been described as one of the masterminds of the *Cole* attack, has been in U.S. military custody since November 2002, when he was captured in a CIA operation. Another leading figure in the *Cole* operation, Walid bin Attash (who also helped plan the 1998 African embassy bombings) has been in U.S. custody since 2003.

But other conspirators served only short prison terms in Yemen before being released, and key figures like Jamal al Badawi have escaped from Yemeni prisons. Some American officials, analysts, and journalists believe that these escapes have been facilitated by Yemeni officials sympathetic to al-Qaeda. "After we worked day and night to bring justice to the victims and prove that these Qaeda operatives were responsible, we're back to square one," stated Ali Soufan, a former FBI agent who took part in the *Cole* bombing investigation. "Do they have laws over there or not? It's really frustrating what's happening."[10]

Under ordinary circumstances, the United States might have taken a harder line against Yemen's government. And at another time, American defense and intelligence agencies might have approved new operations to kill bin Laden and other top al-Qaeda leaders. But the *Cole* bombing took place at the tail end of the Clinton administration, only one month before the 2000 presidential election and three months before President George W. Bush entered the Oval Office. Some observers believe that the attack on the *Cole*, as horrible as it was, simply got lost in the transition between the two administrations. "It was the forgotten attack," summarized Roger Cressey, a counter-terrorism official who served in both the Clinton and Bush administrations.[11]

Bin Laden was surprised that the United States did not launch a major offensive against al-Qaeda in response to the *Cole* attack. He viewed America's inaction as further evidence that for all its wealth and power, the United States was a weak and easily intimidated nation. This same perspective was shared by the Taliban leadership, which suffered no adverse consequences from harboring bin Laden. Left undisturbed, bin Laden turned his full attention to a new terrorist plot that had been simmering for the past several months—a plan to strike deep in the heart of America itself.

Notes

[1] Coll, Steve. *Ghost Wars: The Secret History of the CIA, Afghanistan, and bin Laden, from the Soviet Invasion to September 10, 2001*. New York: Penguin, 2004, p. 341.

[2] Jenkins, Brian M. "The Organization Men: Anatomy of a Terrorist Attack." In *How Did This Happen? Terrorism and the New War.* Edited by James F. Hoge Jr. and Gideon Rose. New York: Public Affairs, 2001, p. 13.

[3] Wright, Lawrence. *The Looming Tower: Al-Qaeda and the Road to 9/11.* New York: Vintage Books, 2006, p. 297.

[4] National Commission on Terrorist Attacks Upon the United States [The 9/11 Commission]. *The 9/11 Commission Report.* New York: Norton, 2004, p. 66.

[5] *Der Spiegel* Writers and Editors. *Inside 9-11: What Really Happened.* New York: St. Martin's Press, 2002, p. 175.

[6] Plett, Barbara. "Egypt Tries to Understand the Luxor Massacre," *BBC News,* December 1, 1997. Retrieved from http://news.bbc.co.uk/2/hi/programmes/from_our_own_correspondent/34587.stm.

[7] "Al-Qaeda's Fatwa," *PBS NewsHour,* February 23, 1998. Retrieved from http://www.pbs.org/newshour/terrorism/international/fatwa_1998.html.

[8] Wright, p. 123.

[9] Quoted in Gutman, Roy. *How We Missed the Story: Osama bin Laden, the Taliban, and the Hijacking of Afghanistan.* Washington, DC: U.S. Institute of Peace, 2008, p. 144.

[10] Whitlock, Craig. "Probe of USS Cole Bombing Unravels," *Washington Post,* May 4, 2008. Retrieved from http://www.washingtonpost.com/wp-dyn/content/article/2008/05/03/AR2008050302047.html?sid=ST2008050400049.

[11] Whitlock, "Probe of USS Cole Bombing Unravels."

Chapter Four

THE SEPTEMBER 11
ATTACKS ON AMERICA

───※───

We have some planes. Just stay quiet and you will be O.K.

—Hijacker of American Airlines Flight 11 to passengers,
21 minutes before the airliner hit the North Tower of the
World Trade Center

In early 1999 Osama bin Laden gave Khaled Sheikh Mohammed his formal stamp of approval for the airplane hijacking proposal Mohammed had first pitched back in 1996. Mohammed immediately began devising plans for the operation. Over the next several months, he and bin Laden and another al-Qaeda deputy named Mohammed Atef settled on a scheme to hijack several U.S. passenger planes and fly them into strategically vital targets along America's eastern seaboard. Preliminary targets included the White House and the U.S. Capitol Building (where the Senate and House of Representatives meet) in Washington, D.C.; the Department of Defense's Pentagon headquarters in northern Virginia, directly across the Potomac River from Washington, D.C.; and New York City's World Trade Center, a symbol of American high finance that Mohammed's nephew had nearly destroyed in a 1993 bombing attack.

Preparing for the "Planes Operation"

Under the plan first conjured up by Mohammed, Atef, and bin Laden, al-Qaeda warriors from Afghanistan would be sent to the United States, where they could enroll in any number of flight schools and learn the basics of airplane piloting. In early 2000, in fact, two such men—Nawaf al-Hazmi and Khalid al-Mihdhar—entered the United States and took up residence in San Diego, California, where they began taking flight lessons.

Over the second half of 2000 and the early months of 2001, Atta and his fellow hijackers trained in small planes and flight simulators at various flight schools and small airports up and down the East Coast. They showed particular dedication to learning how to execute turns and other mid-air maneuvers.... The men showed much less interest in learning how to take off or land airplanes.

Despite sending these operatives to America, however, bin Laden worried that jihadists from Tora Bora and Kandahar were poor candidates for the "planes operation," as it came to be known within bin Laden's inner circle. Most of his followers in the Arab world knew only fragments of English, and they were largely unfamiliar with daily life and culture in the West. Bin Laden and Mohammed recognized that such men could easily draw unwanted attention from the FBI or other law enforcement authorities. And even if they avoided detection, their gaps in knowledge and education might prove too great for them to carry out their mission successfully.

The plotters found a way around these potential stumbling blocks in November 1999, when four radical Islamists arrived in Kandahar from Hamburg, Germany. These men—Mohamed Atta, Ramzi Binalshibh, Marwan al-Shehhi, and Ziad Jarrah—were all active members of the Hamburg al-Qaeda cell, and they passionately hated the United States. More importantly for bin Laden's purposes, the Hamburg men could speak fluent English. In addition, their years as students in Germany—a country that shared many cultural trends and lifestyle similarities with America—had prepared them for living in the United States. "The new recruits from Germany possessed an ideal combination of technical skill and knowledge that the original 9/11 operatives, veteran fighters though they were, lacked," summarized the 9/11 Commission. "Bin Laden and Atef wasted no time in assigning the Hamburg group to the most ambitious operation yet planned by al-Qaeda."[1] Atta was selected as the tactical commander of the group.

As bin Laden had feared, al-Hazmi and al-Mihdhar could not handle the rigors of pilot training. By mid-2000 both men had dropped out of flight school in San Diego. But the emergence of the Hamburg cell saved the plot from unraveling. In early 2000 Atta and the other Hamburg radicals returned to Germany, where they promptly applied to flight schools in the United States (they also considered flight schools in Europe, but determined that flight training in America was less expensive and required less time). By mid-

2000 Atta, al Shehhi, and Jarrah had all obtained travel visas, entered the United States, and begun taking flight training, mostly in Florida.

The fourth Hamburg cell member, Binalshibh, was unsuccessful in his efforts to obtain a U.S. visa. His application was repeatedly turned down because he was a citizen of Yemen, and Yemenis were notorious among U.S. immigration officials for overstaying their visits and becoming illegal aliens. The al-Qaeda leadership responded to this setback by changing Binalshibh's assignment. They made him a courier for the 9/11 attacks, then started looking for someone to replace him as the fourth suicide pilot. After considering a variety of options, including a French Muslim radical named Zacarias Moussaoui (see "The Twenti-eth Hijacker?" sidebar, p. 60), bin Laden, Mohammed, and Atef selected a Saudi Arabian radical named Hani Hanjour to take Binalshibh's place as the fourth pilot. Hanjour had actually earned a commercial pilot's license in Arizona in 1999, so he did not have the learning curve that most other candidates faced.

Over the second half of 2000 and the early months of 2001, Atta and his fellow hijackers trained in small planes and flight simulators at various flight schools and small airports up and down the East Coast. They showed particular dedication to learning about how to execute turns and other mid-air maneuvers. Conversely, several of their flight instructors acknowledged in post-9/11 inter-views that the men showed much less interest in learning how to take off or land airplanes. The hijackers were supported financially during this time by a steady stream of secret payments from al-Qaeda operatives and supporters overseas.

After the four pilots completed their training, al-Qaeda sent a larger group of jihadists to America to help them carry out the planned hijackings. These "strongmen" had orders to help Atta and the other pilots take over the cockpits of the hijacked planes and kill any passengers or crew members who threatened the mission. The arrival of these fanatics on American shores between March and June 2001 was coordinated by al-Mihdhar and al-Hazmi, who remained part of the hijacking plot despite their disastrous flight train-ing experiences in California.

The strongmen entered America in small groups from the United Arab Emirates (UAE), a country that had long been friendly to the United States. Only one of the strongmen was a UAE citizen, however; the rest were from Saudi Arabia. All told, in fact, fifteen of the nineteen terrorists who participat-ed in the September 11 hijackings hailed from Saudi Arabia, bin Laden's native country. The operation's high percentage of Saudis has since been

The Twentieth Hijacker?

Although Zacarias Moussaoui did not participate directly in the September 11 attacks, he has acquired a certain infamy because he was identified by U.S. investigators as a possible "twentieth hijacker" who might have taken part in the attacks if he had not already been in U.S. custody. Born on May 30, 1968, near Narbonne, France, to Moroccan parents, Moussaoui had converted to the fundamentalist Wahhabi strain of Islam as a young man. In 1998 he went to Afghanistan to receive training in Osama bin Laden's al-Qaeda camps, where his devotion to the jihad cause caught the attention of instructors.

In mid-2000 Moussaoui allegedly was selected by bin Laden and Khaled Sheikh Mohammed to serve as a pilot in their coalescing "planes operation" against America. He would replace Ramzi Binalshibh, who had been denied entry into the United States by immigration officials. Over the next several months, al-Qaeda's leadership became sufficiently concerned about Moussaoui's stability that they picked another man to serve as the fourth pilot. Nonetheless, Moussaoui was still sent to the United States to take flight training, and he remained in contact with—and received financial support from—several of the same al-Qaeda figures that coordinated the September 11 attacks.

Moussaoui arrived in the United States in February 2001 with a three-month visa. After flunking out of a flight school in Oklahoma, he enrolled in another flight training program in Eagan, Minnesota, in August. Within

attributed both to the great number of Saudi recruits in al-Qaeda and to the relative ease with which Saudi citizens could obtain U.S. travel visas.[2]

The Hijackers Take Their Places

By the end of July 2001 all nineteen hijackers were in the United States. Most of the strongmen joined Atta and his fellow pilots in Florida, where they tried to blend into the general population. They opened bank accounts, worked out at local gyms, and found housing in modest apartment complexes.

days of entering the program, however, Moussaoui was identified by instructors as a potentially dangerous character. The instructors later told investigators that the student behaved strangely, and that he only wanted to learn to fly a Boeing 747. He also asked them about how cockpit doors operated and inquired about the explosive impact of a Boeing 747 with full fuel tanks. They alerted a Minneapolis FBI field office, and on August 16, 2001, Moussaoui was arrested for remaining in the United States with an expired visa. The Minneapolis agents then asked permission from FBI headquarters to carry out a search of his belongings, but their request was turned down by officials who insisted that they did not have enough evidence to request a search warrant. After September 11, this decision by FBI officials would be heavily criticized by observers who thought that a prompt and full investigation of Moussaoui might have uncovered the terrorist plot before the attacks took place.

Following 9/11, American federal prosecutors charged him with a range of serious crimes, including preparing acts of terrorism, conspiracy to hijack an aircraft, and using weapons of mass destruction against American citizens. Moussaoui initially claimed that he was not involved in the September 11 plot, insisting that he had been working on an entirely separate terrorist scheme. The evidence of his involvement with September 11 was not strong, but prosecutors insisted on going forward. In April 2006, midway through his trial, Moussaoui abruptly admitted guilt to all charges. He was sentenced to life in prison on May 4, 2006. He is currently serving out his sentence in solitary confinement in a maximum security facility in Colorado.

The pilots, meanwhile, took first-class trips on cross-country flights across the United States in order to acquaint themselves with the layouts of the planes they intended to hijack (each pilot made a point of booking his flight on the same type of aircraft he would pilot on September 11).[3] "There were no slip ups," testified FBI Director Robert Mueller months after the 9/11 attack. "Discipline never broke down. They gave no hint to those around them what they were about. They came lawfully. They lived lawfully. They trained lawfully.... They simply relied upon everything from the vastness of the Internet to the openness of our society to do what they wanted to do without detection."[4]

In this still photo taken from security camera footage, two men later identified by authorities as hijackers Mohamed Atta (right) and Abdulaziz Alomari pass through security at a Portland, Maine, airport. They then boarded a plane to take them to Boston, from where they carried out their suicide hijacking of American Airlines Flight 11.

Atta also conducted a meeting in Madrid, Spain, in July with Binalshibh to finalize details of the coming attack. Atta informed Binalshibh that he thought that striking the White House with one of the planes would probably be too difficult, since the target was relatively small. He told the Yemeni terrorist that he and Shehhi intended to fly their planes into the twin towers of the World Trade Center. He also stated that he had assigned Jarrah to take out the Capitol and Hanjour to strike the Pentagon.[5]

Upon returning to the United States from Madrid, Atta and his fellow suicide hijackers began their final preparations. In mid-August Atta selected the date of September 11 for the attacks. On August 26 the hijackers began buying tickets for four separate cross-country flights scheduled to depart from various East Coast airports between 7:45 and 8:14 A.M. on September 11. They selected cross-country flights because the planes would be carrying huge fuel loads—and thus serve as more potent bombs when the hijackers plowed them into their targets. As September 11 approached, the four hijacking teams—each one led by a pilot—checked into hotels near the airports out of which they would be flying.

The lone exceptions to these preparations were Atta and one of the musclemen, Abdulaziz Alomari. Atta spent the last few days going from city to city to meet up with the teams one final time. On September 10 he picked up Alomari at a Boston hotel and drove to Portland, Maine, for unknown reasons. Early the following morning, the two hijackers boarded a commuter flight that took them from Portland to Boston's Logan International Airport, where they had reservations on American Airlines (AA) Flight 11 from Boston to Los Angeles. They arrived in Boston in time to pass through the airport's security checkpoints and make their flight, but one of Atta's travel bags did not get checked through in time to get tossed on Flight 11. It remained behind at Logan, where it sat until 9/11 investigators found it and began sorting through its chilling contents.

American Airlines Flight 11 Hits the North Tower

Atta and Alomari were joined on AA Flight 11 by three familiar faces: Waleed al-Shehri, Wail al-Shehri, and Satam al-Suqami. The five terrorists sat quietly in their seats (which were scattered between the plane's business class and first-class sections) as AA 11 lifted off from Logan Airport at 7:59 A.M. with ninety-two people on board. The airliner, which was helmed by Captain John Ogonowski, was a Boeing 767.

The first fifteen minutes of the flight unfolded in normal fashion. Air traffic controllers monitored AA 11 as it steadily climbed toward its assigned cruising altitude of 29,000 feet. At 8:14, however, the flight's pilots failed to acknowledge new instructions to go to 35,000 feet. At the same time, air traffic controllers began to notice that AA 11 was straying off its assigned flight path. Controllers attempted to communicate with the plane over the next several minutes, but all of their messages were met with silence.

The anxious atmosphere on the ground turned to outright dread and horror at 8:19, when the American Airlines Reservations Control Center received an emergency call from a flight attendant using one of AA 11's airphones. The attendant, Betty Ong, reported in a calm but frightened voice that hijackers had forced their way into the cockpit and taken control of the plane. She also reported that the hijackers had stabbed two flight attendants and cut the throat of a passenger, and she identified the seat numbers of the hijackers.

At 8:22 the Boeing 767's transponder, a type of tracking device for aircraft, stopped emitting signals. This development meant that the flight's altitude could no longer be monitored on the ground. Radar imagery became the only method by which air traffic controllers could track the flight's progress. At 8:24 air traffic controllers heard the voice of a hijacker come in over the air traffic control channel: "We have some planes. Just stay quiet and you will be O.K. We are returning to the airport. Nobody move, everything will be O.K. If you try to make any moves, you'll endanger yourself and the airplane. Just stay quiet." Authorities believe this message was actually intended for the AA 11 passengers, but that the hijackers accidentally broadcast it over the air traffic control communication system rather than the Boeing's cabin public address system. The message confirmed the worst fears of Boston air traffic controllers, who immediately informed other regional air traffic control centers that a hijacking was in progress.

At 8:28 the plane abruptly changed course to the south. Four minutes later, another AA 11 flight attendant, Amy Sweeney, was able to establish contact with the American Airlines Flight Services Office in Boston after several failed attempts. She confirmed Ong's account of the hijacking, and over the next several minutes Ong (who was still on her line) and Sweeney both provided descriptions of the hijackers as well as harrowing firsthand impressions about the plane's "erratic" flight path. Meanwhile, air traffic controllers watched helplessly as the plane's radar image moved down the Hudson River Valley toward New York City.

At 8:44 American Airline officials lost their phone connection to Ong. At the same time, Sweeney reported that "something is wrong. We are in a rapid descent.... We are all over the place." She then peered out one of the windows and stated, "We are flying low. We are flying very, very low. We are flying way too low." She paused briefly, then exclaimed, "Oh my God we are way too low."

Civilians in the North Tower of the World Trade Center jump to their deaths to escape the flames after a hijacked plane hit their building.

A few seconds later, at 8:46:40 A.M., American Airlines Flight 11 smashed into the North Tower of the World Trade Center at a speed of nearly 400 miles per hour. The Boeing 767 hit the north side of the 110-story tower at about the level of the 96th floor. The plane obliterated three floors above and below the point of impact, and it created an enormous fireball that erupted out of the west and east sides of the building. Fragments of airplane and shattered construction girders also "cut through stairwells, severed elevator cables, and displaced entire stairway sections," according to one account of the tragedy. "For everyone above the point of impact at this moment, the tower had become a death trap."[6]

United Airlines Flight 175 Hits the South Tower

At 8:14 A.M.—approximately the same moment that American Airlines Flight 11 was being hijacked by Atta and his henchmen—United Airlines (UA) Flight 175 lifted off from Boston's Logan International Airport. Also bound for Los Angeles, the Boeing 767 was piloted by Captain Victor Saracini and carried 10 other crew members and 61 passengers. Among the tourists and businesspeople on board were five al-Qaeda terrorists—Fayez Banihammed, Ahmed al-Ghamdi, Hamza al-Ghamdi, Mohand al-Shehri, and pilot Marwan al-Shehhi.

Within twenty minutes of liftoff, UA 175 had climbed to its assigned cruising altitude of 31,000 feet and was streaking toward California. At 8:42 the crew reported to air traffic controllers that they had heard a "suspicious transmission" from another plane. This report—which was a reference to the transmission that the AA 11 hijackers had erroneously made over their jet's air traffic control communication system—was the last contact that air traffic controllers had with UA 175.

Sometime between 8:42 and 8:46 A.M., the terrorists aboard UA 175 revealed themselves and wrested control of the airplane from its crew. According to panicked calls made by passengers and crew members, the hijackers used Mace and knives to kill the pilots, attack at least one flight attendant, and herd the remaining crew and passengers to the back of the aircraft. At 8:47 UA 175 changed its transponder signal several times. When controllers asked the plane to go back to its assigned code, they received no response. Over the next few minutes, several passengers managed to make calls to family members or United Airlines offices. It was at this time that the

This photograph shows the hijacked United Airlines Flight 175 just before it slammed into the South Tower of the World Trade Center

New York air traffic control center realized that UA 175 had been hijacked, and at 9:01 the office notified the FAA's national air traffic command center in Herndon, Virginia, that a second hijacking had taken place that morning.

At 8:58 the plane abruptly changed course and turned its wings for New York City. One minute later, a UA 175 passenger named Brian Sweeney used his cell phone to leave a message at home for his wife: "Hi Jules, it's Brian. I'm in a plane being hijacked and it does not look good. I just wanted to let you know that I love you and that I hope to see you again. If I don't, please have fun in life and live your life the best you can."[7] He then called his mother and told her that several passengers were weighing whether they could storm the cockpit and retake control of the plane from the terrorists. At 9:00, passenger Peter Hanson, who was traveling with his wife and two-year-old daughter, called his father. "It's getting bad, Dad," he said. "They seem to have knives and Mace.... Passengers are throwing up and getting sick—The plane is making jerky movements—I don't think the pilot is flying the plane—I think we are going down—I think they intend to go to Chicago or someplace and fly into a building—Don't worry, Dad—If it happens, it'll be very fast—My God, my God."[8]

As Sweeney and Hanson made these final calls to their loved ones, the plane in which they were trapped was descending out of the sky toward downtown Manhattan at a rate of more than five thousand feet per minute. At two different times it nearly collided in midair with other passenger jets, which were forced to take evasive maneuvers. New York Center air traffic controller Dave Bottiglia later stated that he and his colleagues "were counting down the altitudes, and they were descending, right at the end, at 10,000 feet per minute. That is absolutely unheard of for a commercial jet. It is unbelievable for the passengers in the back to withstand that type of force as they're descending. [The hijackers are] actually nosing the airplane down and doing what I would call a 'power dive.'"[9]

The plane crashed into the southeast corner of the South Tower of the World Trade Center at 9:03:11 A.M. The impact and explosion wiped out a huge swath of the tower from the 77th to the 85th floors. But by hitting the extensive steelworks at the corner of the building instead of one of its broad faces, as AA 11 had done to the North Tower, the Boeing's progress was halted before it could demolish all of the stairwells in the interior. One stairwell was left sufficiently intact for eighteen people working on the floors above impact to make it down to the streets below. Investigators who examined amateur videotapes of the UA 175 crash later reported that the Boeing was in the midst of a sharp turn when it plowed into the corner of the South Tower—an indication that al-Shehhi and his fellow hijackers nearly missed the tower altogether.

American Airlines Flight 77 Crashes into the Pentagon

The third American passenger jet that fell into the grip of bin Laden's murderous gang was American Airlines Flight 77, which departed Washington Dulles International Airport (located in Dulles, Virginia, just outside Washington, D.C.) at 8:20 A.M. The Boeing 757, which was piloted by Charles Burlingame, held a total of six crew members and fifty-eight passengers—including five terrorists scattered throughout first class and coach—when it took off that morning on its flight to Los Angeles. The lead terrorist was pilot Hani Hanjour. His strongmen were Khalid al-Mihdhar, Majed Moqed, Nawaf al-Hazmi, and Salem al-Hazmi.

The first half hour or so of the flight passed without incident, and at 8:46 the plane reached its assigned cruising altitude of 35,000 feet. Five minutes later, the crew issued a routine radio transmission to air traffic controllers. Between 8:51 and 8:54, however, the hijackers seized AA 77 using knives (one passenger using a phone also reported that the hijackers possessed box cutters). At 8:54 the plane began drifting south from its assigned course, and at 8:56 air traffic controllers on the ground lost AA 77's transponder signal.

As evidence mounted that a third passenger jet might have been hijacked—a horrifying realization that was underscored at 9:03, when UA 175 crashed into the South Tower—both American Airlines and United Airlines ordered all of their flights that had not yet taken off to be grounded. In other respects, however, both the airlines and the Federal Aviation Administration (FAA)—the government agency responsible for overseeing air transportation in the United States—seemed overwhelmed by the scale of the tragedy that was unfolding. "No one at the FAA or the airlines that day had ever dealt with multiple hijackings,"

"No one at the FAA or the airlines that day had ever dealt with multiple hijackings. Such a plot had not been carried out anywhere in the world in more than 30 years, and never in the United States. As news of the hijackings filtered through the FAA and the airlines, it does not seem to have occurred to their leadership that they needed to alert other aircraft in the air that they too might be at risk."

Firefighters work to put out flames moments after a hijacked jetliner crashed into the Pentagon on September 11.

wrote the 9/11 Commission. "Such a plot had not been carried out anywhere in the world in more than 30 years, and never in the United States. As news of the hijackings filtered through the FAA and the airlines, it does not seem to have occurred to their leadership that they needed to alert other aircraft in the air that they too might be at risk."[10]

Over the next several minutes a number of passengers aboard AA 77 were able to make phone contact with loved ones. They anxiously reported that hijackers had taken control of their plane, employing the same general tactics (such as using knives and forcing passengers to the back of the cabin) as the hijackers of the planes that had struck the World Trade Center. One of the callers was Barbara Olson, who managed to reach her husband, Ted Olson, the solicitor general of the United States. During their conversation Barbara Olson learned of the hijackings and World Trade Center attacks that had already taken place that morning.

At 9:25 air traffic controllers reported that AA 77 was heading straight toward Washington, D.C. Four minutes later, the Boeing 757's autopilot was disengaged and the hijacker pilot (assumed to be Hani Hanjour) took manual control of the airplane. At 9:34 air traffic controllers warned the Secret Service that the hijackers might be targeting the White House, even though President George W. Bush was not there at the time. A few seconds later, the plane executed a wide 360-degree turn, just south of the Pentagon. It then picked up speed and roared over the streets of Washington, shearing off the tops of trees and streetlights. At 9:37:46 it blasted into the southwest side of the Pentagon, instantly killing dozens of people there and all of the plane's passengers and crew.

Passengers Strike Back on United Airlines Flight 93

The last hijacking of September 11 took place aboard a Boeing 757 that departed from Newark, New Jersey, at 8:42 with seven crew members and thirty-seven passengers (including four hijackers) on board. This flight, United Airlines Flight 93, was captained by Jason Dahl and was bound for San Francisco, California. The hijackers on board consisted of pilot Ziad Jarrah and three strongmen—Saeed al-Ghamdi, Ahmed al-Haznawi, and Ahmed al-Nami—all of whom occupied seats in first class. UA 93 was the only flight that was hijacked with a four-man team. Investigators later concluded that this team was short-handed because its likely fifth member, a radical named Mohamed al Kahtani, had been denied entry into the United States by a suspicious immigration inspector at Florida's Orlando International Airport one month earlier.

The first forty-two minutes of UA 93's flight proceeded in a routine fashion. At 9:24, though, Dahl received a message from UA flight dispatcher Ed Ballinger, who on his own initiative had begun transmitting warnings to UA's in-progress transcontinental flights about the possibility of cockpit intrusions from hijackers (at this point neither the airlines nor the FAA had begun issuing official warnings about hijackings). At 9:26 Ballinger received a reply seeking confirmation of his warning: "Ed, confirm latest mssg. [message] pls—Jason." Two minutes later, just before the UA 93 crew could institute additional security measures to defend the cockpit, the hijackers made their move. FAA air traffic controllers listened helplessly on the ground as they received radio transmissions of a fierce struggle for control of the cockpit. They could hear Dahl or co-pilot Leroy Homer shouting "Mayday" and "Get out of here!" as well as the sounds of physical violence. By 9:32 the hijackers

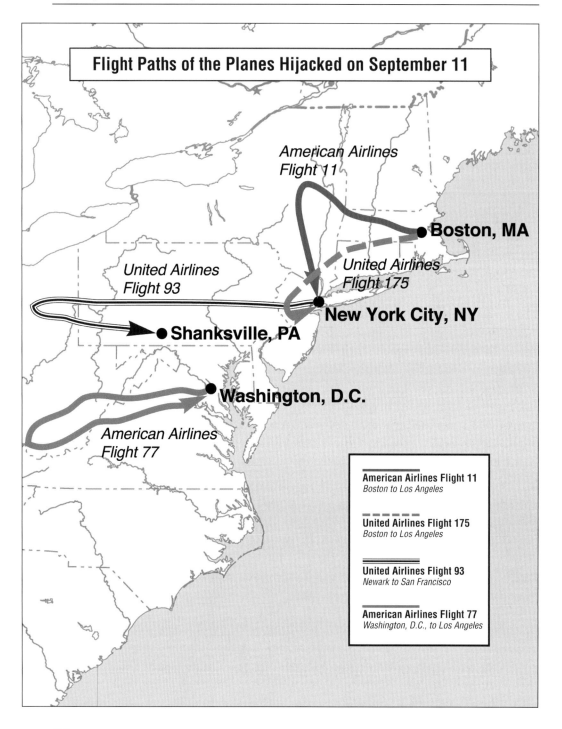

Flight Paths of the Planes Hijacked on September 11

American Airlines Flight 11

● Boston, MA

United Airlines Flight 93

United Airlines Flight 175

● Shanksville, PA

New York City, NY

● Washington, D.C.

American Airlines Flight 77

American Airlines Flight 11
Boston to Los Angeles

United Airlines Flight 175
Boston to Los Angeles

United Airlines Flight 93
Newark to San Francisco

American Airlines Flight 77
Washington, D.C., to Los Angeles

had won this grim struggle. One of the hijackers, most likely Jarrah, broadcast a message into the cabin: "Ladies and Gentlemen: Here the captain, please sit down keep remaining sitting. We have a bomb on board. So, sit."[11]

Most of the passengers and crew members were subsequently pushed toward the rear of the main cabin by the hijackers. It was here that passengers and crew members began making telephone calls to friends, family, and colleagues. According to a number of the passengers, the confident hijackers made no effort to halt these calls. During these conversations, however, many of the passengers learned that hijacked planes had already been flown into the towers of the World Trade Center. Armed with the knowledge that the hijackers almost certainly intended to use their plane as a fuel-laden missile against a vital American target, several brave hostages agreed to take action. They decided to mount an assault against the terrorists and either regain control of the plane or force it down before the hijackers reached the target of their suicide mission.

"We talked about how much we loved each other and our children," recalled the husband of Flight 93 attendant Sandra Bradshaw. "Then she said: 'Everyone is running to first class, I've got to go. Bye.' Those were the last words I heard from her."

The leaders of this rebellion were business executive Tom Burnett, small business owner Mark Bingham, and website sales manager Jeremy Glick, but they were joined by an unknown number of other passengers and crew as well. "The passengers and crew members aboard Flight 93 were not ordinary citizens placed in an extraordinary situation," wrote *New York Times* reporter Jere Longman.

> As a group, these were people who were on top of their game, who kept score in their lives and who became successful precisely because they were assertive and knew how to make a plan and carry it out. The people aboard the plane had varied skills. Not everyone could rush the cockpit, but I am convinced that each person offered whatever resources he or she had available in the final moments of the flight. I heard tapes of a couple of the phone calls made from the plane and was struck by the absence of panic in their voices.[12]

One participant in the counter-attack was flight attendant Sandra Bradshaw, who was on the phone to her husband just before the passengers made their charge. "We talked about how much we loved each other and our children," recalled her husband, Phil Bradshaw. "Then she said: 'Everyone is running to first class, I've got to go. Bye.' Those were the last words I heard from her." Another passenger who participated was sales executive Todd Beamer. He was on the phone with a telephone company operator named Lisa Jefferson when Glick, Bingham, and Burnett signaled that they were preparing to attack. The last words Jefferson heard from Beamer were directed at his fellow passengers: "You ready? OK, let's roll."[13]

The UA 93 passengers launched their attack on the hijackers at 9:57 A.M. The plane's cockpit voice recorder documented the desperate struggle that ensued between the hijackers and the passengers. The device recorded how Jarrah urged the strongmen to hold the passengers off as they tried to force their way into the cockpit, but the Americans refused to give up. Over the next few minutes the recorder filled with the sounds of crashing, shouting, cursing, screaming, and shattering glass. Jarrah pitched the plane up and down and side to side in an effort to disrupt the attack, and at one or two points it appeared that the hijackers managed to fight the unarmed passengers off. Each time, however, the determined passengers simply regrouped and renewed their assault. At 10:02:23, a hijacker could be heard on the recorder saying "Pull it down! Pull it down!" According to the 9/11 Commission, the hijackers probably realized that the passengers were only seconds away from defeating them. The airplane went into a deep dive and turned onto its back as one of the hijackers started screaming "Allah is the greatest, Allah is the greatest." A few seconds later, at 10:03, the Boeing crashed into an empty field just outside of Shanksville, Pennsylvania, about twenty minutes' flying time from Washington, D.C.[14]

The Collapse of the Towers

At the same time that UA 93 passengers and hijackers were fighting for control of that plane, the South Tower of the World Trade Center collapsed. It began to fall in on itself at 9:58:59 A.M., and over the next ten seconds the entire magnificent structure plummeted to the streets below. The collapse, which came fifty-six minutes after the building had been hit by UA 175, killed all civilians and emergency personnel inside the tower, as well as a number of people in the surrounding area. The ruined building was obscured, though, by a massive cloud of debris and dust that billowed up around the tangled steel and concrete. Engineering experts believe that the South Tower collapsed first, even though the North Tower had actually been

The South Tower begins its horrifying collapse as the neighboring North Tower continues to burn.

struck seventeen minutes earlier, for two reasons: UA 175's collision with one of the South Tower's corners had badly damaged its central support structure; and the South Tower had been struck at a lower point than the North Tower, so its impact zone was forced to bear more weight.

The sudden collapse of the South Tower stunned thousands of people in Manhattan who were eyewitnesses to the tragedy. As the ashy cloud billowed forth, covering block after block, countless people fled from the downtown district in panic. It also horrified millions of Americans who watched live television coverage of the tower's fall.

Thirty minutes later, at 10:28:25 A.M., the North Tower collapsed from the top down with a tremendous roar, unleashing a second monstrous cloud of smoke and debris. The loss of this second majestic icon of American capitalism triggered a second wave of grief and disbelief among viewers all across the United States and around the world

The collapse of the twin towers caused extensive damage to the surrounding area. The smaller buildings in the World Trade Complex were destroyed or heavily damaged, and several other adjoining facilities and buildings suffered extensive damage. These losses, though, paled next to the shocking human toll of the attacks. All told, an estimated 2,996 people (excluding terrorists) lost their lives in the al-Qaeda terrorist attacks of September 11. More than 2,700 of these casualties occurred in New York City.

The majority of these losses were innocent civilians, but a staggering number of deaths came from the ranks of the city's "first responders"—emergency personnel who rushed to the towers in rescue operations. The Fire Department of New York (FDNY) suffered 343 fatalities that day, the largest loss of life of any emergency response agency in history. The Port Authority Police Department (PAPD), which provides law enforcement services to bridges, tunnels, seaports, and airports in and around New York Harbor, lost 37 officers on September 11. The carnage also claimed the lives of 23 members of the New York Police Department (NYPD). The deaths of so many valiant firefighters and police officers—men and women who had put their lives on the line every day for the people of New York—gave the day an even more nightmarish hue.

President Bush Learns of the Attacks

When the dark events of the morning of September 11 took place, President George W. Bush was hundreds of miles away from the Oval Office. He

President George W. Bush listens as his chief of staff, Andrew Card, informs him during an appearance at a Florida elementary school that a second plane crashed into the World Trade Center—a sure indication that America was under terrorist attack.

was visiting Emma E. Booker Elementary School in Sarasota, Florida, to publicize and drum up support for some of his education policies. Before entering a class of second graders, Bush had been informed that a plane had hit the North Tower of the World Trade Center. Bush and his staff had no evidence at that point that the incident was anything but a tragic accident, so they decided to go ahead with the event. At 9:05 A.M., though, Bush's chief of staff, Andrew Card, entered the classroom where the president was preparing to participate in a reading lesson. Card leaned down and whispered: "A second plane hit the second tower. America is under attack." Bush's expression became tight and drawn. He spent the next eight minutes sitting silently in the classroom as the second graders made a presentation, then excused himself to talk with his staff. Bush was harshly criticized in some quarters for this delay, but he later said that he had not wanted to frighten the children in the classroom. The Secret Service, which is responsible for the president's safety, has never responded to questions about why it delayed taking Bush to safety despite clear evidence that terrorists were launching spectacular strikes against America.

Bush left the classroom at 9:16, then hurriedly consulted with advisors about the attacks. He also spoke on the phone with FBI Director Robert Mueller and New York Governor George Pataki. Bush decided that he needed to make a televised address to the nation, but as he and his staff worked on his statement, they kept glancing over to a television that showed the horror unfolding in downtown Manhattan. Turning to his aides, Bush reportedly declared, "We are at war."[15]

At 9:30 Bush delivered a brief televised statement acknowledging the tragedy that was unfolding. He closed his remarks by stating that "terrorism against our nation will not stand." A few moments later Bush left in his presidential motorcade for a nearby airport, where Air Force One awaited. Meanwhile, Vice President Dick Cheney and other top White House officials were taken down to the Presidential Emergency Operations Center, a bunker beneath the building that is designed to withstand nuclear attack.

Air Force One lifted off from Sarasota at 9:55. By this time AA 77 had already crashed into the Pentagon and the valiant passengers of UA 93 were preparing their desperate assault on the terrorists who had hijacked their plane. During this same period, orders to ground commercial and private air traffic began to be issued by a variety of aviation agencies, airports, and airline companies across the country. The skies gradually emptied of planes except for U.S. fighter jets that had belatedly scrambled into action. By shortly after noon, there was not a single private or commercial plane flying over the contiguous United States. Commercial air traffic in the United States remained grounded for the next three days.

The military jets that prowled the skies had been authorized by Vice President Cheney around 10:10 A.M. to shoot down any suspected hijacked commercial airliners before they could reach important targets or population centers. When he gave this order, Cheney was unaware that the last hijacked plane, UA 93, had already crashed in Pennsylvania. In actuality, however, Cheney did not possess the legal authority to give such an order. Only Bush, the nation's commander in chief, was so empowered. The White House later said that Bush authorized a "shootdown" order in a conversation with Cheney earlier that morning. But no record of such a call exists in phone logs maintained that morning at the White House and aboard Air Force One.

Protecting the President

Upon leaving the school in Sarasota, Bush expressed a strong desire to return to Washington, D.C. Instead, Secret Service agents and White House staffers with whom he was traveling managed to convince him to go to a military base as a precaution. Air Force One subsequently charted a course for Barksdale Air Force Base in Shreveport, Louisiana. "It was a time of chaos and confusion that is reflected in the official documents of that day, some public, some classified," wrote journalist Bob Woodward. "Various documents have Bush arriving in Louisiana at 11:48 A.M., 11:57 A.M., 12:05 P.M., and 12:16 P.M.—a range of 28 minutes."[16]

Bush and his aides arranged to issue another televised statement at 12:36 p.m from Barksdale. "It had been more than three hours since the president or any senior administration official had spoken publicly," noted Woodward. "The president's eyes were red-rimmed when he walked in. His performance was not reassuring. He spoke haltingly, mispronouncing several words as he looked down at his notes."[17]

"I'm not going to let some tinhorn terrorist keep the president of the United States away from the nation's capital," said Bush. "The American people want to see their president and they want to see him now."

After concluding his remarks, Bush once again voiced a desire to return to Washington. But the Secret Service insisted that it was safer for him to remain sequestered away for the time being, and this position was supported by Cheney, Card, and other top members of the White House staff. Bush grudgingly approved a plan to fly to Offut Air Force Base in Nebraska, which included a heavily fortified bunker facility. In addition, Offut was home to the

U.S. Strategic Command, which maintains and controls the nation's vast arsenal of nuclear weapons.

Air Force One arrived at Offutt at approximately 2:50 P.M. A short time later, Bush conducted a teleconference with the members of his National Security Council to discuss the tragedy. During this meeting Bush was told by Director George Tenet of the Central Intelligence Agency (CIA), America's main spy agency, that the attacks were almost certainly the work of Osama bin Laden. The meeting wrapped up in less than an hour, at which point Bush overruled the Secret Service and ordered Air Force One to take him back to Washington. "I'm not going to let some tinhorn terrorist keep the president of the United States away from the nation's capital," he reportedly said. "The American people want to see their president and they want to see him now."[18]

Bush left for Washington at 4:36 P.M. and he arrived at the White House at 6:54. At 8:30 he gave his third address of the day to the American people—and to a worldwide audience that had been transfixed by the awful events of the day (see "President Bush Addresses the Nation after the 9/11 Attacks," p. 217). Bush declared in his speech that as the United States moved forward to punish its attackers, "we will make no distinction between the terrorists who committed these acts and those who harbor them." He also issued a statement of national resolve. "A great people has been moved to defend a great nation," he said. "America has stood down enemies before and we will do so this time. None of us will ever forget this day. Yet we go forward to defend freedom and all that is good and just in the world."

After concluding his seven-minute address, Bush spent the next few hours meeting with his full National Security Council, including Tenet, Mueller, Secretary of State Colin Powell, National Security Advisor Condoleezza Rice, and Secretary of Defense Donald Rumsfeld, and other close advisors. There was broad agreement in these meetings that al-Qaeda was the culprit—and that Afghanistan and other countries known for harboring terrorists needed to choose whether they were with the United States or against it.

Bush finally went to sleep in the White House residence, only to be awakened by Secret Service agents. Alarmed by reports of an unidentified airplane in the area, the agents hustled Bush and his wife, Laura, to the building's underground bunker. When the plane sighting turned out to be a false alarm, Bush and his wife returned to the residence. Before going back to bed, however, Bush took out his diary and reflected on the day's events. "The Pearl

Harbor of the 21st century took place today," he wrote. "We think it's Osama bin Laden."[19]

Notes

1 National Commission on Terrorist Attacks Upon the United States [The 9/11 Commission]. *The 9/11 Commission Report.* New York: Norton, 2004, pp. 166-67.
2 National Commission on Terrorist Attacks, p. 234.
3 National Commission on Terrorist Attacks, p. 242.
4 Mueller, Robert III." Statement for the Record, FBI Director Robert Mueller III, Joint Intelligence Committee Inquiry." Retrieved from http://www.fas.org/irp/congress/2002_hr/022602mueller.html.
5 National Commission on Terrorist Attacks, p. 244.
6 *Der Spiegel* Writers and Editors. *Inside 9-11: What Really Happened.* New York: St. Martin's Press, 2002, p. 44.
7 Quoted in *Der Spiegel*, p. 69.
8 Quoted in National Commission on Terrorist Attacks, p. 8.
9 Quoted in "Flight 175: As the World Watched" (TLC documentary). *The Learning Channel.* December 2005.
10 National Commission on Terrorist Attacks, p. 10.
11 National Commission on Terrorist Attacks, p. 12.
12 Longman, Jere. *Among the Heroes: United Flight 93 & the Passengers & Crew Who Fought Back.* New York: HarperCollins, 2002, p. xi.
13 Quoted in Alderson, Andrew, and Susan Bisset. "The Extraordinary Last Calls of Flight UA93," *The Daily Telegraph* (UK), October 20, 2001. Retrieved from http://www.telegraph.co/uk/news /world news/northamerica/usa/1360088/The-extraordinary-last-calls-of-Flight-UA93.html.
14 National Commission on Terrorist Attacks, p. 14.
15 Quoted in Sammon, Bill. *Fighting Back: The War on Terrorism from Inside the Bush White House.* New York: Regnery, 2002, p. 94.
16 Woodward, Bob. *Bush at War.* New York: Simon & Schuster, 2002, p. 18.
17 Ibid, p. 19.
18 "Bush Wanted Quick Return to Washington," Associated Press, September 13, 2001.
19 Quoted in Balz, Dan, and Bob Woodward. "America's Chaotic Road to War," *Washington Post,* January 27, 2002, p. A1.

Chapter Five

HEARTBREAK AND HEROISM ON THE GROUND

My back was turned to the buildings at the moment the first building started to fall, but I heard it. I heard this indescribable roar. I felt it. It was a deep, loud, rumbling, thunderous booming. I heard it happening before I saw anything, and I was already moving.... I turned around, and this black cloud as high as the sky was wailing. It had debris in it, and it was coming down and at me. I was so close, and it was coming so fast, I just dropped the clipboard, turned around, and ran like I've never run before."

—FDNY Captain Janice Olszweski,
in *Tower Stories: An Oral History of 9/11*

For the innocent passengers and crew on board the four planes hijacked by Osama bin Laden's followers, their final moments of life were the stuff of the worst nightmares. The morning of September 11 was similarly terrifying for the men and women who worked at the World Trade Center and the Pentagon—as well as the firefighters, paramedics, and police officers who responded to the attacks on those buildings. But just as the passengers of United Airlines Flight 93 valiantly rose above their fears and forced the hijackers to crash the plane far short of their target, countless civilians and first responders at the World Trade Center and the Pentagon displayed remarkable courage and compassion in the chaotic aftermath of the attacks.

Time and again, ordinary office workers, business executives, and military personnel risked their own lives to help injured or disabled people get to safety. Meanwhile, the firefighters, police officers, and other emergency workers who responded to the tragedies in downtown Manhattan and Arlington carried out their duties with unflinching determination and grit. They earned the undying gratitude of thousands of Americans whose lives hung in the balance after the attacks. Tragically, however, hundreds of these heroic first responders were killed when both of the World Trade Center's so-called Twin Towers collapsed.

Fleeing the North Tower

When the hijacked American Airlines Flight 11 slammed into the North Tower of the World Trade Center at 8:46:40 A.M., it wrecked large sections of floors 93 through 99, including all three stairwells. Hundreds of people were killed instantly, either by the impact itself or by the fireball of jet fuel that exploded across the floors. With elevator service halted and all stairwells severed from the 92nd floor up, everyone who was above the "impact zone" of the 110-story building was trapped. As journalists Jim Dwyer and Kevin Flynn wrote, "their fate was sealed nearly four decades earlier [during construction], when the stairways were clustered in the core of the building, and fire stairs were eliminated as a wasteful use of valuable space."[1]

Unable to descend on foot, these survivors of the initial crash also could not be whisked to safety from the air. The heat and smoke from the blaze made it impossible for helicopters to attempt rooftop rescues. As a result, businesses with offices on these upper floors suffered horrible losses. The investment firm Marsh & McLennan lost 295 people on September 11 (see "A North Tower Survivor Remembers His Narrow Escape," p. 205). Another company, Carr Futures, lost 69 employees that day. The financial company Cantor Fitzgerald suffered the greatest losses of all. By the close of that dark day, 658 of its employees had perished.

Some of the men and women stranded on the top floors became so desperate to escape the dense smoke and intense heat from the fires below that they jumped or fell from the tower. For many first responders, the sight of the jumpers was the worst part of an almost unfathomably awful day. FDNY paramedic Gary Smiley recalled that when he arrived at the scene, it was "already littered with bodies. It almost looked like a graveyard.... People were jumping out of the North Tower. At first, you didn't know what the heck they were doing, and then you realized when you saw one after the other after the other. Two people hit two separate firemen and killed them right before my eyes.... I remember watching fourteen people jump, including a couple that must have jumped from

An emergency worker treats a victim of the terrorist attack on New York City's World Trade Center.

at least the ninetieth floor. They held hands and jumped. That was the most sickening sight I've ever seen in my life, the most helpless feeling."[2]

The attack also wreaked havoc with elevator systems throughout One World Trade Center (WTC One), the official address of the North Tower. Many people became trapped in elevators when AA 11 struck the building. In addition, some civilians below the impact zone—primarily from the 70th floor through the 90th floor, but also on several floors further down—found themselves trapped in their offices as a result of fallen debris and infrastructure damage.

A number of these people were rescued by fellow office workers or building employees. For example, Port Authority construction manager Frank De Martini, whose office was on the 88th floor, helped rescue a number of people on his floor. He then organized fellow Port Authority workers Pete Negron, Carlos Da Costa, and Pablo Ortiz into a rescue mission. Armed with flashlights and crowbars, the men roamed up and down the floors immediately below the impact zone, prying open elevator doors and tearing open walls to free trapped workers. The brave actions of these four men—men who "worked anonymously for a faceless government bureaucracy," as Dwyer and Flynn put it—saved the lives of at least seven more people in the North Tower. "When last heard from, they were on their way to try to free more," they wrote.[3] Tragically, however, all four men perished when the North Tower collapsed.

Rescue Mission at the North Tower

Other office workers in WTC One waited for assistance from emergency personnel—in many cases because that's what they had been told to do when they called 911 and other agencies for guidance.[4] This "stay put" advice did not reflect the beliefs of top emergency response officials. To the contrary, fire and police officials who arrived at the scene within minutes of the attack on the North Tower immediately called for full-scale evacuations. By 8:57 Fire Department of New York (FDNY) chiefs on the scene had instructed WTC complex personnel and the Port Authority Police Department (PAPD) to evacuate both the North and South Towers. Three minutes later, the PAPD commanding officer of the World Trade Center ordered an evacuation of all civilians in the entire complex.

Unfortunately, these orders did not reach many of the agencies that were receiving emergency calls from within the towers or coordinating the rescue effort. The evacuation order from the PAPD commanding officer, for example, was given over a radio channel that could not be heard by the South Tower's deputy fire safety director, who was responsible for carrying out evacuation orders. As a result of these breakdowns in communication, many 911 operators and FDNY dispatchers adhered to standard operating procedures for high-rise fires when responding to calls that morning. According to these procedures, civilians threatened by high-rise fires should remain where they were until emergency personnel could reach them. "Those who called 911 from floors below the impact were generally advised to remain in place," confirmed the 9/11 Commission. "One group trapped on the 83rd floor pleaded repeatedly to know whether the fire was above or below them, specifically asking if 911 operators had any information from the outside or from the news. The callers were transferred back and forth several times and advised to stay put. Evidence suggests that these callers died."[5]

People running from smoke-filled lower Manhattan after the towers were hit.

These discoveries were very difficult for 911 operators and dispatchers to absorb. In most cases these women and men performed their duties as well as they possibly could, given the information at their disposal. But after September 11, FDNY dispatchers grappled with feelings of guilt over sending firefighters, paramedics, and EMTs (emergency medical technicians) into harm's way. Dispatchers and 911 operators also struggled with the knowledge that their advice to panicked civilians calling from the towers had tragic results. "We had Call Receiving Operators telling people on the higher floors above the fires, 'Stay there. They'll come get you. Stay there,'" recalled FDNY dispatcher Doreen Ascatigno. "I know one operator who was watching TV and talking with someone on the 90-something floor and saying, 'You'll be fine. You'll be fine.' Then the Tower fell and the line went dead. She cried like a baby....A part of me died with everybody else that day."[6]

In some cases, 911 operators ignored protocol and strongly advised callers within the North Tower to evacuate if they could. Many of these people survived, as did large numbers of workers who decided on their own that the building was unsafe. They poured into stairwells that became increasingly clogged with fleeing people. But despite the crowded conditions, the presence of smoke and debris, and the overwhelming sense of uncertainty that surrounded the evacuation, most reports indicated that the evacuation was, as the 9/11 Commission put it, "relatively calm and orderly."[7]

Much of the evacuation's success also was due to the heroic efforts of firefighters and police officers. Most of these women and men continued to carry out their life-saving efforts with little or no information about what other agencies were doing—or any knowledge that NYPD helicopter personnel had begun issuing warnings that one or both of the towers might collapse. But a glance in any direction provided ample evidence that the lives of all first responders were in jeopardy.

The danger was especially grave for members of the FDNY. Firefighters carrying about 100 pounds of heavy protective clothing, self-contained breathing apparatuses, and other equipment swarmed up the stairs of the tower, fanning out on different floors in search of people who needed assistance or direction. Several of the fire companies freed civilians who had been stranded in their offices, elevators, or stairways by infrastructure damage. Their actions reflected a recognition that rescue rather than firefighting had to be their top priority. "We knew that at the height of the day there were as

A deputy chief with the New York Fire Department shouts orders to rescue workers, who dealt with devastating challenges during the World Trade Center attacks.

many as 50,000 people in this [North Tower] building," one FDNY chief explained to the 9/11 Commission. "We had a large volume of fire on the upper floors. Each floor was approximately an acre in size. Several floors of fire would have been beyond the fire-extinguishing capability of the forces that we had on hand. So we determined, very early on, that this was going to be strictly a rescue mission. We were going to vacate the building, get everybody out, and then we were going to get out."[8]

Meanwhile, civilians who reached the lobby level of the tower were directed to safety or to hastily established medical stations by NYPD and PAPD officers that had taken up stations all around the base of the building. This guidance was essential, for falling debris and jumpers were a major hazard on the south and west sides of the building.

Chaos in the South Tower

In the first minutes after the North Tower was struck, many people working in the neighboring South Tower remained completely unaware that the attack had taken place. Others, however, saw or heard that a plane had hit the North Tower. Many of these civilians immediately decided to evacuate the South Tower, also known as WTC Two. In addition, security officials with the investment company Morgan Stanley, which occupied more than twenty floors of the South Tower, quickly issued an evacuation order to all of its employees.[9]

At about 8:50 A.M., four minutes after the North Tower was hit, managers of the South Tower issued a public address announcement that an "incident" had occurred at WTC One. But the announcement also indicated that the South Tower tenants were safe and that they could essentially go about their normal business day. "Similar advice was given in person by security officials in both the ground-floor lobby—where a group of twenty that had descended by the elevators was personally instructed to go back upstairs—and in the upper sky lobby, where many waited for express elevators to take them down," reported the 9/11 Commission. "Several South Tower occupants called the Port Authority police desk in 5 WTC [building five in the seven-building WTC complex]. Some were advised to stand by for further instructions, others were strongly advised to leave."[10]

At 9:02 the South Tower's deputy fire safety director finally issued an evacuation advisory over the building's public address system. It remains unknown whether the advisory was issued independently, or whether the director had been informed that both the FDNY and PAPD had ordered full evacuations of the Twin Towers. In any case, a second hijacked commercial airliner—United Airlines Flight 175—slammed into the South Tower one minute later, at 9:03:11. The 9/11 Commission observed that when UA 175 crashed into the tower, "what had been the largest and most complicated rescue operation in city history, instantly doubled in magnitude."[11]

UA 175 did enormous damage to the South Tower and its occupants. It tore a huge gash in the side of the building from the 77th through 85th floors. This impact zone included the sky lobby on the 78th floor, where hundreds of people had congregated to take express elevators to the ground. Some people in the sky lobby survived the crash, but most were not so fortunate. "Around [the survivors] were the remains of people who had been breathing and thinking and chatting a few seconds earlier," wrote Dwyer and Flynn. "Now they were flat on their back or torn apart, dead, or horrifically injured and alive. Inside one elevator, eighteen people were alive but sealed in."[12]

The upper floors of the World Trade Center's South Tower erupt in flame after being hit by a hijacked passenger jet, United Airlines Flight 175.

Unlike the plane that had crashed into the North Tower, however, UA 175 had struck the South Tower at an angle that left some portions of the skyscraper relatively intact from top to bottom. Most importantly, one of the stairwells—stairwell A—remained passable from at least the 91st floor down, and likely from the very topmost floors. The continued usability of this stairwell enabled eighteen people above the impact zone of the South Tower to descend and escape with their lives. They joined the grim parade of civilians below the impact zone who took to stairways to evacuate the building.

As with the rescue effort in the North Tower, evacuation in the South Tower was greatly aided by selfless civilians. Stories abounded of business executives, clerks, and building employees who put their own lives at risk to help pregnant, disabled, injured, or overweight people reach safety. Meanwhile, hundreds of firefighters, police officers, and emergency workers moved in to carry out rescue operations and assist people suffering from broken limbs, burns, smoke inhalation, and other injuries.

Heroic Service to the People of New York City

All told, nearly 2,000 NYPD officers esponded to the WTC crisis, while the FDNY dispatched dozens of companies from all around the city. These firefighters were joined by dozens of off-duty colleagues who had rushed to their fire stations or to the WTC complex when they heard about the crisis. The scene they confronted upon arriving at the towers was chaotic, especially after the second plane hit.

Paramedic Roger Smyth recalled that when he and his partner arrived at the base of the World Trade Center, both towers were still standing but the environment was one of "pandemonium. Things strewn everywhere. Everything from bits of bodies to bodies to furniture—office furniture. Luggage. Shoes. Handbags. Mementos. Personal items. Scattered everywhere, all around from the impact, obviously, and the explosion and the debris and everything blowing everywhere. Bodies falling out of the sky. People scattering in every direction. Emergency workers trying to get people out."[13]

"There was a huge noise like the roar of the ocean and the first tower began to slide down into itself and crumble.... People were screaming, people were crying, people were running. It was madness."

But despite these enormously difficult conditions, New York's police officers, firefighters, medical workers, and other first responders persevered and carried out their duties with resolve. Some participants in the rescue effort, such as NYPD officer Carol Paukner, later acknowledged that they feared for their lives that morning: "'But how could I leave all these people?' I said to another officer, 'I'm going to die today.' I just looked at the building and said, 'This is my day,' and I went back and continued to try to evacuate people without causing them any more alarm."[14]

Tragically, however, the South Tower evacuation effort was plagued by some of the same communications problems that afflicted the North Tower. 911 operators remained in the dark about what was occurring at the Twin Towers, and many of them never learned that a ground order to evacuate the entire WTC complex had been issued. As a result, many 911 callers—including some frightened civilians calling from way up on the 88th and 89th floors of the South Tower—were advised to remain where they were until help arrived.[15] First responders, meanwhile, found that incompatible radio systems and other communication problems made it enormously difficult to coordinate their rescue activities.

The Day Turns Black

It was in the midst of this rescue effort that the unthinkable happened: the South Tower buckled and collapsed into itself. The fall of the South Tower, which had actually been struck seventeen minutes after the North Tower, began at 9:58:59 A.M. In the space of ten seconds it was gone, leaving behind a massive debris cloud that choked the air and blackened the skies of downtown Manhattan. The collapse of WTC Two also devastated surrounding buildings, including the Marriott Hotel (WTC Three), which was nestled at the foot of the two towers.

The collapse of the South Tower was a terrifying event (see "A New York Police Officer Endures the Fall of the South Tower," p. 198). One onlooker who had come to Manhattan for a court appearance recalled that "there was a huge noise like the roar of the ocean and the first tower began to slide down into itself and crumble…. People were screaming, people were crying, people were running. It was madness."[16] Another New Yorker who lived in a high-rise apartment one block away from the World Trade Center recalled that when the South Tower collapsed, she felt the ground vibrate under her feet before the cloud enveloped her building. "It was as though someone had just put a huge sock over our entire building. I mean, it went from that bright crisp morning to just total blackness, and then it felt like an earthquake. I thought I was dead because everything went black inside my apartment. My phone went out, the TV went out, and I was just sort of floating in the room, suspended there."[17] Another New Yorker who lived two blocks from the WTC remembered that the collapsing South Tower made "the most frightening sound I've ever heard, like a thousand helicopters on top of us. And a rumbling like the earth was about to split apart…. Our windows shattered. Smoke started to come in, debris started to come in, and we were completely in darkness."[18]

For firefighters, police officers, emergency workers, and evacuees who were moving around the base of the building, the fall of the South Tower was even more terrifying—and heartbreaking. Firefighter Maureen McArdle-Schulman recalled that in the moments just before the fall of the South Tower, her fire company received an assignment from a crisis response command center that had been set up at the entrance of a parking garage directly across from the WTC. "All of a sudden Tower Two started puffing and jumping," she remembered.

> I don't know how else to explain it. There was a ring of fire around the roof, and the building above the area that was burning just started jumping up and down. Then someone came over to the table and said, 'A firefighter just got hit by a jumper. We need last rites.' So a couple guys ran to the right, and we were still standing there staring at the building. It was mesmerizing. People were still jumping from Tower One, and Tower Two was puffing and jumping. Then someone yelled, 'Run!'
>
> If we'd had our forcible entry tools with us, we would have been in the building already. I came out of my trance, turned around, and started running. All I kept thinking as I was running into the garage was, *I'm going to get crushed....* [A few weeks later], I was talking to a guy from Engine 53 ... and he said to me, "You were at the World Trade Center, weren't you? Engine 91? You came pretty close." I said, "Yeah, I figure 30 or 40 seconds." He goes, "No. It was more like two or three seconds. When you were standing at the Command Center and someone yelled 'Run,' everybody at that table was killed. Everybody who ran to the right was killed. Everybody who ran to the left or into the garage was saved. It really was just a matter of a few seconds."[19]

Some of those who survived the collapse of the South Tower itself struggled to survive in the debris cloud—a dense mix of pulverized concrete, ash, smoke, and dust—that followed. One emergency worker recalled that she and several medical workers and civilians became trapped between the outside wall of a building and a pile of debris from the fallen tower. "We were suffocating. We were literally starting to die, because the air was depleting. No light, nothing. It was completely, completely black." They were only able

The South Tower of the World Trade Center began to collapse at 9:58 A.M.;
the North Tower, shown here, at 10:28 A.M.

to save themselves by breaking windows to get into the building, where they could gulp down fresh air. "We started throwing up, because we had to get whatever we had inhaled out of our lungs. We went out the back of the building and came around the other side. Everybody's eyes were burning, and ash and debris were still coming down. People were coming out of the rubble. It was like a graveyard. People were just sitting up, coming out of the dust, and asking for help."[20]

Meanwhile, civilians from the North Tower continued to pour out into streets that had been transformed into a completely alien landscape. "It felt like we were walking through a huge, dirty snow globe that had just been shaken," recalled one survivor. "The plaza was a minefield of twisted metal, covered by a layer of concrete dust several inches thick. I am grateful for that dust, because it means I didn't see any bodies."[21]

The Second Tower Falls

The North Tower continued to stand for another twenty-nine minutes after the fall of its sister tower, enabling thousands of civilians who had survived the initial attack to flee to safety. But the tower still contained an unknown number of civilians—and hundreds of firefighters—at 10:28:25 A.M., when it too collapsed with a deafening roar. "I heard all the crashing and the steel and [then] the street goes totally black," remembered Joseph Pfeifer, an FDNY battalion chief who was there when the second tower fell. "As a firefighter you kind of expect blackness inside of a burning building. But outside in broad daylight, you don't."[22] Visibility in the area remained extremely poor for hours afterward.

The continued presence of the FDNY personnel in the North Tower—despite the fact that most reachable civilians had already been evacuated—later became a major source of controversy in 9/11 investigations. Most of the firefighters in the North Tower "had been in striking distance of safety when the south building fell," observed Dwyer and Flynn.

> [But] few of the people inside the North Tower, even those who had heard the evacuation orders, knew that the other building had collapsed. Virtually none of them—apart from some police officers and those they encountered—realized that helicopter pilots were predicting the imminent failure of the one they were in. For no good reason, firefighters were cut

People covered in dust stagger through the streets of Manhattan in the aftermath of the collapse of the twin towers.

off from critical information…. Even so, when questions were raised in 2004 by the 9/11 Commission about the Fire Department's tactics, planning, and management, past and present city officials responded with outrage, demanding to know how anyone could challenge the bravery or sacrifices of the firefighters. No one had.[23]

The collapse of the twin towers triggered outpourings of grief from the victims' families, the residents of New York, and people all across the United States and around the world. As agencies launched a grim quest for survivors amid the ruins, the task of comforting a grief-stricken nation seemed almost insurmountable (see "Mourning Lost Firefighters and Police Officers in New York," p. 213).

One of the men charged with trying to meet that challenge was New York Mayor Rudy Giuliani, who had rushed to the WTC complex as soon as he heard about the attacks. He spent the next several hours on the streets of

Solemn Tasks at Ground Zero

In the days and weeks following the September 11 terrorist attacks on the World Trade Center, a massive search, recovery, and clean-up campaign was undertaken by city and federal authorities. Legions of officially designated rescue workers were aided in these rescue and recovery efforts by thousands of volunteers ranging from ironworkers and welders (whose skills in cutting through steel and other debris were highly prized) to ordinary men and women who just wanted to help in any way possible.

Initially, this titanic effort was focused on finding survivors beneath the wreckage. It quickly became clear, however, that the sheer scale of violence had been too much for anyone trapped in the towers to overcome. "After the buildings came down, there were no survivors," said paramedic Roger Smyth. "If the Towers hadn't have fallen, we'd have been busy, busy, busy. But they fell and they crushed everybody and that was it. That's the long and short of it. If 110 stories of concrete and steel is coming down, what's it gonna do to you? I mean, you're human."

Before long, the search at Ground Zero, the name given to the former site of the WTC, shifted to a quest to find bodies. When the bodies of firefighters or police officers were found, workers held special salutes and moments of silence as their remains were carried from the site. Workers at Ground Zero also discovered many other human remains and personal mementos such as wedding rings, wallets, and photographs during the clean-up. In many cases, these discoveries were of enormous comfort to grieving family members.

By May 2002, the main clean-up of the site had been completed and officials and residents of New York City had begun debating future uses of the Ground Zero site. This debate, however, was shadowed by numerous reports that Ground Zero workers had acquired a variety of health prob-

Manhattan, coordinating civilian evacuations, organizing searches for survivors, comforting survivors, and urging city residents to remain calm. Giuliani, however, acknowledged in an afternoon press conference that September 11 ranked as "one of the most difficult days in the history of the city. The

lems as a direct result of their labors at the site. Health experts asserted that they were not given sufficient respiratory safety protection against airborne toxins that had been generated by the violence of September 11. In 2010, for example, the *New England Journal of Medicine* published a major study indicating that lung function among firefighters and other rescue workers had been permanently impaired at Ground Zero.

Rescue workers and their medical allies have in some cases alleged that city officials and the Bush administration knowingly misled the public about the dangers of working and living around the Ground Zero site. Critics claim that when officials offered assurances that the air around Ground Zero was safe to breathe in the days and weeks after the 9/11 tragedy, they did so to minimize the economic impact of the attacks. City officials and the Bush White House denied these allegations, but thousands of Ground Zero workers sued the city of New York for negligence during cleanup operations. In November 2010 most of this litigation was settled in a $625 million agreement. One month later, the U.S. Congress passed a bill that provided financial compensation to Ground Zero survivors and workers with respiratory illnesses. The measure, which was signed into law by President Barack Obama in January 2011, provides $4.2 billion in medical care to those suffering from health problems related to the destruction of the World Trade Center.

Sources

Barry, Ellen. "Lost in the Dust of 9/11," *Los Angeles Times*, October 14, 2006.

Hensley, Scott. "Ground Zero Workers Suffered Permanent Lung Damage," Shots: National Public Radio (NPR) health blog, April 8, 2010. Retrieved from http://www.npr.org/blogs/health/2010/04/by_scott_hensley_with_the.html.

Interview with Roger Smyth. In DiMarco, Damon. *Tower Stories: An Oral History of 9/11.* Retrieved from http://www.towerstories.org/stories.php

Lioy, Paul J. *Dust: The Inside Story of Its Role in the September 11th Aftermath.* Landham, MD: Rowman and Littlefield, 2010.

tragedy that we are undergoing right now is something that we've had nightmares about. My heart goes out to all the innocent victims of this horrible and vicious act of terrorism.... The number of casualties," he said softly, "will be more than any of us can bear ultimately."[24]

Firefighters and emergency medical personnel rushed to the Pentagon on the morning of September 11, after it was struck by the hijacked American Airlines Flight 77.

Rescuing Victims of the Pentagon Attack

Less than 250 miles from Manhattan, meanwhile, a third terrorist strike triggered another frantic rescue effort. American Airlines Flight 77 had slammed into the southwest side of the Pentagon and exploded at 9:37:46 A.M.—fifty-one minutes after the first plane hit the World Trade Center and twenty-two minutes before the first tower fell. The suicide attack claimed the lives of 125 people inside the Pentagon—70 civilians and 55 military personnel. Another 106 Pentagon workers required hospitalization for burns, broken bones, and other injuries suffered in the strike (see "A Survivor Recalls the Attack on the Pentagon," p. 209). The crash itself left a gaping, smoking crater in the side of the Pentagon, which for decades had stood as a potent symbol of U.S. military might. Still, the devastation at the Pentagon received less media attention than the WTC attacks. "If it had happened on any other day," noted the 9/11 Commission, "the disaster at the Pentagon would be remembered as a singular challenge and an extraordinary national story."[25]

The emergency response to the terrorist attack on the Pentagon was greatly aided by the existence of a program called the Incident Command System. This management and coordination system enabled local, state, and federal agencies to effectively communicate with one another and craft a successful rescue strategy.[26] But the effective response also was attributed to Pentagon employees who bravely and selflessly came to the aid of injured civilians and military personnel. "One [memory] that really does stick in my mind is looking across the west lawn [of the Pentagon] and seeing the devastation but at the same time just seeing so many people dedicated to helping others," said Arlington County Fire Chief James H. Schwartz, who served as designated "incident commander" at the Pentagon tragedy.[27] The death toll at the Pentagon also would certainly have been higher had it not been for the heroism of local firefighting companies.

Finally, experts agree that the Pentagon death toll would have been much greater had the target been another high-rise building similar to the World Trade Center towers. Instead, the hijacked plane struck a comparatively low-slung building that had seen recent upgrades and renovations to better shield employees from possible attack. "The incident site was relatively easy to secure and contain," added the 9/11 Commission, "and there were no other buildings in the immediate area."[28] The damage was still horrific, but it was not nearly as overwhelming as the destruction in downtown Manhattan. That is a primary reason why no first responders were injured in the rescue and firefighting efforts at the Pentagon.

Notes

[1] Dwyer, Jim, and Kevin Flynn. *102 Minutes: The Untold Story of the Fight to Survive Inside the Twin Towers.* New York: Times Books, 2005, p. 243.

[2] Quoted in Fink, Mitchell, and Lois Mathias. *Never Forget: An Oral History of September 11, 2001.* New York: Regan Books, 2002, p. 33.

[3] Dwyer and Flynn, pp. 164-65.

[4] National Commission on Terrorist Attacks Upon the United States [The 9/11 Commission]. *The 9/11 Commission Report.* New York: Norton, 2004, p. 286.

[5] National Commission on Terrorist Attacks, p. 296.

[6] Quoted in Hagen, Susan, and Mary Carouba. *Women at Ground Zero: Stories of Courage and Compassion.* Indianapolis: Alpha, 2002, p. 5.

[7] National Commission on Terrorist Attacks, p. 297.

[8] National Commission on Terrorist Attacks, p. 291.

[9] National Commission on Terrorist Attacks, p. 287.

[10] National Commission on Terrorist Attacks, p. 289.

[11] National Commission on Terrorist Attacks, p. 293.

[12] Dwyer and Flynn, p. 95.

[13] Interview with Roger Smyth. In DiMarco, Damon. *Tower Stories: An Oral History of 9/11.* Retrieved from http://www.towerstories.org/stories.php.

[14] Quoted in Hagen and Carouba, pp. 58-59.

[15] National Commission on Terrorist Attacks, p. 295.

[16] Interview with David Rosenberger. In DiMarco, Damon. *Tower Stories: An Oral History of 9/11.* Retrieved from http://www.towerstories.org/stories.php

[17] Quoted in Fink and Mathias, p. 10.

[18] Fink and Mathias, p. 12.

[19] Quoted in Hagen and Carouba, pp. 14, 17.

[20] Hagen and Carouba, pp. 109, 112.

[21] Trevor, Greg. "A Survivor's Story." *Rutgers Magazine,* Fall 2006. Retrieved from http://urwebsrv.rutgers.edu/magazine/article/A%20Survivor%27s%20Story/49/p1.

[22] Quoted in Fink and Mathias, p. 21.

[23] Dwyer and Flynn, p. 252.

[24] Quoted in Powell, Michael. "In 9/11 Chaos, Giuliani Forged a Lasting Image." *New York Times,* September 21, 2007.

[25] National Commission on Terrorist Attacks, p. 311.

[26] National Commission on Terrorist Attacks, p. 314.

[27] Quoted in *Arlington Remembers: An Oral History of 9/11.* Arlington (VA) Public Library website, 2006. Retrieved from http://library.arlingtonva.us/departments/Libraries/history/LibrariesHistoryOralHist911Firefighters.aspx.

[28] National Commission on Terrorist Attacks, p. 315.

Chapter Six

INVESTIGATING 9/11

Everyone had an excuse [for not taking action against Osama Bin Laden]. It sounds terrible, but we used to say to each other that some people didn't get it—it was going to take body bags.[1]

—National Security Council counterterrorism
expert Roger Cressey

In the aftermath of the September 11 terrorist attacks on America, the nation entered into an extended period of mourning for all the men, women, and children who had lost their lives in the despicable attack. Meanwhile, expressions of sorrow and solidarity were offered to the United States by millions of people all around the world. Foreign countries also mourned the loss of their own citizens in the attacks, as people from more than ninety countries were among the victims of the World Trade Center tragedy.

Americans from every walk of life also expressed outrage at the perpetrators. They called for the U.S. government to bring Osama bin Laden and his al-Qaeda terrorist network to justice, and they demanded swift punishment for the Taliban rulers of Afghanistan and anyone else that had provided aid and comfort to bin Laden and his band of radical Islamists.

Amid these expressions of grief and anger, however, the American public and news media also directed a number of pointed questions at the Bush administration and the various intelligence and law enforcement agencies responsible for protecting the nation. Why had the terrorist plot succeeded? Did we know that bin Laden and al-Qaeda posed a mortal threat? Were signs of an impending attack ignored or not investigated thoroughly? Did other Islamic countries or groups in the Middle East help the terrorists? Why did security measures designed to protect commercial airplanes from hijackers fail? Were there other al-Qaeda terrorists still operating in the United States? In the months and years following 9/11, these questions became major subjects of interest—and political controversy—in America.

Investigators Identify Bin Laden as the Mastermind

The primary focus of early investigations into the September 11 terrorist attacks was identifying the culprit. This proved to be a simple matter, especially after authorities at Logan Airport in Boston found a travel bag that belonged to Mohamed Atta, the suicide pilot who flew American Airlines Flight 11 into the North Tower. The bag, which had not made it onto the flight, included instructions for carrying out mass murder and Atta's last will and testament. Since Atta was already known to investigators as an al-Qaeda terrorist—and since the materials mentioned bin Laden by name and echoed many of the terrorist leader's beliefs—investigators quickly turned their attention to al-Qaeda and the radical Islamic movement.

By the time September 11 had come to a close, Americans learned that bin Laden—a name most of them had not heard before that day—and his terrorist network were almost certainly the men responsible for the attack. They learned in subsequent weeks that the country's leading spy and antiterrorism agencies—the National Security Agency (NSA), the Central Intelligence Agency (CIA), and the Federal Bureau of Investigation (FBI)—had issued multiple warnings about the man over the previous few years. They even learned that as the September 11 attacks were unfolding, many individuals within the U.S. intelligence community expressed certainty that bin Laden was the man behind the attacks.

In the weeks and months that followed, investigators with the FBI and CIA pieced together virtually every aspect of the September 11 plot. Many aspects of the scheme were revealed through examination of telephone records, money transfers, flight reservation and visa records, and other data. Other elements of the puzzle were filled in through reviews of old intelligence, analysis of new spy reports, contributions from foreign intelligence agencies, and interrogations of captured al-Qaeda members.

President George W. Bush greets and offers words of encouragement to rescue workers at the site of the collapsed World Trade Center on September 14, 2001.

U.S. investigators were gratified that they were able to figure out how al-Qaeda had carried out the attacks. And as they learned the identities not only of the hijackers, but also of the planners, couriers, hosts, and financial supporters of the terrorists, U.S. intelligence and military officials were able to begin crafting strategies for destroying bin Laden and al-Qaeda. But their investigations also brought a troubling reality to light. "The attacks were hardly the bolt from the blue that they seemed in the early days," wrote Jim Dwyer and Kevin Flynn. "The hijackings were only the latest and most lethal link in a chain of events that stretched back years and had been foretold, in one fashion or another, during the months before them."[2]

Years of Unheeded Warnings

Some of these warnings about possible terrorist attacks on American soil had come from special Washington commissions. In early 1997, for example,

> *"The attacks were hardly the bolt from the blue that they seemed in the early days. The hijackings were only the latest and most lethal link in a chain of events that stretched back years and had been foretold, in one fashion or another, during the months before them."*

a commission on civil aviation security chaired by Vice President Al Gore had called for major new investments in airport security.[3] Most of these recommendations were not implemented. One year later, President Bill Clinton and Republican Speaker of the House Newt Gingrich approved the creation of a Pentagon-chartered panel to study national security issues that the United States would face in the twenty-first century. This commission was co-chaired by two retired senators with strong foreign policy and defense credentials, Republican Warren Rudman and Democrat Gary Hart.

The commission's findings, which were released in three stages from September 1999 to January 2001, became known as the Hart-Rudman Report. According to Hart-Rudman, the United States was in grave danger from terrorist attacks. "Americans will likely die on American soil, possibly in large numbers," reported panel members.[4] The commission also warned that despite the growing threat from adversaries who "will resort to forms and levels of violence shocking to our sensibilities," the United States had thus far made little effort to improve or better coordinate its defense and intelligence-gathering systems.[5]

In early 2001 the Hart-Rudman Commission urged Congress and the Bush administration to move swiftly on a series of antiterrorism measures. These recommendations ranged from increased emphasis on old-fashioned spy work (such as undercover infiltration of terrorist groups) to the creation of a Cabinet-level antiterrorism position that would be responsible for planning and coordinating homeland security across all federal agencies. Commission members hammered home this message in congressional testimony in the spring of 2001. "The prospect of mass casualty terrorism on American soil is growing sharply," asserted Hart in April 3 testimony. "Over the next quarter century, this danger will be one of the most difficult national security challenges facing the United States—and the one we are least prepared to address."[6]

As news stories about Washington's unresponsivenesss to these public warnings proliferated after 9/11, the American public expressed frustration and anger. Demands to know whether the attacks could have been prevented by the FBI, CIA, or FAA became even more widespread, as did criticism of the

Bush administration (mostly from Democrats) and the Clinton administration (mostly from Republicans). It was in this supercharged political environment that two new commissions were created. The first was a special investigative committee of Congress headed by Senator Bob Graham (D-Florida) and Representative Porter Goss (R-Florida). The second was the National Commission on Terrorist Attacks Upon the United States, better known as the 9/11 Commission.

The scope of the bipartisan Congressional investigation, formally known as the "Joint Inquiry into Intelligence Community Activities before and after the Terrorist Attacks of September 11, 2001," was limited from the outset. Graham, Goss, and other Congressional leaders indicated that they were less interested in playing the "blame game" than in identifying holes in America's security net and fixing them.[7] Nonetheless, the committee's final report criticized the FBI and CIA for their failure to "capitalize" on a wide range of intelligence they possessed about bin Laden's goals and activities: "The important point is that the Intelligence Community, for a variety of reasons, did not bring together and fully appreciate a range of information that could have greatly enhanced its chances of uncovering and preventing Usama Bin Ladin's plan to attack these United States on September 11, 2001."[8]

The committee's investigative team, which was headed by director Eleanor Hill and analyst Michael Jacobsen, also found evidence that Saudi Arabian citizens within the Saudi government had provided financial and logistical support to at least two of the hijackers. These two men—Nawaf al-Hazmi and Khalid al-Mihdhar—were the al-Qaeda operatives that had taken flying lessons in California in 2000 before being demoted from suicide pilots to strongmen. The committee wanted to include this classified information in their final report, but the Bush White House refused to declassify the information, citing national security concerns.[9]

Creation of the 9/11 Commission

The final report of the special congressional commission was released in December 2002, but its essential findings were widely known months earlier. Throughout the second half of 2002, the Bush administration and many members of Congress signaled that once the joint commission had completed its inquiry and released its report, the United States should devote all of its attention to the "war on terror" and a possible military showdown with

Former New Jersey governor Thomas Kean served as chair of the 9/11 Commission.

Iraq. By this time President Bush, Vice President Dick Cheney, and other top White House officials were all describing Saddam Hussein's hostile regime as a dire terrorist threat that possessed dangerous chemical and biological weapons.

Some Americans, however, were not satisfied that an adequate investigation of America's pre-9/11 security and intelligence failings was being carried out. Most notably, a coalition of organizations that had been founded by the families of victims of the September 11 attacks pressed the Bush administration and the Republican-led Congress to establish a fully independent commission to investigate America's failure to stop the attacks. These groups included Voices of September 11, Families of September 11, and four 9/11 widows—Kristen Breitweiser, Patty Casazza, Lorie Van Auken, and Mindy Kleinberg—known collectively as the Jersey Girls.

The groups were particularly relentless in demanding a thorough investigation that would not only recommend measures to improve the safety of Americans, but also identify individual officials who had failed to fulfill their national security obligations in the weeks, months, and years prior to 9/11. According to people like Stephen Push, whose wife had been aboard the airplane that hijackers crashed into the Pentagon, individuals *had* to be held accountable. "There are people, people in responsible positions, who failed us on 9/11," he explained. "They didn't just fail us once; 9/11 occurred because they were failing us over a long period of time. Some of these people are still in responsible positions in government. Perhaps they shouldn't be."[10]

The Bush White House and Republican leaders on Capitol Hill insisted that an independent commission was unnecessary, but the 9/11 families refused to give up. Their cause was also taken up by Democratic lawmakers and a handful of prominent Republicans, most notably Arizona Senator John McCain. Negative media coverage eventually convinced the administration to drop its opposition, and on November 27, 2002, Bush signed a bill creating the

National Commission on Terrorist Attacks Upon the United States. The legislation called for the commission to complete its work by May 2004, a mere eighteen months after its formation (in early 2004 the commission managed to obtain a sixty-day extension to this deadline, but this still put the probe on an extremely tight deadline). The bill also limited the commission's budget to only $3 million (in March 2003 the Bush administration agreed to extend another $9 million to the commission for operating expenses). By contrast, the independent commission that had investigated the 1986 explosion of the space shuttle *Challenger* had received $40 million to conduct its work.[11]

The Bush administration initially selected former secretary of state Henry Kissinger to lead the commission. Kissinger resigned, however, after the Jersey Girls and other critics questioned his business ties to clients in Saudi Arabia and other Middle Eastern countries. He was quickly replaced by two men who agreed to share the leadership role: retired Republican New Jersey governor Thomas Kean accepted the position of chairman and retired Democratic Congressman Lee Hamilton took the title of vice-chairman. The remaining eight positions on the 9/11 Commission were filled by four Republicans and four Democrats, none of whom were currently holding political office.

Carrying Out a Politically Explosive Investigation

Kean and Hamilton were keenly aware that their investigation had the potential to draw a lot of political fire in Washington. As journalist Philip Shenon observed, "Democrats saw an opening to blame Bush for September 11; Republicans responded by accusing Bill Clinton of having bungled opportunities throughout the 1990s to kill Osama bin Laden and his henchman, probably because Clinton had been so distracted by sexual scandals."[12] Kean and Hamilton thus urged the other members of the 9/11 Commission to fulfill their duties in a fashion that would be seen as impartial and fair. They repeated these instructions to the panel's investigative staff, which would tackle most of the actual research and writing for the report.

Unfortunately, the 9/11 Commission's work was hampered from the start by a variety of obstacles. For one, it had only a limited number of staff members to wade through mountains of intelligence reports and other materials contained in the files of the FBI, CIA, NSA, and Bush and Clinton administrations. These staff members also carried out their duties without benefit of telephones, computers, and other basic necessities for the first few months due to

Members of 9/11 Commission

The 9/11 Commission charged with investigating the September 11, 2001, terrorist attacks on U.S. soil consisted of ten members. Former Democratic Senator Max Cleland of Georgia was an original member of the panel, but in late 2003 he resigned and was replaced by Bob Kerrey. Following are brief biographical summaries of Kerrey and the other nine commission members who signed off on the final report.

Chair Thomas H. Kean served as Republican governor of New Jersey from 1982 to 1990, when he became president of Drew University. He retired from Drew in 2005.

Vice Chair Lee H. Hamilton served as Democratic representative of the Ninth District of Indiana in the U.S. House of Representatives from 1965 to 1999, when he retired from political office.

Richard Ben-Veniste is an attorney with close ties to the Democratic Party. He served as one of the prosecutors in the mid-1970s Watergate scandal that eventually forced the resignation of Republican president Richard M. Nixon from office.

Fred F. Fielding is a Republican lawyer who served as general counsel to both Ronald Reagan and George H.W. Bush during their presidencies.

bureaucratic red tape. In addition, many researchers had difficulty gaining the necessary security clearance to review classified government files.[13]

Meanwhile, the decision by Kean and Hamilton to appoint Philip D. Zelikow as executive director of the 9/11 Commission staff triggered fierce criticism from some 9/11 families, Democratic lawmakers, and media personalities. Zelikow was a highly regarded historian and political scientist at the University of Virginia. Detractors complained, however, that he had uncomfortably close ties to the Bush administration. These ties included a warm friendship with Condoleezza Rice, who was Bush's national security advisor. The two had even co-authored a book on Germany in 1995. Zelikow had also worked in the administration of the first President Bush, and in 2000-2001 he

Jamie S. Gorelick is an attorney who served as deputy attorney general in the Clinton administration's Justice Department.

Slade Gorton is a former Republican senator from the state of Washington. He served a total of three terms before retiring in 2001.

Bob Kerrey served the state of Nebraska as both a governor (1983-1987) and U.S. senator (1989-2001). In 2001 the Democrat left politics to accept the presidency of The New School, a university in New York City.

John F. Lehman served as secretary of the Navy in the Reagan administration before launching a successful investment banking career.

Timothy J. Roemer is a Democrat who served in the U.S. House of Representatives from 1991 to 2003, representing Indiana's Third District. In 2009 he became U.S. Ambassador to India.

James R. Thompson is a Republican who served as governor of Illinois from 1977 to 1991, winning re-election three times during that span.

Source

National Commission on Terrorist Attacks Upon the United States [The 9/11 Commission]. *The 9/11 Commission Report.* New York: Norton, 2004.

had served on the second President Bush's "transition team"—a group that provides for the orderly transfer of power from one presidential administration to the next. Finally, Rice had chosen Zelikow to write a national security strategy paper in 2002 that justified "preemptive war"—military action against a nation or group that was perceived to be a threat, even if the nation or group had not attacked the United States.[14] This doctrine became the cornerstone of the Bush administration's efforts in late 2002 and early 2003 to build support for a military invasion of Iraq.

Zelikow's critics worried that he would use his position to shield the Bush administration from criticism. Kleinberg pointed out that "as executive director, he has pretty much the most important job on the commission. He hires the staff, he sets the direction and focus, he chooses witnesses at the hearings."[15] After the 9/11 Commission investigation got underway in earnest, these fears did not subside. Instead, critics repeatedly accused Zelikow of directing the investigation in ways designed to minimize the political damage to Rice, Bush, and other administration officials. Midway through the investigation, a leading coalition of 9/11 family groups known as the 9/11 Family Steering Committee even called on Kean and Hamilton to fire Zelikow.

But Kean and Hamilton defended Zelikow's performance. They pointed out, for example, that he hired several investigators for the 9/11 Commission who had made their reputations working for Democrats. And even some of Zelikow's most prominent detractors, such as *New York Times* investigative reporter Philip Shenon, acknowledged that the director pushed the Bush White House very hard for access to sensitive government files. In April 2004, Kean and Hamilton appeared on *Meet the Press* and endorsed Zelikow's directorship. Kean described him as "one of the best experts on terrorism" in the entire country, and Hamilton called him a "serious scholar" who has "played it right down the line. I found no evidence of a conflict of interest of any kind."[16]

Public Hearings and Private Presidential Interviews

From its inception in November 2002 to the release of its final report on July 21, 2004, the 9/11 Commission and its research/investigative staff waded through more than 2.5 million pages of documents and other materials, including more than 1,000 hours of audiotapes.[17] The Commission was favorably impressed by the level of cooperation showed by some top intelligence agencies and officials during this period, such as FBI Director Robert Mueller (who had been in the position for only one week when the September 11 attacks took place). The Commission was much less pleased with people like CIA Director George Tenet, who displayed a hazy memory of many key events, meetings, and documents. Some members and staffers came to feel that Tenet was essentially an uncooperative witness.[18]

The 9/11 Commission also complained of noncooperation from agencies such as the Federal Aviation Administration (FAA) and the North American Aerospace Defense Command (NORAD), a U.S.-Canada military entity that has responsibility for preventing air attacks against the two nations. The 9/11 Commission became so frustrated by the attitude of these two agencies that it secured subpoenas against them. These court orders, which the 9/11 Com-

Longtime counterterrorism official Richard Clarke, seen here being sworn in to testify before the 9/11 Commission on March 24, 2004, became the Bush administration's fiercest critic after the 9/11 attacks.

mission used only as a last resort, forced agency officials to turn over evidence that they had refused to relinquish to the investigators.

The Commission also heard testimony from 160 witnesses during twelve public hearings that it held over the course of its investigation. Witnesses ranged from 9/11 widows and widowers and scholars on Middle Eastern politics to top officials in the Clinton and Bush administrations. Former president Bill Clinton and former vice president Al Gore also submitted to lengthy and separate private interviews with the commission in early April 2004. Three weeks later, on April 29, 2004, Bush and Cheney appeared together before the commission members for a private interview. This arrangement sparked an outcry from administration critics. They asserted that Cheney would feed answers to Bush and shield him from answering tough questions about events leading up to September 11. By all accounts, though, Cheney barely spoke in the interview, which lasted for more than three hours.[19]

Clarke and Rice Clash over the Bush Record

The most explosive and politically charged testimony of the entire investigation came in late March and early April of 2004. On March 24, 2004, a top counterterrorism official in both the Clinton and Bush administrations appeared before the panel and delivered a stunning public rebuke of the Bush administration's record on terrorism in the months prior to September 11.

Richard Clarke had served as the National Security Council's top counterterrorism advisor from 1998 until January 2003, when he resigned. In early 2004 Clarke stepped into the national spotlight with fierce criticisms of the Bush White House and its approach to terrorism in the months leading up to September 11. Many of these serious charges were contained in a 2004 memoir called *Against All Enemies.* According to this account, Clarke had warned the administration time and again that Osama bin Laden and al-Qaeda were poised to strike on U.S. soil, only to have his concerns discounted by Rice and other top intelligence officials. He also pointed out that when Bush took office, Rice downgraded his position—National Coordinator for Counterterrorism—in ways that reduced his access to the president and other top national security decision makers. Clarke further alleged that when he gave Rice a briefing about al-Qaeda in January 2001, "her facial expression gave me the impression she had never heard the term before."[20] He also rejected Bush administration claims that it had not received any proposals for combating al-Qaeda from the outgoing Clinton administration. Clarke pointed out that on January 25, 2001—less than a week after Bush's inauguration—he had sent his Delenda Plan to Rice for her consideration.

Finally, Clarke's memoir accused Bush and his top military advisors of manipulating public horror and anger about September 11 to launch an invasion of Iraq in 2003. "I think they wanted to believe that there was a connection [between Iraq and the 9/11 terrorist attacks], but the CIA was sitting there, the FBI was sitting there, I was sitting there saying we've looked at this issue for years. For years we've looked and there's just no connection" between Iraqi dictator Saddam Hussein and al-Qaeda, Clarke said in an interview with the *60 Minutes* news show that aired three days before his appearance before the 9/11 Commission. "I find it outrageous that the president is running for reelection on the grounds that he's done such great things about terrorism. He ignored it. He ignored terrorism for months when maybe we could have done something to stop 9/11. Maybe. We'll never know."[21]

Since Clarke's memoir and his *60 Minutes* appearance had been extensively covered and debated in American news outlets, his nationally televised appearance before the 9/11 Commission was highly anticipated. His testimony, delivered under oath, was dramatic from the outset. Clark began by issuing a personal apology to all "the loved ones of the victims of 9/11…. Your government failed you. Those entrusted with protecting you failed you. And I failed you. We tried hard, but that doesn't matter because we failed. And for that failure, I would ask—once all the facts are out—for your understanding and for your forgiveness."[22] According to the *Washington Post,* these remarks elicited "sobs and cheers from the front rows of the packed hearing room, which were filled with relatives of victims of the terrorist attacks."[23] Clarke spent the rest of the afternoon repeating his accusations that the Bush administration did not treat terrorism as an "urgent" national security issue. Democratic members of the commission were generally friendly and respectful in their questioning of the former counterterrorism "czar." The panel's Republicans, meanwhile, challenged Clarke's account of events and implied that the recent publication of his memoir gave him a financial motivation to level sensational charges against the Bush White House (see "Richard Clarke's Explosive Testimony Before the 9/11 Commission," p. 226).

"Your government failed you," said Richard Clarke in an apology to the families of 9/11 victims. "Those entrusted with protecting you failed you. And I failed you. We tried hard, but that doesn't matter because we failed."

Clarke's remarks posed a major political threat to the Bush administration. The White House, Republican lawmakers, and conservative media outlets all pushed back hard against Clarke's story. They noted that prior to resigning in 2003, Clarke had actually defended the Bush administration's record on terrorism to journalists. They also asserted that just because Clarke was not present for discussions about al-Qaeda and Islamic terrorism, it did not mean that such meetings were not taking place. It simply meant that he was "out of the loop." Some of Clarke's critics also contended that he exaggerated how much he warned about al-Qaeda in the months leading up to 9/11. This charge, however, was fully refuted by the 9/11 Commission's final

National Security Advisor Condoleezza Rice strongly defended the Bush administration during her testimony before the 9/11 Commission.

report, which documented numerous instances in which Clarke warned the administration and intelligence agencies that Islamic terrorists posed an immediate and serious threat to national security.

Rice took a lead role in defending the Bush national security team against Clarke's attacks, in large part because she herself had been the target of so many of his criticisms. On March 22, 2004, the *Washington Post* ran a guest editorial from Rice, who insisted that the Bush administration had been vigilant against terrorists from the president's first days in office (see "Condoleezza Rice Defends the Bush Administration's Record on Terrorism," p. 222). She also gave interviews to ABC, CBS, NBC, CNN, and Fox rebutting Clark's claims. Then, on April 8, 2004, Rice gave public testimony under oath before the 9/11 Commission. Many White House officials did not want Rice to testify because they thought it eroded the principle of "executive privilege"—the idea that to be effective and successful, American presidents must be able to speak freely with close advisors without worrying about whether their conversations will ever be revealed. But Rice badly wanted to testify, and she convinced Bush to approve her appearance.

In her testimony, Rice claimed that when the Islamic terrorists struck the United States on September 11, 2001, the Bush administration had been in the midst of developing what she called "a new and comprehensive strategy to try and eliminate the al-Qaeda network. President Bush understood the threat, and he understood its importance. He made clear to us that he did not want to respond to al-Qaeda one attack at a time."[24] She also insisted under skeptical questioning from Democratic panel members that the warnings of an attack prior to September 11 were too vague for the CIA, the FBI, or any other agency to act on. "By the end of the hearing," wrote Shenon, "it seemed a draw. Democrats could see in it what they wanted—Rice as duplicitous, eager to hide the truth about her performance, and Bush's, before 9/11. Republicans saw her as heroic, valiantly defending the president, giving as good as she got from ... Democratic 'bullies.'"[25]

The Commission Releases Its Report

The Clarke-Rice showdown on Capitol Hill was the most high-profile example of several politically charged tempests that erupted in the weeks leading up to the July release of the 9/11 Commission's final report. When the report was published, however, much—though not all—of the criticism subsided. Many observers of different political persuasions found the panel's security reform recommendations to be sensible ones. These unanimous recommendations included reforming FBI and CIA operations and information-sharing, changing defense-related procedures for presidential transitions, and creating a national intelligence director with cabinet-level authority to oversee the nation's array of spy agencies and intelligence groups (on February 17, 2005, Bush named diplomat John Negroponte to serve as the nation's first DNI—director of national intelligence).

Criticism of the final report was also muted because the commission found fault with *every* institution that it investigated, from the FBI, CIA, FAA, and other federal agencies to the Clinton and Bush administrations (see "The 9/11 Commission Issues Its Final Report," p. 233). Since no one was spared, neither Democrats nor Republicans could claim that the report was a partisan attack. Afterwards, Hamilton admitted that many Americans were unhappy with the fact that the 9/11 Commission tried to avoid "calling out" specific people. The commission vice-chair argued, however, that the panel really had no choice. "I get a lot of nasty comments ... because people wanted us to point the finger at Bill Clinton or George Bush or Dick Clarke or Condi Rice," he said. "But if we had begun coming up with a list of bad actors, it would have blown the commission apart and it would have blown any credibility we had. If we had a paragraph saying Condi Rice really screwed up, that's all *The New York Times* would have written about. That level of personal accountability would have been a total dead end—there's no end to it."[26]

On the whole, commission members and staff expressed satisfaction about the report and its findings. Several commission members and investigators did admit, however, that they wished they had been given more time. They expressed particular regret that many intelligence files contained in the archives of the National Security Agency (NSA) were never examined due to time constraints.[27]

Notes

[1] Quoted in Mayer, Jane. *The Dark Side: The Inside Story of How the War on Terror Turned into a War on American Ideals.* New York: Doubleday, 2008, p. 24.

[2] Dwyer, Jim, and Kevin Flynn. *102 Minutes: The Untold Story of the Fight to Survive Inside the Twin Towers.* New York: Times Books, 2005, p. 249.

[3] Miller, John J., and Michael Stone, with Chris Mitchell. *The Cell: Inside the 9/11 Plot, and Why the FBI and CIA Failed to Stop It.* New York: Hyperion, 2002, p. 333.

[4] United States Commission on National Security/21st Century. *New World Coming: American Security in the Twenty-First Century,* September 15, 1999, p. 7.

[5] United States Commission on National Security/21st Century, p. 6.

[6] Quoted in Tapper, Jake. "We Predicted It," *Salon.com,* September 12, 2001. Retrieved from http://www.salon.com/news/politics/feature/2001/09/12/bush.

[7] Leiby, Richard. "A Cloak but No Dagger," *Washington Post*, May 18, 2002. Retrieved from http://www.washingtonpost.com/ac2/wp-dyn?pagename=article&node=&contentId=A36091-2002May17.

[8] Joint Inquiry into Intelligence Community Activities before and after the Terrorist Attacks of September 11, 2001. "Abridged Findings and Conclusions," *Report of the Joint Inquiry into Intelligence Community Activities before and after the Terrorist Attacks of September 11, 2001.* Washington, DC: Government Printing Office, 2002.

[9] Graham, Bob. *Intelligence Matters: The CIA, the FBI, Saudi Arabia, and the Failure of America's War on Terror.* New York: Random House, 2004, pp. 103-21, 159-77.

[10] Quoted in Shenon, Philip. *The Commission: The Uncensored History of the 9/11 Investigation.* New York: Twelve, 2008, p. 103.

[11] Shenon, p. 31.

[12] Shenon, p. 19.

[13] Shenon, pp. 98, 105.

[14] Shenon, pp. 38-43.

[15] Quoted in Conason, Joe. "The Widows Are Watching," *Salon.com,* April 2, 2004. Retrieved from http://www.salon.com/news/opinion/joe_conason/2004/04/02/widows.

[16] Transcript of April 4 Interview with Tim Russert, *Meet the Press,* April 4, 2004. Retrieved from http://www.msnbc.msn.com/id/4663767/ns/meet_the_press/t/transcript-april/.

[17] National Commission on Terrorist Attacks Upon the United States [The 9/11 Commission]. *The 9/11 Commission Report.* New York: Norton, 2004, p. 449.

[18] Shenon, p. 403.

[19] Kean, Thomas H, and Lee H. Hamilton, with Benjamin Rhodes. *Without Precedent: The Inside Story of the 9/11 Commission.* New York: Knopf, 2006, pp. 205-11.

[20] Clarke, Richard A. *Against All Enemies: Inside America's War on Terror.* New York: Free Press, 2004, p. 229.

[21] "Richard Clarke Speaks Out," *60 Minutes,* CBS News, March 21, 2004. Retrieved from http://www.cbsnews.com/video/watch/?id=607658n.

[22] Quoted in "Transcript: Wednesday's 9/11 Commission Hearings." *Washington Post,* March 24, 2004. Retrieved from http://www.washingtonpost.com/wp-dyn/articles/A20349-2004Mar24.html.

[23] Eggen, Dan, and Walter Pincus. "Ex-Aide Recounts Terror Warnings," *Washington Post,* March 25, 2004, p. A1.

[24] Rice, Condoleezza. Testimony at Ninth Public Hearing, National Commission on Terrorist Attacks Upon the United States, April 8, 2004. Retrieved from http://govinfo.library.unt.edu/911/archive/hearing9/9-11Commission_Hearing_2004-04-08.htm.

[25] Shenon, pp. 301-02.

[26] Quoted in Shenon, p. 405.

[27] Shenon, p. 373.

Chapter Seven

MISSED CLUES
AND OPPORTUNITIES

The domestic agencies never mobilized in response to the
threat. They did not have direction, and did not have a plan
to institute. The borders were not hardened. Transportation
systems were not fortified. Electronic surveillance was not
targeted against a domestic threat.... The terrorists exploited
deep institutional failings within our government.

—The 9/11 Commission, 2004

From the outset of its investigation, the 9/11 Commission focused on identifying and explaining the failures and flaws of America's intelligence and antiterrorism networks that were supposed to keep events like September 11 from ever happening. Many of the criticisms detailed by the commission in its final report were echoed in a wide variety of other sources, from investigative reports by journalists to interviews with lawmakers, intelligence officials, and individual American spies and intelligence officials who made valiant attempts to uncover and stop the 9/11 plot before it could be carried out.

Intelligence Failures of the FBI

According to the 9/11 Commission and many other observers, the FBI's failure to identify and stop the September 11 terrorist plot stemmed from many factors. One problem was that even though the FBI was America's leading agency for intelligence gathering and crime fighting within U.S. borders, it made virtually no investments in new computer and communications technology during the 1990s and early 2000s. "In 2003, nearly a generation after electronic mail had become routine in American businesses and on college campuses and almost everywhere else, the FBI had no functioning internal e-mail system or easy employee access on the Internet," reported Shenon. "There was no searchable computer database for most FBI case files. FBI agents might go home at night to find their teenagers playing on their laptops, swapping e-mail messages with school friends, or trading MP3 files. But when the agents went back to work at the bureau the next morning, they were returned to the electronic dark ages."[1]

The commission also found that the FBI failed to allocate sufficient resources to antiterrorism activities throughout the directorship of Louis Freeh, who led the bureau from September 1993 to June 2001. Of the 12,500 special agents working in the FBI, only 50 or so worked in the realm of counterterrorism on September 11.[2] This inattention to terrorist activities was felt in a variety of ways. For example, the FBI had a perpetual shortage of translators of Arabic and other common languages of terrorist groups. As a result, the FBI had accumulated a backlog of 100,000 hours of untranslated audiotapes of intercepted communications by suspected terrorists by September 11.[3] "FBI leadership seemed unwilling to shift resources to terrorism from other areas such as violent crime and drug enforcement," concluded the final report.[4]

Freeh did create a division known as I-49 devoted to uncovering terrorist activity in the United States. But the division was perpetually underfunded and unappreciated, even though its work was strongly supported by John O'Neill, who led the FBI's prestigious New York field office. FBI counterterrorism efforts were also hampered by misinterpretation and misunderstanding of procedures for information-sharing across internal divisions. These barriers needlessly reduced the flow of terrorism-related information within the bureau itself.[5]

Problems with information-sharing also extended to other agencies. For decades the FBI had been locked in a nasty rivalry with the CIA for "top dog" status in U.S. intelligence. As a result of this longstanding animosity, the agencies frequently hoarded valuable intelligence information from one another. In many cases, they wasted valuable time and resources to obtain information that the other agency already had in its possession. In Madagascar, for instance, FBI agents with the I-49 program built an antenna aimed at intercepting telephone calls of 9/11 mastermind Khaled Sheikh Mohammed, but the CIA already had this information.[6] Relations were so bad between the agencies that one effort to exchange agents—and thus foster greater intera-

John O'Neill and September 11

In the years and months leading up to the 9/11 attacks on America, FBI agent John O'Neill was among the small number of federal officials who recognized just how deadly Osama bin Laden might be. Born in Atlantic City, New Jersey, in 1952, O'Neill became a special agent of the FBI in July 1976. He steadily moved up through the ranks, and in 1995 he was named to head the bureau's counterterrorism section in New York City. O'Neill quickly focused in on al-Qaeda. By late 1996 he was the FBI's most prominent critic of U.S. counterterrorism policies, which he felt were inadequate to meet the threat posed by bin Laden.

O'Neill played a lead role in the investigations of several al-Qaeda bombings that took place overseas in the late 1990s, including terrorist attacks on U.S. embassies or military personnel in Kenya, Tanzania, and Yemen. During this same time, however, his career in the FBI stalled out. After being passed over for promotion several times, O'Neill decided to retire. He accepted a job as head of security at the World Trade Center. His first day was August 23, 2001. Nineteen days later, O'Neill was sitting in his office on the 34th floor of the North Tower when al-Qaeda hijackers crashed American Airlines Flight 11 into the building. O'Neill was in the tower participating in the rescue effort when the building collapsed. The FBI's leading expert on al-Qaeda thus became a victim of its most brutal and evil terrorist act.

Sources

"The Man Who Knew." PBS Frontline, 2002. Retrieved from http://www.pbs.org /wgbh/pages/frontline/shows/knew/.

Wright, Lawrence. *The Looming Tower: Al-Qaeda and the Road to 9/11*. New York: Vintage Books, 2006.

gency cooperation—was only half-jokingly referred to as a "hostage exchange program."[7] The hostility was particularly strong between O'Neill, the FBI's top counterterrorism official, and his CIA counterpart, Michael Scheuer. Both O'Neill and Scheuer relentlessly pushed their agencies to pay more attention to bin Laden and his minions. But the two men loathed and distrusted one

Less than a month before the 9/11 attacks, Zacarias Moussaoui was arrested in Minnesota by FBI agents. But urgent requests from the Minnesota office to open a full-scale investigation of Moussaoui were turned down by FBI officials in Washington.

another so much that they never found a way to collaborate on counterterrorism efforts.

The FBI has also been heavily criticized for its lack of response to two warnings issued by bureau field agents (agents who work at local offices scattered around the country) in the months prior to 9/11. On July 10, 2001, an FBI agent based in Phoenix, Arizona, named Kenneth Williams sent an urgent memo to FBI supervisors. Williams warned that he had studied intelligence indicating that Osama bin Laden might be sending followers to the United States for flight school training. He urged his superiors to approach all the flight schools in the country and investigate whether any students from Arabic backgrounds posed a national security risk. But Williams's so-called "Phoenix memo" quickly faded from sight without ever reaching top officials. Many observers believe that if Williams's warning had been taken more seriously, the 9/11 plot might have been uncovered. Some FBI agents, however, believe that this accusation is unfair.

"You can't find the hijackers with the Phoenix memo," insisted one former FBI counterterrorism chief. "If we wanted to look at all Arabs at schools in California, Arizona, and Florida? There are 1,625 flight schools, 82,000 flight instructors, and 69,000 ground instructors [in the country to interview]. There's just no way that would have happened."[8]

The other warning came from agents at a Minneapolis FBI field office who had taken an Islamic radical named Zacarias Moussaoui into custody. The agents had been tipped off by a local flight school that Moussaoui might be a potential hijacker. On August 16, 2001, Moussaoui was arrested for remaining in the United States with an expired visa. The Minneapolis agents subsequently asked FBI headquarters for permission to obtain a criminal search warrant to search Moussaoui's laptop computer. The request was turned down, though, to the great frustration of the Minneapolis office. When the supervisor of the Minneapolis office tried to get headquarters to reconsider, he was told he was trying to get people "spun up." The supervisor angrily responded that he was "trying to keep someone from taking a plane and crashing into the World Trade Center."[9] This argument was dismissed at headquarters, and Moussaoui's laptop was left untouched until after the terrorist attacks. Once it was finally examined, investigators found strong evidence of terrorist activity and links with al-Qaeda. The 9/11 Commission report noted that a high-priority investigation of these links "might have brought investigators to the core of the 9/11 plot" before it could be carried out.[10]

Finally, the FBI's failure to detect or stop the 9/11 attacks has been blamed to some degree on the U.S. Justice Department, which is the parent organization for the FBI and other law enforcement agencies such as the Drug Enforcement Agency (DEA) and the Immigration and Naturalization Service (INS). The head of the U.S. Justice Department is the attorney general, who in 2001 was John Ashcroft. Critics assert that Ashcroft and other top officials did not make terrorism a high priority for the FBI and other agencies. They point out that when Ashcroft released a list of his top Justice Department law enforcement priorities in May 2001, terrorism was not on it.[11] Acting FBI Director Thomas Pickard also told the 9/11 Commission that after he delivered two briefings to Ashcroft about the al-Qaeda threat, the attorney general told him he did not want to hear any more about the subject.[12] Ashcroft later denied this charge in sworn testimony before the 9/11 Commission. Detractors have also pointed out that on September 10, 2001—one day before bin Laden struck—Ashcroft rejected a proposed $58 million increase in FBI counterterrorism funding for the next year's budget.

Security Failures of the CIA

Unlike the FBI, the Central Intelligence Agency had shown throughout the late 1990s and early 2000s that Islamic terrorism was a top agency priority. After the 1998 bombings of two U.S. embassies in Africa, CIA Director George Tenet had even issued an agency-wide memo that explicitly identified al-Qaeda as one of the country's most dangerous enemies. The title of this memo was "We Are at War." The CIA also took this message to President Clinton, President Bush, Congress, and other spy agencies. "There were many people in the agency, Tenet among them, who saw al-Qaeda and other terrorist groups as the most serious threat of the new century," wrote Shenon. "A review of Tenet's congressional testimony and his speeches showed that he had warned, time after time before September 11, about bin Laden's inten-

CIA analyst Michael Scheuer recognized that al-Qaeda posed a serious threat to U.S. security.

tions, including the possibility that he would acquire weapons of mass destruction.... CIA had also repeatedly warned against just the sort of terrorist attack that had taken place on 9/11—airplanes as weapons."[13] In 1996 the CIA even established a special department known as Alec Station that was devoted exclusively to Osama bin Laden. The supervisor of this department was Scheuer, who became just as well known as Richard Clarke and John O'Neill for issuing dark warnings about al-Qaeda's desire to shed American blood on American soil.

In other respects, though, the CIA's efforts to combat terrorism were hampered by many of the same internal problems that afflicted the FBI. According to the 9/11 Commission and numerous works of investigative journalism, the CIA failed to allocate sufficient resources to counterterrorism work. It accumulated huge backlogs of intelligence material that needed translation and failed to develop a new generation of "streetwise spies" capable of infiltrating al-Qaeda and other terrorist groups.[14] "In 1995, the low point for recruitment, only twenty-five trainees became clandestine officers," according to scholar Amy B. Zegart. "By the late 1990s, the [CIA] . . had cut by nearly one-third the number of its personnel deployed overseas."[15] In fairness to the CIA, this problem was made worse by Congress, which made major cuts in national security expenditures after the end of the Cold War in 1991.

But there was no excuse for the way that many senior CIA officials treated Scheuer and his mostly young, female staff of analysts at Alec Station. When they warned that intelligence indicated that bin Laden might be planning a major terrorist attack in America, some older male administrators dismissed Scheuer and his "girls" as hysterical alarmists. This attitude infuriated Scheuer, who knew firsthand how much these women sacrificed to try to keep America safe. "We had marriages break up, we had people who delayed operations they needed," he said. "People were working sixteen, seventeen hours a day, some of them seven days a week for years."[16]

CIA divisions also refused to share potentially valuable intelligence with the FBI, foreign intelligence services—and even other CIA divisions—on numerous occasions. The 9/11 Commission admitted that there were instances in which the departments were genuinely worried about the wisdom of information sharing. "Information was compartmented in order to protect it against exposure to skilled and technologically sophisticated adversaries. There were therefore numerous restrictions on handling information and a deep suspicion about sending information over newfangled electronic systems, like email, to other agencies of the U.S. government."[17] In many cases, however, the CIA refused to give the FBI important counterterrorism intelligence because of their interagency rivalry.

On at least one occasion, the interagency pettiness between the FBI and CIA torpedoed one of America's prime opportunities to uncover the September 11 plot before it could take place. In the spring of 2000, the CIA learned that a known al-Qaeda operative, Nawaf al-Hazmi, had entered the United States and settled in San Diego, California. CIA analysts also strongly suspected that an al-Qaeda accomplice, Khalid al-Mihdhar, was at large in the United States. Over the next several months, Al-Hazmi and al-Mihdhar took flight lessons, flunked out, and were reassigned by bin Laden to serve as strongmen for the September 11 hijackings.

All of their movements took place in the United States, where the FBI had full legal authority to investigate these men—and quite possibly uncover the hijacking plot of which they were a part. Since the CIA never informed the bureau about the presence of the two men, however, their activities, travels, and communications were never monitored. Whether the information was withheld intentionally or by mistake, the CIA did not inform the FBI, the State Department, and other agencies about the presence of al-Hazmi and al-Mihdhar in the United States until August 13, 2001, less than a month before the attacks. By that time, acknowledged the CIA, the whereabouts of the two men was unknown.

Security Problems in the FAA

Next to the CIA and FBI, the federal agency that received the most criticism in the wake of 9/11 was the Federal Aviation Administration (FAA). The

FAA bears direct responsibility for security at airports and in airplanes across the country. But the 9/11 Commission found top FAA officials to be shockingly ignorant and unconcerned about the threat of terrorism. Early in its investigation, the commission asked to look at the FAA's official "no-fly" watch list of potential terrorists who are not permitted to board aircraft entering, traveling in, or leaving United States airspace. The FAA list had fewer than twenty names on it on September 11, 2001. By contrast, the U.S. State Department maintained its own TIPOFF watch list of possible terrorists. On September 11, 2001, the TIPOFF list included 61,000 names—including those of Nawaf al-Hasmi and Khalid al-Mindhar. TIPOFF was widely viewed as the U.S. government's most authoritative terrorist watch list, and the State Department urged other agencies to use it. But the FAA's chief of civil aviation security in 2001 admitted to the 9/11 Commission that he did not even know that the TIPOFF list existed until after the terrorists struck.[18]

> *"Each layer [of FAA security] relevant to hijackings—intelligence, passenger prescreening, checkpoint screening, and onboard security—was seriously flawed prior to 9/11," according to the 9/11 Commission.*

Investigators were also stunned by the ease with which the knife-wielding hijackers were able to board the planes. In a number of cases, hijackers set off metal detectors while trying to board their planes on the morning of September 11. In each instance, however, security personnel gave them only a cursory inspection before waving them through to their waiting planes. Even if the knives they were carrying had been detected, however, they might have been able to board with the weapons. Incredibly, pre-9/11 FAA regulations allowed for passengers to carry knives with blades under four inches in length.

The 9/11 Commission acknowledged that the FAA faced a lot of pressure from for-profit commercial airlines and airports not to impose overly expensive security procedures and technology. But the panel kept returning to the basic fact that the FAA's number one priority was supposed to be the safety of America's air transportation system, and that the layers of aviation security rules it had in place had failed miserably. "Each layer relevant to hijackings—intelligence, passenger prescreening, checkpoint screening, and onboard security—was seriously flawed prior to 9/11," wrote the commission. "Taken together, they did not stop any of the 9/11 hijackers from getting on board four different aircraft at three different airports."[19]

The Clinton White House and al-Qaeda

According to the 9/11 Commission's final report and the impressions of many analysts, the United States became very attentive to the threat posed by Osama bin Laden and al-Qaeda during the presidency of Bill Clinton, which lasted from January 1993 to January 2001. "President Clinton was deeply concerned about bin Laden," wrote the panel. "Clinton was a voracious reader of intelligence … [and he] spoke of terrorism in numerous public statements.… President Clinton repeatedly linked terrorist groups and WMD [weapons of mass destruction] as transnational threats for the new global era."[20]

Bin Laden first caught the attention of the administration during his mid-1990s stay in Sudan. From that point forward he and the terrorist network he was crafting became an ever greater focus of the U.S. intelligence community and the Clinton White House. Bin Laden's high profile was due in large part to the efforts of Richard Clarke, George Tenet, and Sandy Berger, Clinton's national security advisor. It was Berger, in fact, who responded to bin Laden's 1998 fatwa against the United States by arranging Clarke's inclusion in cabinet-level intelligence briefings and meetings about counterterrorism policies.

By late 1997 the CIA's one-year-old Alec Station had developed a significant store of intelligence about bin Laden and his desire to commit mass murder against the United States and Israel. According to Scheuer, who ran Alec Station, "we had more information on al-Qaeda [by 1997] than we had on terrorist groups we had been collecting against for twenty years."[21] The CIA used this data to craft a plan to neutralize bin Laden. The scheme, which was thoroughly rehearsed on several occasions in late 1997 and early 1998, called for selected Afghan tribesmen to capture the terrorist leader and deliver him to the CIA for eventual trial.

The plan, though, was never presented to Clinton for final approval.[22] Instead it was quietly shelved—a decision that has been laid primarily at the feet of military officials and senior CIA administrators who thought that the scheme was too risky. Objections included possible heavy civilian casualties and the loss of American soldiers. Another commonly expressed concern was that Arab nations and other parts of the world would react negatively if bin Laden—who had not yet been convicted of any terrorist acts—were killed in the operation. The plan was thus put aside, but no equivalent plan took its place."No capture plan before 9/11 ever again attained the same level of detail and preparation," stated the 9/11 Commission. "The tribals' reported readi-

President Bill Clinton (far right) meets with his foreign policy team in September 1998. Sitting on the opposite side of the table from Clinton, left to right, are CIA Director George Tenet, Secretary of State Madeleine Albright, National Security Advisor Sandy Berger, Secretary of Defense William Cohen, and Chairman of the Joint Chiefs of Staff General Hugh Shelton.

ness to act diminished. And bin Laden's security precautions and defenses became more elaborate and formidable."[23]

Still, 9/11 investigators, journalists, and government officials agree that other plans were crafted to capture or kill bin Laden or otherwise disrupt al-Qaeda during the final years of the Clinton administration. In most cases, however, these operations—such as an August 1998 "Delenda Plan" crafted by Clarke that called for a sustained campaign of missile strikes against al-Qaeda targets—would be delayed or set aside. Conservative media commentators, Republicans, and other critics contend that this inaction stemmed from White House fears of another incident like the 1993 military operation in Somalia that claimed eighteen U.S. lives. Scheuer shared these feelings. He declared that "moral cowardice" on the part of Clinton and Clarke kept the United States from taking out bin Laden.[24]

Clinton administration officials and their supporters flatly rejected this accusation. They argued that Secretary of Defense William Cohen and military leaders at the Pentagon were extremely reluctant to carry out covert operations against bin Laden. The 9/11 Commission provided some confirmation of this view, stating that "at no point before 9/11 was the Department of Defense fully engaged in the mission of countering al-Qaeda.... Within Defense both Secretary Cohen and Secretary Rumsfeld [in the Bush administration] gave their principal attention to other challenges."[25]

Members of the Clinton White House also insisted that Tenet and the CIA frequently pulled the plug on operations themselves. "Anytime anybody [in the CIA] ever brought a proposal to do anything [against bin Laden or al-Qaeda] to the White House, we approved it," said Clarke. "CIA would reject them in-house because in some cases the information was wrong or they thought it was too risky, or whatever."[26] They also point out that under Clinton's orders, the United States did carry out a missile strike against al-Qaeda positions in Afghanistan in retaliation for the 1998 bombings of two U.S. embassies in Africa. Defenders of the administration's counterterrorism record acknowledge that while the missile strikes failed to kill bin Laden, they showed that Clinton at least tried to do so. Investigators with the commission also disclosed that the Clinton administration signed a series of secret orders that authorized the killing of bin Laden by foreign groups allied with the CIA.[27]

It has been more difficult, however, for members of the Clinton administration and their supporters to defend some of the performance problems that flared up in the FBI and the CIA during the 1990s. Detractors point out, for example, that Clinton and Attorney General Janet Reno both had the authority to demand new investments in computers and other communications technology in the FBI, which fell further behind in these areas with each passing day.

The Bush White House and al-Qaeda

The Bush administration's record on counterterrorism has also been clouded by political gamesmanship and posturing. Both defenders and critics of the Bush White House and its stance toward bin Laden and al-Qaeda have plenty of material from which to draw.

Supporters of the Bush White House frequently note that President Bush requested significant increases in the counterterrorism budgets for both the CIA and the FBI in his first year in office. Moreover, both the Pentagon and the State Department operated under high alert levels throughout the spring and summer of 2001, when the CIA and FBI both experienced a surge in vague but frightening intelligence about possible terrorist attacks on U.S. soil.

The president also expressed dissatisfaction with the counterterrorism policies he inherited from the Clinton administration. In Bush's view, bin Laden and his terrorist network needed to be dealt with more aggressively. "I'm tired of swatting at flies," he stated in a March 2001 meeting with Rice and other top national security officials. "I'm tired of playing defense... I want to take the fight to the terrorists."[28] These convictions reportedly prompted Rice and various intelligence officials in the CIA, FBI, State Department, and Pentagon to launch a complete reassessment of U.S. counterterrorism strategy and goals. Many of these officials suggested that the only problem with this approach was that a new plan had not yet been finalized and implemented before September 11. "We weren't going fast enough," admitted Richard Armitage, who served as deputy secretary of state during the first five years of the Bush administration.[29]

Critics, however, have asserted that Bush, Rice, Vice President Dick Cheney, and other important administration officials failed to treat terrorism with the necessary urgency. Former Joint Chiefs of Staff chairman Hugh Shelton told the 9/11 Commission, for example, that the Bush administration pushed terrorism "farther to the back burner" than it had been under President Clinton.[30]

The heaviest criticism of the Bush administration's pre-9/11 performance focused on whether Bush, Cheney, Rice, and other high-level White House figures took warnings of impending terrorist attacks as seriously as they should have. Many of the most strongly worded warnings came from Richard Clarke, who Rice had effectively demoted in early 2001 so that he no longer attended cabinet-level meetings on terrorism issues. According to the 9/11 Commission and Clarke himself, the counterterrorism czar tried to compensate for his diminished access by penning a blizzard of memos to Rice and other key decision makers. Clarke repeatedly warned that Americans were going to suffer mightily at al-Qaeda's hands in the near future if the Bush White House did not get "serious" about bin Laden.[31] Clarke's mounting frustration could be seen in several of the memos, including a May 29 letter to Rice: "When these attacks occur, as they likely will, we will wonder what more we could have done to stop them."[32]

Warnings about the murderous intentions of al-Qaeda were also frequently included in the president's daily briefing throughout 2001. This CIA

President George Bush (center), Vice President Dick Cheney, and National Security Advisor Condoleezza Rice reviewing an intelligence report after 9/11.

briefing, also known as the PDB, is a specially prepared summary of intelligence developments and concerns gathered from all of America's spy agencies. The PDB is only seen by the president, the vice president, and a handful of top White House officials. A nearly identical summary, known as the senior executive intelligence brief or SEIB, is also distributed to a few hundred top-level security officials (including the FBI director and attorney general) and members of Congress.

The 9/11 Commission discovered in its investigation that from January 2001 through September 10, 2011, more than forty PDBs presented to Bush contained references to Bin Laden. One of these PDBs, dated August 6, 2001, was even titled "Bin Ladin Determined to Strike in US" (see "The CIA Warns of al-Qaeda Attacks on American Soil," p. 196) These foreboding intelligence briefings were also contained in the SEIBs, under headings such as "Bin Ladin

Planning Multiple Operations" (April 20), "Bin Ladin Public Profile May Presage Attack" (May 3), "Bin Ladin Attacks May Be Imminent" (June 23), and "Bin Ladin Planning High-Profile Attacks" (June 30).

Throughout this period and well into August, CIA counterterrorism officials pressed the administration for authority to launch an operation in Afghanistan that would take out bin Laden, but to no avail. By most accounts, they were simply unable to convince skeptical national security decision makers that a strike on U.S. soil was coming. "Most of the intelligence community recognized in the summer of 2001 that the number and severity of threat reports were unprecedented," explained the 9/11 Commission. "Many officials told us that they knew something terrible was planned, and they were desperate to stop it. [But] despite their large number, the threats received contained few specifics regarding time, place, method, or target."[33]

Four months after the September 11 terrorist attacks, Bush himself tacitly acknowledged that he wished he had focused more on bin Laden and his terrorist organization in the spring and summer of 2001. "There was a significant difference in my attitude [about Bin Laden] after September 11," he told the *Washington Post*. "I was not on point, but I knew he was a menace, and I knew he was a problem. I knew he was responsible, or we felt he was responsible, for the previous bombings that killed Americans. I was prepared to look at a plan that would be a thoughtful plan that would bring him to justice, and would have given the order to do that. I have no hesitancy about going after him. But I didn't feel that sense of urgency, and my blood was not nearly as boiling."[34]

A System-wide Failure

In its examination of the September 11 terrorist attacks in the United States, the 9/11 Commission admitted that it is easy to find fault in the aftermath of a terrible event. The panel quoted from historian Roberta Wohlstetter, who had studied America's failure to anticipate Japan's surprise attack on Pearl Harbor in December 1941. "[It] is much easier *after* the event to sort the relevant from the irrelevant signals," she wrote. "After the event, of course, a signal is always crystal clear; we can now see what disaster it was signaling since the disaster has occurred. But before the event it is obscure and pregnant with conflicting messages."[35]

The 9/11 Commission and virtually all journalists, scholars, and analysts who have studied the September 11 attacks agree that President Clinton and

President Bush were genuinely concerned about the danger posed by al-Qaeda.[36] They also agree that the men and women charged with the duty of protecting America from attack were committed to those responsibilities. And a few souls fought valiantly to save the nation from that horrible day. "Heroic individual efforts led to the identification of obscure Islamist suspects, including some of the eventual hijackers, yet time and again nothing came of such feats," lamented the authors of a 2004 investigative report in *Vanity Fair.* "Rivalries, interagency squabbling, and countless bureaucratic hurdles kept essential pieces of information from being shared."[37]

The 9/11 Commission's final report famously declared that America's inability to detect the September 11 plot reflected a failure of imagination. This perspective is shared by many others. "Almost no one took [the threat of al-Qaeda] seriously," wrote Lawrence Wright. "It was too bizarre, too primitive and exotic. Up against the confidence that Americans placed in modernity and technology and their own ideals to protect them from the savage pageant of history, the defiant gestures of bin Laden and his followers seemed absurd and even pathetic."[38]

Notes

[1] Shenon, Philip. *The Commission: The Uncensored History of the 9/11 Investigation.* New York: Twelve, 2008, p. 268.

[2] Zeman, Ned, David Wise, David Rose, and Brian Burrough. "The Path to 9/11: Lost Warnings and Fatal Errors." *Vanity Fair,* November 2004. Retrieved from http://www.vanityfair.com/politics /features/2004/11/path-to-9-11-200411.

[3] Shenon, p. 272.

[4] National Commission on Terrorist Attacks Upon the United States [The 9/11 Commission]. *The 9/11 Commission Report.* New York: Norton, 2004, p. 77-78.

[5] National Commission on Terrorist Attacks, p. 78-80.

[6] Wright, Lawrence. *The Looming Tower: Al-Qaeda and the Road to 9/11.* New York: Vintage Books, 2006, p. 388.

[7] Mayer, Jane. *The Dark Side: The Inside Story of How the War on Terror Turned into a War on American Ideals.* New York: Doubleday, 2008, p. 15.

[8] Quoted in Zeman, Wise, Rose, and Burrough.

[9] National Commission on Terrorist Attacks, p. 275.

[10] National Commission on Terrorist Attacks, p. 276.

[11] Shenon, p. 246.

[12] National Commission on Terrorist Threats, p. 265.

[13] Shenon, p. 139, 140.

[14] Zeman, Wise, Rose, and Burrough.

[15] Zegart, Amy B. *Flying Blind: The CIA, the FBI, and the Origins of 9/11.* Princeton, NJ: Princeton University Press, 2007, p. 40.

[16] Quoted in Shenon, p. 190.

[17] National Commission on Terrorist Attacks, pp. 91-92.

[18] Shenon, pp. 114-15.

[19] Shenon, p. 83.

[20] National Commission on Terrorist Attacks, pp. 174, 500 (footnotes 1, 2).

[21] Quoted in Shenon, p. 188.

[22] National Commission on Terrorist Attacks, p. 114.

[23] National Commission on Terrorist Attacks, p. 114.

[24] Scheuer, Michael. "Bill and Dick, Osama and Sandy," *Washington Times,* July 4, 2006. Retrieved from http://www.washingtontimes.com/news/2006/jul/4/20060704-110004-4280r/.

[25] National Commission on Terrorist Attacks, pp. 351-52.

[26] Quoted in Zeman, Wise, Rose, and Burrough.

[27] Eggen, Dan, and Walter Pincus. "Ex-Aide Recounts Terror Warnings," *Washington Post,* March 25, 2004, p. A1.

[28] Quoted in National Commission on Terrorist Attacks, p. 202.

[29] Quoted in Kean, Thomas H, and Lee H. Hamilton, with Benjamin Rhodes. *Without Precedent: The Inside Story of the 9/11 Commission.* New York: Knopf, 2006, p. 171.

[30] Kean and Hamilton, p. 171.

[31] National Commission on Terrorist Attacks, pp. 201-04, 212-14, 256-60.

[32] Quoted in National Commission on Terrorist Attacks, p. 256.

[33] National Commission on Terrorist Attacks, p. 262.

[34] Woodward, Bob, and Dan Balz. "Bush and His Advisors Set Objectives, but Struggled With How to Achieve Them," *Washington Post,* January 28, 2002.

[35] Wohlstetter, Roberta. *Pearl Harbor: Warning and Decision.* Palo Alto, CA: Stanford University Press, 1962, p. 387.

[36] National Commission on Terrorist Attacks, p. 349.

[37] Zeman, Wise, Rose, and Burrough.

[38] Wright, p. 8.

Chapter Eight

LEGACY OF THE SEPTEMBER 11 ATTACKS

That day of fire is a distant memory for some of our citizens. The youngest Americans have no firsthand knowledge of the day. Eventually, September 11 will come to feel more like Pearl Harbor Day—an honored date on the calendar and an important moment in history, but not a scar on the heart, not a reason to fight on.

—Former President George W. Bush
in his memoir *Decision Points,* 2010

The world that Americans woke up to after September 11, 2001, was much different than the one to which they were accustomed. As journalist Jonathan Schell (who lived six blocks from the World Trade Center) wrote, "in an instant and without warning on a fine fall morning, the known world had been jerked aside like a mere slide in a projector, and a new world had been rammed into its place.... Has the eye of the world ever shifted more abruptly or completely than it did on September 11?"[1]

Confronted by the twisted wreckage at Ground Zero—the name given to the site of the fallen World Trade Center towers—and the Pentagon and a field in rural Pennsylvania, the United States took decisive and far-reaching steps to punish al-Qaeda. The Bush administration also embraced sweeping new measures meant to prevent another 9/11-type attack from ever occurring again. These measures were praised by many Americans as necessary and prudent. But they were heavily criticized by other Americans—as well as by other nations—as betrayals of fundamental American ideals.

The U.S. Invasion of Afghanistan

U.S. intelligence networks quickly identified al-Qaeda and its leader, Osama bin Laden, as the terrorists responsible for the 9/11 carnage. On September 18, 2001, President Bush signed into law a joint resolution passed by Congress that authorized the use of force against those responsible for attacking the United States. On October 7 the United States launched a massive bombing campaign—Operation Enduring Freedom—against al-Qaeda and Taliban positions throughout Afghanistan. The Bush administration asserted that these air strikes, which were undertaken with British support, were legal under the terms of the Congressional joint resolution. In the months ahead, the Bush White House would also cite the joint resolution as the legal rationale for other sweeping measures the U.S. government took to combat terrorism. These measures ranged from eavesdropping on U.S. citizens without a court order to holding suspected terrorists without trial at an American military base in Guantanamo Bay, Cuba.

The Operation Enduring Freedom bombing campaign was followed by the arrival of U.S. ground forces in Afghanistan in late October. The Taliban government and military quickly crumbled before this onslaught, and in December Taliban leader Mullah Omar Mohammad was forced to flee into hiding. Osama bin Laden and some of his top lieutenants also managed to escape, most likely into the mountainous wilds of neighboring Pakistan. Bin Laden's disappearance was a source of tremendous frustration to Bush and the American people (see "Osama bin Laden Taunts America after September 11," p. 219).

With the Taliban seemingly vanquished, a new interim government was installed in Kabul under the guidance of the United Nations. Over the next two years U.S. military and diplomatic personnel worked with the North Atlantic Treaty Organization (NATO)—which was responsible for international peacekeeping forces in Afghanistan—humanitarian groups, and the Afghan people to build a viable new society. Meanwhile, the Bush administration began shifting military and intelligence resources away from Afghanistan toward Iraq, which the president described as the next front in America's "war on terror."

In January 2004 Afghan lawmakers approved a new constitution, and in October 2004 Hamid Karzai became the first democratically elected president of the country. In 2006, though, revitalized Taliban forces struck back in

U.S. Army soldier Johnny Nguyen and other American forces patrolling a street in Qalat City, Afghanistan, in 2011.

many parts of the country. Many of these Taliban fighters were based in Pakistan, a nominal ally of the United States that was nonetheless riddled with pockets of Islamic radicalism. Over the ensuing months it became clear that the American military forces remaining in Afghanistan were not large enough to handle the uprising.

Territorial gains by the Taliban, rising American casualties, and news reports detailing corruption and incompetence in Karzai's administration all sapped the American public's support for the war effort in Afghanistan. In 2009, though, President Obama announced that he was sending more U.S. troops to Afghanistan to turn back the Taliban. This infusion of new soldiers stopped the Taliban advance, but the country remained vulnerable and weak. Obama has since promised to carry out a total withdrawal of American troops from Afghanistan, beginning with a withdrawal of 33,000 soldiers in the summer of 2012. American diplomats and military leaders hope that by the time that withdrawal is complete, the foundation for a safe and stable Afghanistan will be in place.

Iraq and the War on Terror

The other country on which the United States trained its gunsights after September 11 was Iraq, which was still ruled by the dictator Saddam Hussein. Even before 9/11, Bush and influential foreign policy advisors like Vice President Dick Cheney, Secretary of Defense Donald Rumsfeld, and Deputy Secretary of Defense Paul Wolfowitz had viewed Hussein as a dangerous and unpredictable force on the world stage. Their desire to see Hussein overthrown intensified after bin Laden's deadly attack. By the first anniversary of the 9/11 attacks, the Bush administration was clearly positioning itself to carry out a full-scale military invasion of Iraq.

This shift in focus away from Afghanistan—the home of bin Laden and al-Qaeda—toward Iraq has been the subject of intense debate over the years. Leading Bush administration officials and their supporters on Capitol Hill and conservative news outlets argued that the United States possessed ironclad evidence that Hussein was trying to develop deadly chemical, biological, or nuclear weapons. Spokespeople ranging from Cheney and Rice to Secretary of State Colin Powell asserted that such "weapons of mass destruction," also known as WMDs, might very well be used against American targets. In addition, the Bush administration and many influential foreign policy experts believed that if Hussein's dictatorship could be replaced with a more democratic government, its example might spark democratic movements in other parts of the Middle East.

Critics of the push to invade Iraq, though, claimed that the Bush White House wanted to overthrow the Iraqi dictator for other reasons. Skeptics pointed out that Bush apparently believed allegations that Hussein had tried to plot the assassination of Bush's father, former President George H.W. Bush, when he visited the Middle East in 1993. They also charged that Bush and Cheney, both of whom had strong oil industry ties, wanted to invade Iraq to gain control of its large oil reserves. Opponents of war with Iraq also complained that America had no business going into Iraq before it was sure that al-Qaeda and Taliban forces in Afghanistan and neighboring Pakistan had been permanently crushed.

A final factor that played into the Bush administration's aggressive stance toward Iraq, though, was a conviction that Hussein had to have played *some*

In February 2003 U.S. Secretary of State Colin Powell insisted in an appearance before the UN Security Council that the United States had ironclad evidence that Iraq possessed so-called "weapons of mass destruction."

part in the September 11 terrorist attacks. As journalist Peter Beinart put it, Bush, Cheney, Wolfowitz, and Rumsfeld all "genuinely believed that Saddam had a hand in the attack, and they didn't much care that the administration's terrorism experts thought they were nuts."[2] Beginning in late 2002, Cheney and other administration officials strongly implied in public remarks that Iraq might have been involved in the 9/11 plot. As a result, U.S. public opinion polls showed a big spike in the number of Americans who believed in a Hussein-9/11 link. The 9/11 Commission reported in 2004, however, that it never found any evidence "that Iraq cooperated with al-Qaeda in developing or carrying out any attacks against the United States."[3]

Still, the Bush administration might never have taken on the task of invading Iraq if it had not experienced so much initial success in Afghanistan. When the Taliban government collapsed in November 2001, enthusiasm within the Bush administration for action against Iraq increased dramatically.

"Eight days after the capture of Kabul, Bush told Rumsfeld to develop a strategy for toppling Saddam," wrote Beinart. "By February 2002, the U.S. military was shifting forces from Afghanistan to the Persian Gulf. The Iraqi threat had not grown as a result of America's apparent victory over the Taliban, but the Bush administration's self-confidence had."[4]

In late 2002 and early 2003 the United Nations Security Council demanded that Iraq open all of its facilities to UN weapons inspectors to see whether Hussein was in possession of WMDs. The Bush administration expressed deep reservations about the effectiveness of these inspections, and on March 17, 2003, Bush announced that "Saddam Hussein and his sons must leave Iraq within 48 hours. Their refusal to go will result in military conflict commenced at a time of our choosing." When Hussein responded with defiance, Bush ordered a full military invasion of Iraq on March 20.

American military analysts expected a brutal conflict that would inflict mass casualties on both sides, but the war was a rout. Buoyed by powerful air strikes on Iraqi military targets, a coalition of mostly American and British ground forces swept across Iraq, encountering only fitful resistance. By April 9 coalition forces had seized control of the capital of Baghdad and sent Hussein fleeing from capture. He was eventually captured in a U.S. military operation outside the city of Tikrit on December 13, 2003. Hussein was later convicted of crimes against humanity by an Iraqi court, and he was executed by the new Iraqi government on December 30, 2006.

The Occupation of Iraq

On May 1, 2003, President Bush announced an end to major combat operations in Iraq from the deck of the aircraft carrier USS *Abraham Lincoln*, which was adorned with a huge banner that read "Mission Accomplished." In reality, though, America's military challenges in Iraq were just beginning. When U.S. forces took control of the country, they were unable to stop a massive wave of looting and lawlessness. Critics claimed that the deployment of American troops in Iraq was too small to maintain order, especially after U.S. authorities disbanded the existing Iraqi military and police forces. Subsequent efforts to build a democratic government faltered due to violent clashes between different religious factions, and living conditions in many parts of Iraq dramatically worsened. These problems were further exacerbated by al-Qaeda, which left its bloody mark in numerous cities and towns across Iraq.

American soldiers on patrol in Iraq.

A Jordanian terrorist named Abu Musab al-Zarqawi organized numerous al-Qaeda attacks on American military forces and Iraqi civilians and security personnel who dared to cooperate with the "infidels" (al-Zarqawi was killed by a U.S. air strike on June 7, 2006).

The American occupation of Iraq also revealed that the Hussein regime had not possessed any weapons of mass destruction. After conducting an extremely thorough survey, a U.S.-led investigative team reported that Iraq had ended all of its WMD programs more than a decade earlier. This news was deeply embarrassing to the Bush administration, which had based its arguments for an invasion on the WMD issue. The absence of WMDs also sparked heavy criticism from other countries—including many that had extended heartfelt words of sympathy to the United States after 9/11. "People don't realize in America how little underlying credibility the United States now has in the world, especially on this matter of WMDs," said Vahid Majidi, a high-ranking official in an FBI division devoted to WMD issues. "We went to war—the most important thing a country does—based on WMD, and we were wrong. That means either we're amazingly incompetent or we lied. Take your pick."[5] America's international reputation took another hit in 2004, when it was revealed that American soldiers had abused Iraqi prisoners at Baghdad's Abu Ghraib prison.

By 2005 the American occupation of Iraq had all the appearances of an unfolding disaster. The economic cost of the war was skyrocketing with each passing week, and American soldiers were being killed or wounded in ever-growing numbers by roadside bombs, snipers, and other forms of terrorism. Ordinary Iraqis also suffered enormously from high rates of poverty, violence, hunger, and dislocation from their homes. In 2007, however, the Bush administration approved a major military "surge" in Iraq. This massive infusion of new troops dramatically improved security across Iraq and gave the citizenry a much-needed infusion of stability.

The improved economic and security outlook gave President Barack Obama the opportunity to prepare a withdrawal upon taking office in January 2009. In August 2011—by which time the occupation had cost an estimated $1 trillion and claimed the lives of more than 4,400 American soldiers—all U.S. combat troops left Iraq. The Obama administration has promised a complete military withdrawal by the close of 2012. At that point Iraqi security will be the sole responsibility of the Iraqi government, which is led by Nouri al-Maliki. Al-Maliki became the first leader of Iraq after Hussein's ouster, and in November 2010 he was elected to a second term as prime minister.

The Search for bin Laden

It is widely believed that U.S. military forces nearly captured or killed Osama bin Laden in the opening weeks of the 2001 invasion of Afghanistan. But when bin Laden eluded capture in the mountains of Tora Bora, he seemed to vanish into thin air. Most analysts believe that he took up residence in some cave deep in the mountainous wilderness that marks the border region of Afghanistan and Pakistan, but American intelligence and military officials were unable to find him. By March 2002, Bush indicated in a news conference that his top priority was Iraq, not the al-Qaeda leader. "We haven't heard from him in a long time. The idea of focusing on one person really indicates to me people don't understand the scope of the mission. Terror is bigger than one person.... I really just don't spend that much time on him, to be honest with you."

By 2006 the manhunt for bin Laden had gone completely cold. "The clandestine U.S. commandos whose job is to capture or kill Osama bin Laden have not received a credible lead in more than two years," reported the *Washington Post* in September of that year. "Nothing from the vast U.S. intelligence world—no tips from informants, no snippets from electronic intercepts, no points on any satellite image—has led them anywhere near the al-Qaeda leader, according to U.S. and Pakistani officials."[6]

The search for bin Laden remained quiet for another five years. Late in the evening of May 1, 2011, though, President Barack Obama made a dramatic television appearance to declare that bin Laden had been killed by U.S. Navy SEALS (Sea, Air, and Land special forces) in a raid on a compound in the quiet town of Abbottabad, Pakistan (see "President Obama Announces the Death of Osama bin Laden," p. 237).

The story of how America finally brought bin Laden to justice came out over the next several days. In June 2009 Obama issued a directive to the CIA to intensify its efforts to find and take out the al-Qaeda leader. In August 2010 CIA Director Leon Panetta told Obama that agents believed that they had identified bin Laden's personal courier, who might be able to lead the United States to the elusive terrorist. The CIA tracked the courier to the Abbottabad compound. As analysts studied activities in and around the tight cluster of buildings, they became increasingly confident that bin Laden was hiding inside. In late 2010 the Obama administration began weighing options for a military strike against the compound. Obama ultimately approved a helicopter assault on the target, but he decided not to tell Pakistan about the operation because of CIA fears that sympathizers within the Pakistani government might tip off bin Laden. On April 29 Obama gave final approval for the assault, which was successfully executed on the evening of May 1 (no Americans were lost in the firefight). After killing bin Laden, the SEALS took his body to waiting U.S. officials. They prepared it for burial in accordance with Muslim religious tradition, then buried it at sea in a secret location.[7]

As Americans across the country rejoiced at the news that the architect of the 9/11 tragedy could no longer threaten the nation, Obama cautioned that the terrorist network bin Laden had spawned still remained a danger.

"The clandestine U.S. commandos whose job is to capture or kill Osama bin Laden have not received a credible lead in more than two years. Nothing from the vast U.S. intelligence world—no tips from informants, no snippets from electronic intercepts, no points on any satellite image—has led them anywhere near the al-Qaeda leader."

President Barack Obama, Vice President Joe Biden (far left), and other members of the Obama administration's national security team monitor the progress of the top-secret military mission that killed Osama bin Laden on May 1, 2011.

Counterterrorism experts acknowledge that Ayman al-Zawahiri, who succeeded bin Laden as the leader of al-Qaeda, is still at large. And some individual cells, such as one based in Yemen, have attempted bombings of U.S. targets in recent years. In December 2009, for example, Yemeni members of al-Qaeda tried to bring down a Detroit-bound commercial airliner with a bomb.

Some analysts, however, believe that al-Qaeda might actually be on the verge of collapse. They point out that many members of the group have been captured or killed by CIA "drone strikes"—missiles fired by unmanned aircraft into terrorist hideouts in Afghanistan and Pakistan. U.S. officials believe that drone strikes killed as many as 1,200 al-Qaeda terrorists from 2004 to mid-2011. In addition, numerous al-Qaeda leaders have been killed by American forces in the past few years. On August 22, 2011, for example, a drone strike in Pakistan took the life of Abd al-Rahman, Zawahiri's second in command. Finally, they note that bin Laden's death struck a severe blow to the morale of an organization that had been under siege from U.S. forces for a solid decade.

The Arab Spring

Changes in Arab countries have contributed to the declining influence of al-Qaeda and other Islamic extremist groups. According to many scholars and counterterrorism experts, the murderous perversions of Islam that sprouted from the minds of bin Laden and other terrorists in the late twenti-eth century might never have taken root in the hearts of so many young Arab men if their homelands had been less cruel and repressive. "The typical Arab citizen, with few exceptions, has felt humiliated in recent decades by his or her government," wrote Rami G. Khouri, an American-born journalist of Palestinian-Jordanian heritage.[8]

Hundreds of millions of Arabs feel they have been denied both their human rights and their citizenship rights, the result of decades of socioeco-nomic stresses and political deprivations. These include petty and large-scale corruption; police brutality; abuse of power; favoritism; unemployment; poor wages; unequal opportunities; inefficient or nonexistent public services; lack of freedom of expression and association; state control of media, culture, and education; and many other dimensions of the modern Arab security state. At the same time, ordinary men and women in countries across the region have seen small groups of families in the ruling elite grow fabulously rich simply because of their connections.

In December 2010, though, a remarkable event in rural Tunisia rocked the Arab world. A poor vegetable peddler named Mohamed Bouazizi became so distraught when police confiscated his vegetables that he set himself on fire in protest on December 17, 2010. Bouazizi's action sparked a massive wave of youthful protests against Tunisia's repressive regime. The government tried to crush the rebellion, but the demonstrations continued to grow. The uprising became so great that Tunisia's dictatorial president, Zine al-Abidine Ben Ali, was forced to flee the country in mid-January 2011.

Around the same time that Ben Ali was chased out of office, a string of sui-cides similar to the one carried out by Bouazizi took place in Algeria and Egypt. These dramatic suicides triggered huge anti-government demonstrations led by young people, many of whom used Facebook, Twitter, and other social media technology to organize protests and defy crackdowns by the police. The protests in Algeria forced the government to implement significant political and social reforms. In Egypt the demonstrations had an even more stunning impact: they forced longtime Egyptian strongman Hosni Mubarak to resign the presidency on February 11, 2011. He was subsequently arrested by the Egyptian military, which pledged to hold power only until a "legitimate" government had formed. Mubarak has been charged with the murder of protestors. Prosecutors have also discussed opening an investigation into whether Mubarak played any role in the 1981 assassination of Egypt's previous president, Anwar Sadat.

Since the rebellions erupted in Tunisia, Algeria, and Egypt, brave and frustrated young men and women have led major demonstrations and rallies against unpopular regimes throughout the Arab world, including those in Yemen, Syria, Iraq, Jordan, Morocco, Oman, Lebanon, Libya, and Saudi Arabia. These powerful protests, which have come to be known collectively as the Arab Spring, have ranged in their impact from country to country. Some of the protestors managed to wrest only minor reforms from their governments. But other rebellions, which have been led by moderate Muslims rather than radical Islamists, have attracted so much energy and popular support that they have forced their governments to make major concessions. And in some places, pro-reform and pro-democracy movements are threatening ruthless regimes that once seemed invincible. In Libya, for example, armed rebels backed by NATO forces ousted dictator Muammar Qaddafi, who had ruled the North African nation with an iron fist since 1969. And in Syria, President Bashar Assad was barely clinging to power in early 2012, despite the fact that, according to a January UN estimate, his security forces had massacred over 5,000 protestors during the course of the previous year.

Activists, scholars, and politicians around the world acknowledge that they do not know how the Arab Spring will turn out. Perhaps the unrest sweeping across the Arab world in 2011 will create governments that are just as repressive and uncaring as the ones they replaced. But perhaps the demonstrations mark the leading edge of reforms that will finally unleash the talents and ambitions of peoples that have long wanted more out of life for themselves and their loved ones. "At present we are in a period of transition," wrote Moroccan novelist Tahar Ben Jelloun. "It is a difficult time, marked by the impatience and disappointment of the people in rebellion. How to explain to them that it takes time to rebuild a country and put the state back on its feet when a dictator has pillaged, spoiled, and dishonored it? Despite the present disorder, though, and the more or less fortunate improvisations in Tunisia and Egypt, the wind of this spring continues to blow over all of the Arab world.… Fear has changed sides. The dictators in power, men without legitimacy, are now the fearful ones."[9]

Life in America after 9/11

One of the most important steps that President Bush took after the September 11 terrorist attacks was to emphasize to his fellow citizens that bin Laden and his murderous minions were not representative of the Islamic faith. "All Americans must recognize that the face of terror is not the true face of Islam," he declared. "Islam is a faith that brings comfort to a billion people around the world. It's a faith that has made brothers and sisters of every race. It's a faith based upon love, not hate." These words provided comfort to millions of loyal Americans of the Islamic faith, as well as to Muslim peoples around the world who had been horrified by the events of 9/11. But they failed to stop an upturn in violence and vandalism against Muslim families, businesses, and places of worship in some parts of America.

The events of September 11 increased tensions between Americans in other ways as well. The Bush administration and the Republican leadership of Congress responded to 9/11 by crafting a slate of ambitious new homeland security policies. The urgency of this activity was further underscored in late September and early October, when mysterious letters containing deadly anthrax bacteria were received at the offices of two Democratic senators and several news organizations. Within two years of the 9/11 tragedy, the United States had passed a wide range of new domestic and foreign surveillance measures, beefed up airport security, approved extremely harsh new methods for interrogating suspected terrorists, and created a Cabinet-level Department of Homeland Security to defend against new terrorist plots. The CIA also established a "secret detention" or "extraordinary rendition" program in which suspected terrorists were housed and interrogated in foreign countries that were known to torture prisoners. All of these new weapons in the war on terror were given a stamp of legality by lawyers inside the White House and the U.S. Department of Justice.

"All Americans must recognize that the face of terror is not the true face of Islam," said President Bush. "Islam is a faith that brings comfort to a billion people around the world.… It's a faith based upon love, not hate."

Many of these policies enjoyed broad support, especially within Bush's Republican Party. After all, Americans wanted to feel more safe and secure. Large numbers of

149

A mourner traces the name of a victim of the September 11 terrorist attacks during a ceremony marking the tenth anniversary of the attacks at the World Trade Center site in New York City.

them viewed the new homeland security and counterterrorism programs as legitimate and sensible tools, especially given the bloodthirsty nature of al-Qaeda and other terrorist groups prowling the planet. But other Americans were horrified by these new policies. Conservatives joined liberals in expressing profound reservations about the CIA's expanded powers to spy on American citizens. Some Americans also raised objections about waterboarding and other "harsh interrogation" methods used by American officials against suspected terrorists. Critics said that these methods amounted to torture, which the United States had always previously opposed as barbaric and immoral. In their eyes, the Bush administration's "enhanced interrogation" and "extraordinary rendition" policies were doing tremendous damage to America's reputation around the world. Some opponents even described Vice President Cheney as a war criminal for his lead role in developing and implementing these policies on the treatment of prisoners.

The Bush White House and its supporters angrily rejected these characterizations and charged that their critics had no understanding of the type of enemy America faced in the war on terror. In some instances they also implied that such criticism amounted to providing aid and comfort to the terrorists. Not surprisingly, these insinuations sparked further howls of outrage from critics who argued that they were defending America's honor, reputation, and civil liberties from an administration that had lost its moral bearings.

This furious debate sputtered on inconclusively until Bush and Cheney left office in January 2009. Bush's successor, Barack Obama, promptly signed executive orders that dramatically curtailed the extraordinary rendition program and outlawed waterboarding and other "enhanced interrogation" techniques altogether. But he rejected calls for the creation of an independent commission to investigate whether Bush, Cheney, or other officials were guilty of criminal conduct in carrying out their antiterror policies.

This political warfare saddened many Americans—conservatives and liberals alike—who remembered how the country had spoken with one proud and united voice in the days and weeks after 9/11. "Spontaneous acts of generosity, a spirit of voluntarism and charity, and a coming together in the face of tragedy permeated the country" in those days, wrote scholar Elaine Tyler May. "People reached out to their family members across the country and the world, contacted friends and kinfolk, offered assistance to people they hardly knew, donated generously to charities to help the families of victims."[10]

Marking a Somber Anniversary

In September 2011 people across the United States held numerous ceremonies to mark the tenth anniversary of the 9/11 attacks. Some of these ceremonies were large and attracted national attention, such as services conducted at the Pentagon, in downtown Manhattan, and in Shanksville, Pennsylvania. Others were smaller, community-organized affairs that nonetheless meant a lot to their participants. All of them, large and small, paid tribute to the memories of the men, women, and children who lost their lives on that horrible day.

In New York, Obama and Bush appeared together with their wives for special ceremonies at Ground Zero, where the World Trade Center towers once stood. "On September 12, 2001, we awoke to a world in which evil was closer at hand, and uncertainty clouded our future," Obama acknowledged in remarks at the site, where a National September 11 Memorial and Museum now stands.

> In the decade since, much has changed for Americans. We've known war and recession; passionate debates and political divides. We can never get back the lives we lost on that day, or the Americans who made the ultimate sacrifice in the wars that followed.
>
> Yet today, it is worth remembering what has not changed. Our character as a nation has not changed. Our faith—in God and each other—that has not changed.... These past ten years tell a story of resilience. The Pentagon is repaired, and filled with patriots working in common purpose. Shanksville is the scene of friendships forged between residents of that town, and families who lost loved ones there. New York remains a vibrant capital of the arts and industry, fashion and commerce. Where the World Trade Center once stood, the sun glistens off a new tower that reaches toward the sky. Our people still work in skyscrapers. Our stadiums are filled with fans, and our parks full of children playing ball. Our airports hum with travel, and our buses and subways take millions where they need to go. Families sit down to Sunday dinner, and students prepare for school. This land pulses with the optimism of those who set out for distant shores, and the courage of those who died for human freedom.[11]

These sentiments were echoed by speakers at many other 9/11 anniversary events. At a special "evening of remembrance and reflection" at New York's Kennedy Center, journalist Leon Wieseltier spoke for millions of Americans when he declared that "the obscenities of September 11, 2001 exposed the difference between builders and destroyers. We are builders. Let us agree, on this anniversary, that it is an honor to be an American and it is an honor to be free."[12]

Whether America can permanently recapture the sense of unity it experienced in the days following September 11 is an open question. But thousands of Americans who experienced the terror of that day firsthand believe that *they* were forever changed by the experience. Many of the firefighters, police officers, emergency paramedics, and ordinary citizens who survived the attacks on New York City and the Pentagon say that they gained a newfound appreciation for their family and friends on that dark day. These same sentiments are echoed by many of the families who lost loved ones at the World Trade Center, the Pentagon, and the Pennsylvania field where Flight 93 went down. "It's such a shame that something like this had to happen before people realize that they should try to live each day," said one New York City detective who participated in the rescue effort in downtown Manhattan.

> Why complain about everything? Why walk through the streets miserable, hating the world, hating everybody else? I think I've learned to appreciate life more. I see this sunrise, I appreciate this day for what it is, and I'm glad I'm here. We should feel lucky we're alive, because we don't know when this life will be taken away from us. There are 3,000 people who didn't know that September 11 was going to be their last day. I thought it was going to be mine, too.[13]

Notes

[1] Schell, Jonathan. "Letter from Ground Zero: The Power of the Powerful," October 15, 2001. Retrieved from http://www.thenation.com/article/letter-ground-zero-38.

[2] Beinart, Peter. *The Icarus Syndrome: A History of American Hubris.* New York: HarperCollins, 2010, p. 330.

[3] National Commission on Terrorist Attacks Upon the United States [The 9/11 Commission]. *The 9/11 Commission Report.* New York: Norton, 2004, p. 83.

⁴ Beinart, p. 338.

⁵ Quoted in Suskind, Ron. *The Way of the World: A Story of Truth and Hope in an Age of Extremism.* New York: Harper, 2008, pp. 169-70.

⁶ Priest, Dana, and Ann Scott Tyson. "Bin Laden Trail 'Stone Cold,'" *Washington Post,* September 10, 2006. Retrieved from http://www.washingtonpost.com/wp-dyn/content/article/2006/09/09/AR20060 90901105.html.

⁷ Schmidle, Nicholas. "Getting Bin Laden: What Happened that Night in Abbottabad," *New Yorker,* August 8, 2011. Retrieved from http://www.newyorker.com/reporting/2011/08/08/110808fa_fact_ schmidle.

⁸ Khouri, Rami G. "The Arab Awakening," *The Nation,* September 12, 2011. Retrieved from http:// www.thenation.com/article/162973/arab-awakening.

⁹ Ben Jalloun, Tahar. "When Dictators Shoot Back." *Newsweek,* July 25, 2011. Retrieved from http:// www.thedailybeast.com/newsweek/2011/07/24/has-arab-spring-become-arab-hell.html.

¹⁰ May, Elaine Taylor. "Echoes of the Cold War." In *September 11 in History: A Watershed Moment?* Edited by Mary L. Dudziak. Durham, NC: Duke University Press, 2003, p. 51.

¹¹ "Text of Obama's Speech Commemorating Sept. 11," ABCNews.com, September 12, 2001. Retrieved from http://abcnews.go.com/Politics/wireStory?id=14496866

¹² Wieseltier, Leon. From "9/11: An Evening of Remembrance and Reflection," *NewRepublic.com,* September 8, 2011. Retrieved from http://www.tnr.com/article/94774/leons-remarks-911-event.

¹³ Quoted in Hagen, Susan, and Mary Carouba. *Women at Ground Zero: Stories of Courage and Compassion.* Indianapolis: Alpha, 2002, p. 266.

154

BIOGRAPHIES

Mohamed Atta (1968-2001)
Egyptian-born al-Qaeda Member Who Led the 9/11 Hijackings

Mohamed Mohamed el-Amir Awad el-Sayed Atta was born at Kafr el-Sheikh, an Egyptian town in the Nile Delta. He spent most of his adolescence in Giza, a middle-class suburb of the national capital of Cairo. His father, Mohamed el-Amir Awad el-Sayed Atta, was a lawyer. His mother was Bouthayna Mohamed Mustapha Sheraqi, who had two daughters before she gave birth to her only son. Atta's sisters grew up to become a professor and a doctor, and some people who have studied Atta's life believe that he often felt overshadowed by his older siblings when he was growing up.

Atta enrolled at the University of Cairo to study architecture in 1985. He spent the next five years at the school, where friends remembered him as shy and modest. "I could never imagine him on a plane threatening people, killing people," said one of Atta's best friends from his university days. "He would be scared to death.... Mohamed was well liked because he never offended or bothered anyone."[1] Atta also joined an engineering society at the school that was sponsored by the Muslim Brotherhood, an Islamic group that often clashed with Egypt's authoritarian rulers.

In October 1992 Atta began studying architecture and city planning at the Technical University of Hamburg in northern Germany. Atta was reportedly anxious about the intensely competitive business environment in Cairo. He hoped that a graduate degree from Hamburg would give him a career advantage over other young Egyptians when he completed his studies and returned home.

A Mysterious Transformation

Atta's first few years in Hamburg were quiet ones. He studied hard and supported himself with a part-time architectural drafting job in the city. Classmates, professors, and fellow employees remembered him as a well-mannered young man who was quietly devoted to his Islamic faith. Over time, however, Atta became more outspoken about his religious beliefs. He also became active in a Muslim student group on campus. During this same period, he expressed growing anger and frustration with the corrupt nature of many Arab governments and the influence of the United States over Middle Eastern affairs.

In mid-1997 Atta was laid off from his drafting job. Shortly thereafter, he took an extended break from his studies. He vanished in June 1997, and when he returned to Hamburg in the fall of 1998 he seemed to be an entirely different person. Atta was sporting the sort of big, bushy beard that was favored by some Islamic fundamentalists, and he seemed to walk around with a perpetual scowl on his face. Atta reported that he had spent much of his absence on a religious pilgrimage, but such trips typically only take a fraction of the time that he was gone. Several months later, Atta requested a new passport to replace his old one. He claimed to have lost his old passport, but passport replacement is a common tactic employed by criminals and terrorists who wish to erase evidence of their travel patterns.[2]

Atta led an increasingly secretive existence in late 1998 and 1999. He abandoned his studies and found work at a shipping warehouse with a number of other young Muslim men who shared his increasingly hateful religious and political beliefs. They shared an apartment as well, and investigators believe that this was probably the time that Atta and his friends coalesced into an actual al-Qaeda cell group.

In November 1999 Atta and three other radical Islamists from Hamburg traveled to Afghanistan to visit Osama bin Laden. The four men—Atta, Ramzi Binalshibh, Marwan al-Shehhi, and Ziad Jarrah—were selected by bin Laden and 9/11 mastermind Khaled Sheikh Mohammed to serve as the suicide pilots in a malevolent plot to hijack American planes and crash them into various targets on U.S. soil (Binalshibh was eventually replaced by Hani Hanjour). Bin Laden also selected Atta to serve as the operation's field commander, meaning that he was in charge of directing and organizing the other al-Qaeda hijackers involved in the plot.

Atta and the other suicide pilots then went to the United States for flight training in late 2000 and early 2001. Atta had several flight instructors and landlords during these months, and they all later described the Egyptian terrorist as a serious and arrogant man who displayed an intense dislike for women. The hijackers paid for housing, food, transportation, clothing, and flight lessons during this time through secret payments from al-Qaeda. Once the four pilots completed their training in Florida, they were joined by the rest of the al-Qaeda jihadists. By July 2001 nineteen al-Qaeda terrorists were quietly biding their time in sunny Florida. During this same month, Atta traveled to Madrid, Spain, and met with Binalshibh to finalize the details of the planned hijackings.

Carrying Out the Attacks

In mid-August Atta selected the date of September 11 for the attacks. On August 26 the hijackers began buying tickets for four separate cross-country flights scheduled to depart from various East Coast airports on the morning of September 11. Atta made all the hijacker assignments for the attack. He reserved the suicide pilot duties on American Airlines (AA) Flight 11, which was departing from Boston, for himself. Atta and four fellow hijackers boarded AA 11 without incident, but one of Atta's bags was left behind at Logan International Airport. The contents of this bag included Atta's last will and testament and several al-Qaeda documents. All of these materials helped 9/11 investigators piece together elements of the attack and identify al-Qaeda as the culprit.

The AA 11 hijackers seized control of the plane within twenty minutes of its 7:59 A.M. liftoff, and Atta settled in to steer the plane. He set a new course for downtown Manhattan, and at 8:46 A.M. Atta plowed the jet into the side of the World Trade Center's North Tower. This awful event stunned people in New York and across the country, but Americans would soon learn that it was only the first salvo in what would become the worst terrorist attack on U.S. soil in American history.

Since that dark day, investigators have thoroughly documented Atta's role as the lead hijacker in the September 11 attacks. But his metamorphosis into a cold-blooded assassin will always remain a mystery to the family and friends who knew him during his youth. "When Atta brought hell to the north tower of the World Trade Center, when he perished in the flames and had his picture beamed around the world, friends back in Egypt were dumbfounded," wrote journalist John Cloud. "They looked and looked again at the photos, trying to find the kid they once knew.... 'Let each find his blade for the prey to be slaughtered,' reads a passage of the letter found in Atta's luggage. How Atta found his blade may never be known."[3]

Sources

Cloud, John. "Atta's Odyssey," *Time,* September 30, 2001. Retrieved from http://www.time.com/time/magazine/article/0,9171,176917-1,00.html.

Hooper, John. "The Shy, Caring, Deadly Fanatic," *The Guardian (UK),* September 23, 2001. Retrieved from http://www.guardian.co.uk/world/2001/sep/23/september11.education.

McDermott, Terry. *Perfect Soldiers: The 9/11 Hijackers: Who They Were, Why They Did It.* New York: HarperCollins, 2005.

Notes

[1] Quoted in Cloud, John. "Atta's Odyssey," *Time,* September 30, 2001. Retrieved from http://www.time.com/time/magazine/article/0,9171,176917-1,00.html.
[2] McDermott, Terry. *Perfect Soldiers: The 9/11 Hijackers: Who They Were, Why They Did It.* New York: HarperCollins, 2005, p. 57-58.
[3] Cloud, "Atta's Odyssey."

Osama bin Laden (1957-2011)
Founder and Leader of the al-Qaeda Terrorist Organization

Osama bin Muhammad bin Awad Laden was probably born in March 1957 in Riyadh, Saudi Arabia. According to some journalists, however, bin Laden himself stated on a number of occasions that he was born in January 1958. His mother was Alia (Ghanem), who hailed from a family of Syrian citrus farmers. His father was Muhammad bin Laden, a native of Yemen who moved to Saudi Arabia as a young man. An ambitious and talented builder, the elder bin Laden created a mighty construction empire in his new homeland. He became the royal family's favorite builder for all sorts of huge projects, including royal palaces, highways, and renovations to Islamic holy sites at Medina and Mecca. By the 1960s, bin Laden had become such a favorite of King Faisal that all major government construction contracts were automatically sent to his company.

A Privileged Upbringing

Osama bin Laden was his father's seventh son and seventeenth child (Muhammed took numerous wives and reportedly fathered well over fifty children). Osama was a young boy when his father divorced his mother, but this event did not cast them into poverty. Muhammed arranged for Alia to marry Mohammad al-Attas, who was an executive in his construction empire. The couple eventually had four other children. Osama, meanwhile, remained a fully recognized member of his father's clan. Osama lived in Jeddah with his mother and stepfather, but he spent many weekends with his half-brothers and half-sisters. Osama also attended classes at the finest private schools with princes of the royal family.

In 1967 Muhammed bin Laden perished in a helicopter crash. His fabulous wealth was distributed among Osama and his many siblings. According to some accounts, Osama's share of the inheritance was as much as $80 million. Whatever the exact amount, it enabled him to lead an almost royal life of leisure and privilege. He owned his own stable of racing horses by age fifteen, and he traveled freely in the Arab world. But unlike many other wealthy Saudi students—including almost all of his siblings—he never traveled outside the Middle East. "That lack of exposure to Western culture would prove a crucial distinction," observed the *New York Times.* "The other siblings went on to lead lives that would not be unfamiliar to most Americans. They took over the family business, estimated to be worth billions, distributing Snapple drinks, Volkswagens and Disney products across the Middle East."

The shy and conservative bin Laden, by contrast, immersed himself in Wahhabism, a severe strain of Islam that was deeply anti-Western in its orientation. Bin Laden's turn toward fundamentalist Islamic teachings intensified at King Abdul Azia University in Jeddah, where he earned a degree in engineering. It was here that bin Laden became exposed to the ideas of the radical Muslim Brotherhood and the teachings of anti-Western scholars like Sayyid Qutb.

Forming al-Qaeda

By the early 1980s bin Laden had become obsessed with the idea of using jihad—holy war—to rid the Middle East of foreign influences and restore Islam to its central place in Arab life. He first put these ideas into practice in Afghanistan, a Muslim nation that had been invaded by the Soviet Union in 1979. In the mid-1980s bin Laden used his money to recruit young jihadists and train them for combat against the Soviet army. He also spent months at a time in Afghanistan, overseeing his training camps and conjuring up plots against enemy forces. During this same period he met the radical Islamist Ayman al-Zawahiri in neighboring Pakistan. Both men shared the same fanatical religious views, and before long they became close allies. By the time the Soviets withdrew from Afghanistan in 1989, bin Laden had gained a reputation among radical Islamists as a true holy warrior—a man who used his wealth to advance the cause of Islam, not to engage in decadent behavior. In addition, his Afghan training camps had become the basis for a frightening new organization known as al-Qaeda.

After the Soviet retreat, bin Laden returned to Saudi Arabia. Bursting with self-confidence, he became openly critical of the Saudi government and the royal family that sat at its head. His attacks became even more scathing after the 1991 Gulf War, when Saudi authorities allowed U.S. troops—initially deployed to help drive Iraq out of Kuwait—to remain in the country. The continued presence of American soldiers in Saudi Arabia, which housed Islam's holiest sites, put bin Laden in a cold fury. From this point forward he saw the United States as a corrupt and evil presence that had to be destroyed in order to usher in a new age of Islamic fundamentalism.

In 1992 bin Laden relocated with his many wives and children to Sudan, a country in northeastern Africa led by a radical Islamic government. He spent the next four years in Sudan, where he worked on various construction and agricultural projects, continued developing al-Qaeda, and lobbed vicious verbal attacks at the Saudi government, Israel, the United States, and other "enemies" of Islam. Bin Laden's incendiary statements burned his last ties to Saudi Arabia, which stripped him of his citizenship. They also ruined his relationship with his extended family. Cut off from the family fortune, bin Laden became increasingly dependent on gifts from wealthy benefactors to maintain al-Qaeda.

In 1996 Sudanese authorities became increasingly anxious about their worldwide reputation as a willing host to terrorists. They thus pressed bin Laden to find somewhere else to live. Bin Laden reluctantly complied. Fully aware that most Arab states viewed him as a troublemaker, he ended up back in Afghanistan. By this time the Afghan people were living under the rule of the Taliban, an exceedingly cruel and radical Islamic movement led by a mysterious cleric named Mullah Mohammed Omar. Bin Laden set out to charm Mullah Omar, and within a matter of months the terrorist leader's position in Afghanistan was secure. He then turned his attention to al-Qaeda, which became a leading sponsor and organizer of terrorist attacks against secular Arab regimes and U.S. targets, including embassies, naval ships, and military personnel. The organization steadily expanded during this period, as young recruits answered repeated calls from bin Laden for a global jihad against the United States and Israel.

Bin Laden and the September 11 Attacks

In 1999 bin Laden gave his approval to a terrorist scheme to hijack several U.S. airplanes and fly them into American buildings that held special symbolic or strategic importance. Over the next several months he worked closely on the plot with Khaled Sheikh Mohammed, who had first suggested the idea to the al-Qaeda leader back in 1996. They selected pilots and other hijackers for the attack, provided money to train and house them in the United States, and gave them logistical support.

The terrorist plot was unveiled on the morning of September 11, 2001. The al-Qaeda members hijacked four U.S. airplanes flying out of three different East Coast airports. Two of the planes were steered by hijackers into New York City's World Trade Center and another was driven into the Pentagon in Arlington, Virginia. Counterterrorism experts believe that the fourth plane's target was probably the capitol building in Washington, D.C., or perhaps even the White House. But when brave passengers tried to wrest control of the plane from the hijackers, the flight—United Airlines Flight 93—crashed in a field in Pennsylvania.

The United States responded quickly to the horrible attacks of September 11. American military forces invaded Afghanistan and swept the Taliban from power. Bin Laden narrowly avoided capture or death, however, and he disappeared into the mountainous border country between Afghanistan and Pakistan. Al-Qaeda operatives occasionally released videotapes of their leader, but it was difficult to tell when some of these videos had been recorded.

The Bush administration continued to search for bin Laden, but the trail grew cold. By the five-year anniversary of the September 11 attacks, some Americans despaired that he would ever be brought to justice for his crimes. Others wondered if, unbeknownst to the outside world, he was already lying dead in a cave from some injury or illness.

In the meantime, the organization that bin Laden had created—al-Qaeda—came under years of punishing attacks from the administrations of both George W. Bush and Barack Obama. By 2011 some U.S. counterterrorism officials were expressing cautious optimism that al-Qaeda had been broken. But the inability to find the organization's chief merchant of death remained a source of tremendous frustration to U.S. military and intelligence forces, as well as millions of ordinary Americans. On May 2, 2011, however, Obama made a dramatic late-night television appearance to announce that U.S. special forces had, only a few hours earlier, found and killed bin Laden in a compound in the village of Abbottabad, Pakistan. This news was greeted across much of America with spontaneous celebrations and expressions of grim satisfaction. It also provided a measure of comfort and relief to the thousands of families who lost loved ones in bin Laden's murderous September 11 attack.

Sources

Coll, Steve. *The Bin Ladens: An Arabian Family in the American Century.* New York: Penguin, 2008.
Wright, Lawrence. *The Looming Tower: Al-Qaeda and the Road to 9/11.* New York: Vintage Books, 2006.
Zernike, Kate, and Michael T. Kaufman. "The Most Wanted Face of Terrorism," *New York Times,* May 2, 2011.

George W. Bush (1946-)
*President of the United States during the
September 11 Terrorist Attacks*

George Walker Bush was born on July 6, 1946, in New Haven, Connecticut. His parents were Barbara Pierce Bush and George Herbert Walker Bush, an oil industry executive who later became U.S. ambassador to the United Nations, director of the Central Intelligence Agency (CIA), and the forty-first president of the United States. Young George was raised mostly in Texas, but in 1961 he enrolled at Phillips Academy, a prestigious prep school in Andover, Massachusetts. In 1964 he enrolled at Yale University in New Haven, Connecticut, which his father had also attended. He did not distinguish himself academically at Yale, but he was president of his fraternity and he earned a bachelor's degree in history in 1968.

Bush's studies at Yale enabled him to secure a student deferment from a national military draft that the United States had instituted to obtain soldiers for the Vietnam War. As his time at Yale drew to a close, Bush applied for a pilot position in the Texas Air National Guard (members of the National Guard were much less likely to be sent to fight in Vietnam than soldiers who enlisted or were drafted). Bush received a spot, and he was commissioned a second lieutenant in July 1968. He fulfilled his training and became a certified fighter pilot in June 1970. Over the next three years, however, records indicate that Bush missed many months of duty while he was nominally assigned to a base in Alabama. The controversy over whether Bush fulfilled all his military obligations during this period flared up on numerous occasions over the next few decades—and especially during the 2000 and 2004 presidential election campaigns. In 1973 Bush was discharged from the Texas Air National Guard and transferred to the Air Force Reserve. He received an honorable discharge from the Air Force Reserve on November 21, 1974.

Making His Mark in Texas

In 1975 Bush received a master's degree in business administration from Harvard University. He then made an unsuccessful bid in 1978 to represent

Texas in the U.S. House of Representatives. Shaking off this disappointment, Bush moved to Midland, Texas, and began working as an executive in the oil industry. In 1986 Bush stopped drinking alcohol after he determined that it was becoming an unhealthy force in his life. Bush credits this decision, along with a renewal of his Christian religious faith, as essential to his later personal happiness and professional success. In 1988 he worked on his father's successful election campaign to win the White House. Shortly thereafter, he organized a group of investors to purchase the Texas Rangers baseball franchise.

In 1994 Bush resigned from his position with the Rangers to run for governor of Texas. A Republican like his father, Bush won his party's nomination. He then defeated incumbent Democratic governor Ann Richards. When he easily won re-election four years later, many Republicans around the country began touting Bush as someone capable of winning the White House.

In 2000 Bush accepted the grueling challenge of a presidential campaign. He held off Arizona Senator John McCain for the Republican nomination, then faced off against the Democratic nominee, Vice President Al Gore, in the general election. The November 2000 presidential election was the closest in U.S. history. Gore actually won the popular vote, garnering half a million more votes than Bush. But Bush became the forty-third president of the United States after a controversial U.S. Supreme Court decision ended a ballot recount of the popular vote in Florida, which had given its decisive electoral college votes to Bush by a razor-thin margin. This ruling, issued despite widespread evidence of voting irregularities and ballot confusion in Florida, preserved Bush's narrow margin in the electoral college. Bush took office on January 20, 2001.

During Bush's first months as president, he received numerous warnings about the threat of terrorist attacks by al-Qaeda from U.S. intelligence officials. Bush responded by ordering national security and counterterrorism departments in his administration to prepare new strategies for neutralizing al-Qaeda and its leader, Osama bin Laden. But these instructions failed to reassure officials like counterterrorism czar Richard Clarke or CIA Director George Tenet. By August 2001, in fact, Tenet had become so concerned about the danger posed by al-Qaeda that he personally took a group of CIA analysts to Crawford, Texas, where Bush was vacationing. The August 17 briefing did not, however, result in any changes in government security or counterterrorism policies. Bush's mild reaction to the special briefing did not escape the notice of the 9/11 Commission, which was charged with investigating why

America was unable to stop the al-Qaeda attacks from taking place on September 11, 2001. "Both Presidents Bill Clinton and George Bush and their top advisors told us they got the picture—they understood Bin Ladin was a danger. But given the character and pace of their policy efforts, we do not believe they fully understood just how many people al-Qaeda might kill, and how soon it might do it. At some level that is hard to define, we believe the threat had not yet become compelling."[1]

Responding to September 11

Bush was appearing at an event at an elementary school in Sarasota, Florida, on the morning of September 11, 2001. News of the terrorist hijackings and the collapse of the World Trade Center towers triggered a chaotic day for the president, who was whisked from military base to military base before finally returning to Washington, D.C., on the evening of the 11th. He delivered a brief nationally televised address to the American people about the terrorist attacks that night, but most of his time was spent huddled with military and intelligence advisors. They soon devised a strategy for carrying out an international "war on terror" that focused first on Afghanistan, where bin Laden was based. In October 2001 the United States launched a major military invasion of Afghanistan. This offensive succeeded in toppling the Taliban, the Islamic fundamentalist rulers of Afghanistan. It also destroyed al-Qaeda camps in many parts of the country. But the mission failed to capture or kill bin Laden, who escaped and disappeared.

In March 2003 the Bush administration launched a military invasion of Iraq, which it repeatedly described as a looming threat to U.S. security. Bush and various top White House officials warned that Iraqi dictator Saddam Hussein maintained a secret program to develop weapons of mass destruction (WMD). On some occasions they also implied that Iraq had played a role in the September 11 attacks. Both of these charges were later proven to be untrue. The U.S. invasion of Iraq, meanwhile, succeeded in ousting Iraqi dictator Saddam Hussein. But the subsequent American occupation of the country proved far more expensive and violent than the Bush administration had anticipated. The main factor in these grim trends was a steady barrage of attacks against U.S. soldiers and Iraqi citizens by "insurgents"—armed rebels who refused to recognize the authority of the United States or the new Iraqi government. By 2007 Bush's decision to invade Iraq had become tremendously unpopular with the American people. That same year, however, he approved a military "surge" in Iraq. This campaign greatly reduced insurgent activity and improved security conditions across much of the country.

Bush left office on January 20, 2009, after serving two full terms in the White House (he narrowly defeated Democratic nominee John Kerry in the 2004 presidential election). He retired to his ranch in Crawford, Texas, where he has kept a relatively low profile. In 2010, however, he published a memoir of his years in the White House. In this book, titled *Decision Points*, Bush described the September 11 terrorist attacks as the single most important event of his presidency. "September 11 redefined sacrifice," he wrote. "It redefined duty. And it redefined my job. The story of that week is the key to understanding my presidency. There were so many decisions that followed, many of them controversial and complex. Yet after 9/11, I felt my responsibility was clear. For as long as I held office, I could never forget what happened to America that day. I would pour my heart and soul into protecting the country, whatever it took."[2]

Sources

Bush, George W. *Decision Points*. New York: Crown, 2010.

Frum, David. *The Right Man: The Surprise Presidency of George W. Bush*. New York: Random House, 2003.

Rich, Frank. *The Greatest Story Ever Sold: The Decline and Fall of Truth, from 9/11 to Katrina*. New York: Penguin Press, 2006.

Notes

[1] National Commission on Terrorist Attacks Upon the United States [The 9/11 Commission]. *The 9/11 Commission Report*. New York: Norton, 2004, pp. 342-43.

[2] Bush, George W. *Decision Points*. New York: Crown, 2010, p. 151.

Richard A. Clarke (1951-)
Top Counterterrorism Official in the Clinton and Bush Administrations

Richard Alan Clarke was born on October 27, 1951, in Dorcester, Massachusetts. His father died when he was very young, and he was raised in the Boston area by his widowed mother, who worked as a nurse. Clarke graduated from Boston Latin High School in 1968 and earned a bachelor's degree from the University of Pennsylvania in 1972. A few months later he accepted a position in the Department of Defense as a nuclear weapons analyst. This 1973 posting marked the beginning of a career of government service that spanned thirty years. It was interrupted only by a brief break in 1978, when he earned a master's degree from the Massachusetts Institute of Technology.

Rising Through the Ranks of the Intelligence Community

In the late 1970s Clarke moved over to the State Department, where he worked as a foreign intelligence analyst. By this time he was building a reputation as a brilliant but prickly expert on spycraft and foreign affairs. The Reagan administration recognized his talents, and by the mid-1980s he had risen to the influential position of Assistant Secretary of State for Intelligence in the Republican-led administration.

Clarke stayed on board at the State Department when another Republican, George H.W. Bush, succeeded Ronald Reagan as president in early 1989. During Bush's four-year term Clarke was Assistant Secretary of State for Political-Military Affairs. In this capacity he played an important role in coordinating America's successful efforts to build and support an international military response to Iraq's 1990 invasion of Kuwait. The Gulf War ended in a decisive victory for the American-led military coalition, which forced Iraqi dictator Saddam Hussein to withdraw his army from Kuwait in the fall of 1991.

Clarke's status as one of the State Department's top-ranking intelligence officials remained unchanged even after Democrat Bill Clinton defeated Bush in the 1992 presidential election. Clinton named Clarke to head up a special Counterterrorism Strategy Group (CSG), and from 1995 to 1998 he served as Assistant Secretary of State for Intelligence. In May 1998 Clinton promoted him again, making Clarke the nation's first-ever National Coordinator for Security, Infrastructure Protection, and Counterterrorism. The American news media quickly shortened that title to "counterterrorism czar." The title did not account for Clarke's many responsibilities that were not related to terrorism, but administration officials say that it accurately reflected Clarke's deep passion for counterterrorism issues. As early as 1996, in fact, Clarke was one of only a handful of intelligence analysts sounding the alarm about a fanatical anti-American Saudi citizen named Osama bin Laden, who was building a private army of radical Islamists in Afghanistan.

Issues Repeated Warnings about al-Qaeda

By mid-1998 the Clinton White House had become sufficiently concerned about bin Laden that it decided to include Clarke in the administration's highest-level discussions about counterterrorism and national security. In many instances, in fact, Clarke was a major presence in counterterrorism meetings attended by Clinton and his top aides. From this point forward he repeatedly urged the United States to take stronger measures to protect itself from al-Qaeda, from beefing up homeland security to approving military strikes against bin Laden and his terrorist training camps. In Clarke's view, the need for tougher policies was further underscored by events such as the 1998 attacks on U.S. embassies in Tanzania and Kenya and the 2000 suicide attack against the USS *Cole* in Yemen. Virtually every proposal to take out bin Laden remained untried, however. Most of them were shelved because they were viewed as too risky by the Central Intelligence Agency (CIA) or U.S. military officials.

In January 2001 Republican George W. Bush was inaugurated as the forty-third president of the United States. The Bush White House decided to keep Clarke on as the head of the National Security Council's Counterterrorism Strategy Group. But National Security Advisor Condoleezza Rice and other top aides decided to downgrade his position. Instead of meeting directly with President Bush, Secretary of State Colin Powell, Rice, CIA Director George Tenet, and other top national security officials, Clarke was told to meet with deputy officials who did not have the same authority to make decisions about counterterrorism policies.

The demotion angered Clarke, who felt that the administration did not appreciate just how much of a threat al-Qaeda posed. In meetings and memos throughout the spring and summer of 2001 he urged Rice and other top officials to speed up their review of American counterterrorism policies and take new security precautions. "Are we serious about dealing with the Al Qaeda threat?" he wrote in a memo to Rice one week before the September 11 attacks. "Decision makers should imagine themselves on a future day when the CSG has not succeeded in stopping Al Qaeda attacks and hundreds of Americans lay dead in several countries, including the U.S. What would those decision makers wish that they had done earlier? That future day could happen at any time."[1] Clarke eventually became so frustrated by the tepid response to his terrorism warnings that he requested a transfer to cybersecurity issues in mid-2001.

Clark was still the nation's counterterrorism czar, however, when bin Laden's hijackers struck America on the morning of September 11. Clarke took a lead role in coordinating the national government's response to the attacks that had taken place in New York and Washington. Concerned about possible other attacks, he issued dozens of counterterrorism instructions to people ranging from Secretary of Defense Donald Rumsfeld to Director Tenet on that day. In the weeks following, he also helped map out strategies for capturing or killing bin Laden and smashing al-Qaeda. He later said, however, that none of these actions might have been necessary if the Bush administration had taken the threat of al-Qaeda more seriously.

At the Center of a Political Firestorm

Clarke resigned from his position in February 2003. Upon leaving the government, he immediately began speaking out against the Bush administration's antiterrorism performance in the weeks and months prior to September 11. He also condemned the Bush White House for its decision to invade Iraq in 2003. According to Clarke, the U.S. invasion of Iraq was falsely sold to the American public as an anti-terrorism campaign. He also asserted that by focusing so much attention and military strength on Iraq, the Bush administration failed to remove bin Laden and al-Qaeda as a threat.

Clark delivered his sharp criticisms in television interviews, a bestselling book called *Against All Enemies: Inside America's War on Terror* (2004), and nationally televised testimony before the 9/11 Commission. His statements triggered a tremendous backlash from the Bush administration, its allies in Congress, and conservative media outlets. Clarke was painted by some detractors as an embittered bureaucrat who refused to take responsibility for his own failures. Some Republicans tried to discredit him by calling him a liar who manufactured anti-Bush charges to sell books. Impartial observers such as the 9/11 Commission, however, have generally supported Clarke's claims that he issued many warnings about bin Laden and the danger he posed—and that these warnings were not treated with the necessary urgency.

After leaving government service, Clark founded Good Harbor Consulting, a strategic planning and corporate risk management firm. He has also taught at Harvard's Kennedy School of Government and the Belfer Center for Science and International Affairs. He is a frequent commentator on counterterrorism, foreign policy, and computer security issues, and has become a published novelist as well.

When Clarke learned in May 2011—fifteen years after he had first begun sounding the alarm about bin Laden—that the al-Qaeda leader had finally been killed by U.S. Special Forces in Pakistan, the former counterterrorism official admitted that he "did not feel any sense of satisfaction at all. I put it this way: if you order a pizza that arrives 15 years late you are not going to find it satisfying…. I thought that closure would happen. But really it did not help. It just sort of reminded me it had taken 15 years."[2]

Sources

Clarke, Richard A. *Against All Enemies: Inside America's War on Terror.* New York: Free Press, 2004.
Coll, Steve. *Ghost Wars: The Secret History of the CIA, Afghanistan, and bin Laden, from the Soviet Invasion to September 10, 2001.* New York: Penguin, 2004.
Kaplan, Fred. "Dick Clarke Is Telling the Truth: Why He's Right About Bush's Negligence on Terrorism." *Slate.com*, March 23, 2004. Retrieved from http://www.slate.com/id/2097685/

Notes

[1] National Commission on Terrorist Attacks Upon the United States [The 9/11 Commission]. *The 9/11 Commission Report.* New York: Norton, 2004, p. 212.
[2] Quoted in Harris, Paul. "Living with 9/11: The Anti-Terror Chief," *The Guardian (UK),* September 5, 2011. Retrieved from http://www.guardian.co.uk/world/2011/sep/05/living-with-911-richard-clarke.

Khaled Sheikh Mohammed (1964?-)
Chief Architect of the September 11
Terrorist Attacks

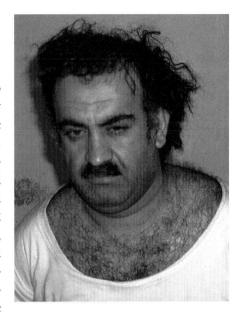

Khaled Sheikh Mohammed, who is also widely referred to in media reports by his initials, KSM, is believed to have been born in either 1964 or 1965 in Kuwait. His family, though, came from the large Pakistani province of Baluchistan, a rugged region located along the country's northern border with Afghanistan. Mohammed spent most of his childhood and youth in Kuwait, although he reportedly spent time in Pakistan as well. By age sixteen he had joined the Muslim Brotherhood, a Middle East-based organization that urged Arab states to adopt the Koran as the basis for all laws.

In the 1980s Mohammed traveled to the United States to continue his academic studies. In 1986 he earned a bachelor's degree in engineering from North Carolina A&T. He reportedly developed a negative attitude toward many aspects of American life during this time, but the 9/11 Commission stated in 2004 that much of the hatred that Mohammed later showed toward the United States stemmed from American policies that were supportive of Israel.[1]

In 1987 Mohammed went to Pakistan and settled in Peshawar. The city was a central gathering place for radical Islamists who wanted to join neighboring Afghanistan's jihad against the Soviet army, which had invaded the country back in 1979. It was during this time that Mohammed became acquainted with Osama bin Laden, who was emerging as one of the best-known "holy warriors" of the radical Islamic underworld.

Mohammed and the September 11 Plot

After the Soviets retreated from Afghanistan in 1989, Mohammed resumed his globe-trotting ways, traveling under dozens of false identities. By 1994 he had landed in the Philippines, where he began plotting terrorist strikes with his nephew, Ramzi Yousef, who one year earlier had tried to topple New York's World Trade Center towers with a van packed with explosives. Over a period of months Mohammed and Yousef devised what came to be known as the Bojinka Plot—a scheme to simultaneously blow up as many as twelve U.S. jetliners over the Pacific with smuggled bombs. The Bojinka Plot was uncovered in January 1995, however, and Yousef was captured in Pakistan one month later and turned over to U.S. authorities. Mohammed promptly went underground to avoid the same fate.

Mohammed's whereabouts became a mystery to U.S. intelligence agents for the next several years. After 9/11, though, investigators learned that in 1996 he traveled to Afghanistan and told bin Laden about the foiled Bojinka Plot. The plan reportedly intrigued the al-Qaeda leader, but he was noncommittal about approving something similar for his own organization. Mohammed, meanwhile, gradually fell deeper and deeper into al-Qaeda's orbit. The terrorist had always prided himself on being able to move freely among numerous jihadist groups, but he was very impressed when bin Laden's group carried out deadly suicide bombings against two American embassies in Africa in 1998. Now convinced that bin Laden had both the means and the desire to strike major blows against America, Mohammed agreed to become a full member of al-Qaeda in early 1999. From this point forward Mohammed was one of bin Laden's chief lieutenants.

Sometime in 1999 bin Laden also gave formal approval to a "planes operation" similar to the Bojinka Plot. Mohammed became the chief architect of the plot, though bin Laden and another high-ranking member of al-Qaeda named Mohammed Atef also contributed ideas. Under Mohammed's guidance, the plot gradually evolved into the September 11, 2001, plane hijackings and attacks on the World Trade Center and Pentagon.

After 9/11 Mohammed continued to dream up acts of terrorism against the United States and other "enemies of Islam." He reportedly confessed after his 2003 capture to being a central figure in the 2002 bombings of nightclubs in Bali, the failed December 2001 effort by "shoe bomber" Richard Reid to blow up a U.S. passenger plane in mid-flight, the 2002 kidnapping and murder of American journalist Daniel Pearl, and plots to attack high-value targets in Israel, England, and the United States.

In March 2003 Mohammed was captured by Pakistani intelligence officers in the city of Rawalpindi. He was promptly turned over to U.S. authorities. His exact whereabouts then became a mystery until late 2006, when

Bush administration officials moved him from a secret prison location to the U.S. naval base at Guantanamo Bay, Cuba, where several other prominent suspected terrorist leaders are also detained. In 2008 the Central Intelligence Agency (CIA) publicly acknowledged that during Mohammed's first few months in U.S. custody he was subjected to "waterboarding" a total of 183 times. This interrogation technique, which makes the prisoner feel like he is drowning, had historically been shunned by the United States as a form of torture. The Bush administration asserted, however, that this form of "enhanced interrogation" did not meet the definition of torture. In April 2009 President Barack Obama banned the controversial practice from being used in the interrogation of terrorist suspects.

That same year, the Obama administration recommended that Mohammed and several other 9/11 plotters receive civilian jury trials in New York City on war crimes charges. The Obama White House explained that such a move would show the world—including Arabic peoples—the transparency and fairness of the U.S. justice system. The administration also emphasized that prosecutors had an extremely strong case against the 9/11 suspects.

This decision, however, was met with a firestorm of objections. Critics alleged that a trial in New York might attract new terrorist attacks. Some also expressed concerns that since civilian courts had tighter standards for admissible evidence than military courts, Mohammed and his fellow terrorists might be able to obtain more lenient sentences or acquittal on some charges. In April 2011 the administration reluctantly reversed course and announced that Mohammed would be tried before a U.S. military tribunal at Guantanamo Bay.

Sources

Mayer, Jane. *The Dark Side: The Inside Story of How the War on Terror Turned into a War on American Ideals.* New York: Doubleday, 2008.

McDermott, Terry. *Perfect Soldiers: The 9/11 Hijackers: Who They Were, Why They Did It.* New York: HarperCollins, 2005.

"Profile: Khalid Sheikh Mohammed," *Sunday Times Online (UK),* March 15, 2007. Retrieved from http://www.timesonline.co.uk/tol/news/world/us_and_americas/article1517893.ece.

Notes

[1] National Commission on Terrorist Attacks Upon the United States [The 9/11 Commission]. *The 9/11 Commission Report.* New York: Norton, 2004, p. 147.

Condoleezza Rice (1954-)
National Security Advisor and Secretary of State to President George W. Bush

Condoleezza "Condi" Rice was born on November 4, 1954, in Birmingham, Alabama. Her father, John Wesley Rice Jr., was a Presbyterian minister and high school guidance counselor at one of the city's segregated black public schools. Her mother, Angelena (Ray), was a high school teacher and organist at her husband's church. Condi was an only child.

Rice spent her earliest years in a city that was one of the major flashpoints in America's civil rights struggles of the 1950s and 1960s. Racial segregation and blatant discriminatory treatment of African Americans and other minorities was commonplace in many parts of the United States, and especially in the Deep South. Nonetheless, Rice's parents worked hard to give her a quality education, expose her to the wider world, and teach her to follow her dreams and aspirations. She showed a talent for the piano at an early age, and as a youth she gave recitals and other performances all across the city. Rice also learned Spanish and French through private lessons, and she became an accomplished figure skater as well. Amid all of these extracurricular activities Rice also posted excellent academic marks.

The Rice family left Birmingham in 1965. After a brief stint in Tuscaloosa, Alabama, where John Rice worked as a college administrator, the family moved on to Denver, Colorado, in 1967. It was in Denver that Rice attended an integrated school for the first time. She earned her high school diploma in Denver at age fifteen. Rice's next stop was the University of Denver, where her father was employed as vice chancellor. She earned a bachelor's degree in political science (with top academic honors) in 1974. Rice then enrolled at Notre Dame University in Indiana, where she earned master's degrees in government and international studies in one year. In 1981 the twenty-six-year-old Rice received a Ph.D. in political science from the University of Denver.

Making a Mark in Washington

Rice's dazzling academic qualifications resulted in a fellowship offer from Stanford University's prestigious Center for International Security and

Arms Control. She became a professor of political science at Stanford as well, teaching courses on the history and political ideology of the Soviet Union. By 1987, when Rice became a tenured professor at Stanford, her reputation as a brilliant scholar and expert on Soviet affairs had attracted the attention of some of the country's leading politicians and diplomats. In 1989 she was approached by Brent Scowcroft, who had accepted an appointment to be national security advisor in the new administration of President George H.W. Bush. Scowcroft asked if she would be willing to become a deputy advisor with the National Security Council, an agency that helps the White House develop American foreign policy. Rice accepted the offer, and she quickly became known as the council's top expert on the Soviet Union and the Communist regimes of Eastern Europe. She also became a Special Assistant to the President for National Security Affairs.

From 1989 to 1991 Rice helped guide U.S. foreign policy through an exciting and turbulent period of world history. The Soviet Union crumbled and fell apart during these years, as did numerous Communist governments in Eastern Europe that the Soviets had long dominated. Years later, Rice acknowledged that she was stunned by the sudden collapse of America's longtime Cold War foe. "I felt joy for the Russian people, though I knew life would be tough for them," she said in a 2002 interview. "I also felt amazement at how it happened.... This was a state with 5 million men under arms and 30,000 nuclear weapons. But on December 25, 1991, [Soviet President Mikhail] Gorbachev sat on television and simply said never mind, after 75 years of communism. They brought down the hammer and sickle and ... it was over. We should be grateful to Gorbachev for the graceful exit of the Soviet Union, because I'm not sure that every leader would have made that choice."[1]

In late 1991 Rice returned to a teaching position at Stanford, but she continued to advise the Bush White House and corporate clients about Russia and other countries that had once been part of the Soviet empire. In 1993 she became the first woman and first African American to serve as provost at Stanford. This position gave her primary responsibility for the university's academic programs and budget. Rice served as Stanford's provost from 1993 to 1999.

America's First Female National Security Advisor

In December 2000 Rice agreed to join the incoming administration of George W. Bush, the son of former president George H.W. Bush, as his national security advisor. Rice became the first woman ever to hold the position, which calls for a complete command of all potential national security issues facing America. Once Bush took office in January 2001, Rice quickly became known as one of his closest and most trusted advisors on foreign policy and national security issues.

Rice's performance as national security advisor came under heavy scrutiny after the September 11 terrorist attacks on America by Osama bin laden and his Al-Qaeda terrorist organization. Critics inside and outside of government accused her of not taking the threat of bin Laden seriously, despite repeated warnings from the CIA and other counterterrorism agencies about the danger he posed. Detractors also ridiculed some of her efforts to defend the Bush White House against charges that it should have been better prepared for an Al-Qaeda attack. On May 16, 2002, for example, she told reporters that "I don't think anybody could have predicted that these people would take an airplane and slam it into the World Trade Center, take another one and slam it into the Pentagon—that they would try to use an airplane as a missile."[2] These remarks triggered a firestorm of anger from critics who pointed out that counterterrorism officials like Richard Clarke had repeatedly warned the administration about exactly that sort of attack. The most scathing assessment of Rice came from David Kay, who headed the U.S. WMD (weapons of mass destruction) search unit in Iraq after American military forces invaded that country. He called Rice "probably the worst national security adviser in modern times since the office was created."[3]

Rice and her many defenders strongly rejected these charges. They insisted that the Bush administration took the threat of terrorism very seriously from the moment President Bush took office, and they emphasized that many of the warnings they received from intelligence officials about Al-Qaeda were extremely vague. "There was no silver bullet that could have prevented the 9/11 attacks," she said in 2004 testimony before the 9/11 Commission. Rice acknowledged that the warnings were "troubling," but she said that "they don't tell us when [attacks will occur]. They don't tell us where."[4]

In January 2005 Rice left her position as national security advisor to become President Bush's secretary of state. Although she was the sixty-sixth secretary of state in U.S. history, she was only the second woman—and the first African-American woman—to hold the post. She served her country in this capacity until January 2009, when Bush left office.

Rice subsequently returned to Stanford, where she accepted professor-ships of political science and political economy. In addition to her teaching responsibilities at Stanford, Rice is a Senior Fellow on Public Policy at the Hoover Institution. In addition, she serves on the board of directors of a wide range of corporations and philanthropic organizations, including the John F. Kennedy Center for the Performing Arts, and the Boys and Girls Clubs of America.

Sources

Kessler, Ronald. *The Confidante: Condoleezza Rice and the Creation of the Bush Legacy.* New York: St. Martin's Press, 2007.

Mabry, Marcus. *Twice as Good: Condoleezza Rice and Her Path to Power.* New York: Rodale/Modern Times, 2007.

Rice, Condoleezza. *Extraordinary, Ordinary People: A Memoir of Family.* New York: Crown, 2010.

Rice, Condoleezza. "Oprah Interviews Condoleezza Rice." *O, The Oprah Magazine,* February 2002. Retrieved from http://www.oprah.com/omagazine/Oprah-Interviews-Condoleezza-Rice/1.

Woodward, Bob. *State of Denial.* New York: Simon & Schuster, 2006.

Notes

[1] Rice, Condoleezza. "Oprah Interviews Condoleezza Rice." *O, The Oprah Magazine,* February 2002. Retrieved from http://www.oprah.com/omagazine/Oprah-Interviews-Condoleezza-Rice/1.

[2] Quoted in Bumiller, Elizabeth. *Condoleezza Rice: An American Life.* New York: Random House, 2007, p. 180.

[3] Quoted in Woodward, Bob. *State of Denial.* New York: Simon & Schuster, 2006, p. 330.

[4] "Transcript: Testimony of Condoleezza Rice Before 9/11 Commission." *New York Times,* April 8, 2004. Retrieved from http://www.nytimes.com/2004/04/08/politics/08RICE-TEXT.html.

George Tenet (1953-)
Director of the Central Intelligence Agency (CIA) from 1997 to 2004

George John Tenet was born on January 5, 1953, in Queens, New York. He and his twin brother Bill were the sons of Greek immigrants who owned a neighborhood diner. Tenet worked as a busboy in his family's diner and attended public schools in Queens. In 1976 he earned a bachelor's degree in foreign service from Georgetown University. Two years later Tenet received a master's degree in international affairs from New York's Columbia University.

In 1978 Tenet accepted a job as research director for the American Hellenic Institute, a lobbying organization devoted to policy issues that affect Greek Americans and U.S. relations with Greece. In 1979 he began a four-year stint working for the Solar Energy Industries Association. Tenet's career in government service began in 1982, when he joined the staff of Republican U.S. Senator H. John Heinz III of Pennsylvania. Tenet specialized in national security and energy issues for Heinz, and by 1985 he was the senator's top aide.

Becoming America's Spymaster

In 1985 Tenet joined the staff of the U.S. Senate's Select Committee on Intelligence (SSCI). This special committee is responsible for providing congressional oversight of spying and other intelligence-gathering operations conducted by the Central Intelligence Agency (CIA) and other government agencies. Tenet's hard work, talent, and outgoing personality all made a favorable impression on committee members, and in 1989 he was promoted to the position of SSCI staff director. Tenet served his country in that capacity for the next four years, during which time he became widely known in Washington as one of the country's leading experts on spycraft and other intelligence-gathering activities.

In 1993 President Bill Clinton selected Tenet to serve as director of intelligence programs at the National Security Council (NSC), a special group that provides counsel to the White House on major foreign policy issues. In July 1995 Tenet was transferred to the CIA to take a position as deputy director under CIA Director John Deutch. When Deutch resigned in December 1996, Clinton made Tenet the agency's acting director. The Clinton White House then nominated Anthony Lake to succeed Deutch. When Lake's nomination was blocked by Republicans in Congress, however, Clinton made Tenet his nominee. Tenet's long history of working with Republicans and Democrats on intelligence issues made his nomination a popular one, and he was unanimously confirmed in the Senate. He officially began his duties as CIA director on July 11, 1997.

Tenet has been credited with improving the agency's morale, which had suffered from losses of funding and personnel over the previous several years. He also pushed the CIA to pay more attention to the threat of terrorism. Several important counterterrorism initiatives were founded or expanded under Tenet's watch in the late 1990s, including Michael Scheuer's Alec Station, which was devoted to tracking Osama bin Laden and al-Qaeda, and Cofer Black's Counterterrorism Center, which monitored terrorism threats in the Middle East and around the world.

The Threat of al-Qaeda

During the late 1990s Tenet became extremely concerned that bin Laden and his terrorist network posed a genuine threat to American lives, both at home and overseas. Other counterterrorism officials in the Clinton administration echoed these fears, and various proposals to capture or kill bin Laden were considered. Most of these schemes were eventually shelved, though—at least in part because Tenet and some other CIA officials expressed misgivings about them. According to journalist Jane Mayer, "some of Tenet's underlings in the Agency grew increasingly frustrated with what they regarded as an overabundance of caution at the CIA. This was particularly true of Black. But despite pressure from the counterterrorism staff, Tenet himself never advised either President Clinton or President Bush to approve the use of lethal force against Al Qaeda. To him, it seemed drastic and politically risky."[1]

When George W. Bush became president in early 2001, he decided to keep Tenet at the helm of the CIA. During the spring and summer of 2001 Tenet and other counterterrorism officials expressed deep anxiety to the Bush White House about indications that al-Qaeda was plotting to stage a big attack on American soil. By July of 2001, Tenet later wrote, the U.S. national security system "was blinking red."[2] In other respects, though, the CIA's performance in the months leading up to the September 11 attacks was deeply flawed.[3] Most notably, the CIA failed to inform the Federal Bureau of Investigation (FBI), the State Department, or other intelligence agencies after it learned that two known al-Qaeda operatives (Nawaf al-Hazmi and Khalid al-Mihdhar, who would later participate in the 9/11 hijackings) had entered the United States in the spring of 2000. Critics say that if this information had been shared, an FBI investigation might have uncovered the 9/11 plot before it could be executed.

After the September 11 attacks took place, Tenet and the CIA played a lead role in identifying the terrorists and planning campaigns to eradicate al-Qaeda. But his directorship continued to be dogged by controversy. When the 9/11 Commission was convened to determine why America had fallen victim to bin Laden's diabolical scheme, many commission members and staff became frustrated with Tenet's inability to recall details of meetings and conversations about al-Qaeda prior to the attacks.

Tenet was also mocked and criticized for telling Bush in a December 2002 meeting that the CIA possessed "slam-dunk" evidence that Iraq possessed weapons of mass destruction.[4] Tenet's remarks almost certainly contributed to Bush's decision to invade Iraq a few weeks later. After the invasion took place, however, investigators learned that Iraq did not possess a program for producing chemical, biological, or nuclear weapons.

In June 2004 Tenet resigned his post as CIA director, citing personal reasons. His directorship was the second-longest in the agency's history, ranking only behind Allen Welsh Dulles (who served from February 1953 to November 1961). In December 2004 Bush awarded him the Presidential Medal of Freedom, the highest honor that the federal government can bestow on a civilian.

Since leaving the CIA Tenet has worked in the private sector as an executive for several financial firms and software companies. In 2007 Tenet also published a memoir, *At the Center of the Storm: My Years at the CIA*, in which he gave his perspective on the war on terror and the 2003 invasion of Iraq.

Sources

Coll, Steve. *Ghost Wars: The Secret History of the CIA, Afghanistan, and bin Laden, from the Soviet Invasion to September 10, 2001*. New York: Penguin, 2004.

Schorn, Daniel. "George Tenet: At the Center of the Storm." CBSNews.com, February 11, 2009. Retrieved from http://www.cbsnews.com/stories/2007/04/25/60minutes/main2728375.shtml.

Notes

[1] Mayer, Jane. *The Dark Side: The Inside Story of How the War on Terror Turned into a War on American Ideals.* New York: Doubleday, 2008, p. 20.
[2] Tenet, George. *At the Center of the Storm: My Years at the CIA.* New York: HarperCollins, 2007, p. 198.
[3] National Commission on Terrorist Attacks Upon the United States [The 9/11 Commission]. *The 9/11 Commission Report.* New York: Norton, 2004, pp. 86-92, 254-77.
[4] Quoted in Woodward, Bob. *Plan of Attack.* New York: Simon and Schuster, 2004, p. 249.

Ayman al-Zawahiri (1951-)
Egyptian Leader of Al-Jihad and Major Figure in al-Qaeda

Ayman Muhammad Rabaie al-Zawahiri was born on June 19, 1951, in Maadi, a suburb of the Egyptian capital of Cairo. He was raised in an atmosphere of wealth, privilege, and scholarly pursuits. His father was a well-known professor and physician, and his paternal grandfather served for a time as the Imam of al-Azhar mosque, the highest authority in the Sunni branch of Islam.

Radicalized at a Young Age

Serious and studious, al-Zawahiri was pulled into the current of Islamic fanaticism at a young age. In his early teens he became obsessed with the political and religious ideas of radical Islamic writers like Sayyid Qutb, a fellow Egyptian. At age fourteen he even joined an Islamic group dedicated to the overthrow of the secular (non-religious) Egyptian government. Al-Zawahiri's extreme beliefs further hardened in the late 1960s, when Israel defeated the armies of several Arab nations in the Six-Day War. From this point forward, al-Zawahiri was convinced that the pathway to a new age of Arab glory lay in jihad—holy war against secular Arab rulers, Israel, and the heathens of the Western world.

Al-Zawahiri continued his academic studies throughout this period of political radicalization. He graduated from Cairo University's medical college in 1974 and earned his master's degree in surgery from the school in 1978. One year later he married and started a family. Throughout these years, however, al-Zawahiri dove deeper into the world of Islamic fundamentalism. He was one of the primary founders of al-Jihad (also known as Egyptian Islamic Jihad), a terrorist organization dedicated to the overthrow of Egyptian President Anwar Sadat and the establishment of a new government founded on strict interpretations of the Koran, the holy book of Islam.

On October 6, 1981, Sadat was killed by al-Jihad assassins. He was replaced by Hosni Mubarak, whose security forces swept across Egypt to find the killers and stamp out their radical Islamic sympathizers. Al-Zawahiri was caught in this dragnet. Although he was not personally implicated in the Sadat assassination, he was convicted of other charges, including illegal weapons dealing. Imprisoned in 1981, he was reportedly tortured repeatedly by Egyptian authorities until his release in 1984. The brutality he experienced in jail further fueled his rage, and after his release he became even more dedicated to his violent and strict brand of Islam.

Al-Zawahiri left Egypt for a hospital job in Saudi Arabia in 1986. Before long, however, he decided to go to Pakistan, which had become a major entry point into Afghanistan for radical Islamists wishing to help Afghan fighters in their war against Soviet military occupation. He rebuilt al-Jihad in the Pakistani city of Peshawar, where he also met Osama bin Laden. The two men quickly became allies, and terrorism experts believe that al-Zawahiri's bloodthirsty vision of Islamic revolution had a big impact on bin Laden's beliefs and goals. In 1988 bin Laden formed al-Qaeda with assistance from al-Zawahiri and a handful of other trusted "true believers."

Bin Laden's Right-Hand Man

After the Soviet Union withdrew from Afghanistan in 1989, al-Zawahiri landed briefly in Europe before joining bin Laden again in Sudan. From there he orchestrated terrorist activities against Mubarak's government throughout the mid-1990s. The deadliest of these attacks was a suicide bombing attack on the Egyptian embassy in Islamabad, Pakistan, that killed sixteen people. Egyptian authorities responded to this bombing with a sweeping counterattack that badly damaged al-Jihad's operations. In late 1996 al-Zawahiri was arrested by Russian authorities when he tried to cross the border into Chechnya, a Russian republic where Islamic rebels had launched a fight for independence. He was held in custody for several months but was eventually released.

In 1998 al-Zawahiri returned to Afghanistan, where he merged his fading al-Jihad organization with bin Laden's thriving al-Qaeda network. That same year he was sentenced to death "in absentia" (despite not being in custody) for helping to plan the so-called Luxor Massacre of November 17, 1997. This terrorist attack by Islamic radicals claimed the lives of seventy foreign tourists and native workers at a popular vacation spot in Egypt.

After formally joining his group to al-Qaeda, al-Zawahiri acted as bin Laden's chief counselor and strategic advisor. He also helped bin Laden hone his fanatical beliefs to an even sharper edge. Scholars and counterterrorism

185

experts speculate that al-Zawahiri's support for targeting civilians and other innocents for terrorist attacks played an important role in shaping al-Qaeda's murderous agenda.

Al-Zawahiri played a major role in the planning of the September 11, 2001, terrorist attacks on the United States. He helped develop the hijacking scheme used on 9/11, and he also was involved in the selection of the terrorists who were used in the operation. In the wake of those attacks, he became one of the most hunted men on the entire planet. American intelligence and military forces were unable to capture or kill him, however, and he disappeared. Most experts believe that he is still hiding somewhere in the wilderness border region of Afghanistan and Pakistan.

After bin Laden was found and killed by American military forces in May 2011, al-Zawahiri became the new leader of al-Qaeda. Counterterrorism experts, though, say that al-Zawahiri lacks the charisma and popularity of his predecessor. They speculate that al-Zawahiri—who is still being relentlessly hunted by U.S. forces—will face a steep challenge to keep the battered al-Qaeda organization from fading into oblivion.

Sources

Musharbash, Yassin. "Loss of Bin Laden Threatens al-Qaeda 'Brand,'" *Spiegel Online,* September 2, 2011. Retrieved from http://www.spiegel.de/international/world/0,1518,783655,00.html.

Naughton, Philippe. "The Man They Call Osama bin Laden's Brain," *The Sunday Times (UK),* August 4, 2005. Retrieved from http://www.timesonline.co.uk/tol/news/uk/article551544.ece.

Wright, Lawrence. *The Looming Tower: Al-Qaeda and the Road to 9/11.* New York: Vintage Books, 2006.

PRIMARY SOURCES

Osama Bin Laden and the World Islamic Front Call for a "Holy War" Against Jews and Crusaders

During the late 1990s Osama bin Laden issued two "fatwas" in which he urged devout Muslims to wage war against the United States and Israel. The first of these declarations came in August 1996. The second, which is reprinted here, was issued on February 23, 1998, through a London-based Arabic newspaper. In it, he claims that U.S. occupation of Arab lands following the 1991 Persian Gulf War and U.S. support for Israel justify a jihad, or holy war. Although the 1998 fatwa was viewed as bin Laden's fatwa, it was also co-signed by Ayman al-Zawahiri and several other radical Islamic leaders. These terror chieftains agreed to release the jihad under the banner of the World Islamic Front, but American intelligence officials recognized that it was primarily bin Laden's creation.

Praise be to Allah, who revealed the Book, controls the clouds, defeats factionalism, and says in His Book: "But when the forbidden months are past, then fight and slay the pagans wherever ye find them, seize them, beleaguer them, and lie in wait for them in every stratagem (of war)"; and peace be upon our Prophet, Muhammad Bin-'Abdallah, who said: I have been sent with the sword between my hands to ensure that no one but Allah is worshipped, Allah who put my livelihood under the shadow of my spear and who inflicts humiliation and scorn on those who disobey my orders.

The Arabian Peninsula has never—since Allah made it flat, created its desert, and encircled it with seas—been stormed by any forces like the crusader armies spreading in it like locusts, eating its riches and wiping out its plantations. All this is happening at a time in which nations are attacking Muslims like people fighting over a plate of food. In the light of the grave situation and the lack of support, we and you are obliged to discuss current events, and we should all agree on how to settle the matter.

No one argues today about three facts that are known to everyone; we will list them, in order to remind everyone:

First, for over seven years the United States has been occupying the lands of Islam in the holiest of places, the Arabian Peninsula, plundering its riches, dictating to its rulers, humiliating its people, terrorizing its neighbors, and turning its bases in the Peninsula into a spearhead through which to fight the neighboring Muslim peoples.

If some people have in the past argued about the fact of the occupation, all the people of the Peninsula have now acknowledged it. The best proof of this is the Americans' continuing aggression against the Iraqi people using the Peninsula as a staging post, even though all its rulers are against their territories being used to that end, but they are helpless.

Second, despite the great devastation inflicted on the Iraqi people by the crusader-Zionist alliance, and despite the huge number of those killed, which has exceeded 1 million … despite all this, the Americans are once again trying to repeat the horrific massacres, as though they are not content with the protracted blockade imposed after the ferocious war or the fragmentation and devastation.

So here they come to annihilate what is left of this people and to humiliate their Muslim neighbors.

Third, if the Americans' aims behind these wars are religious and economic, the aim is also to serve the Jews' petty state and divert attention from its occupation of Jerusalem and murder of Muslims there. The best proof of this is their eagerness to destroy Iraq, the strongest neighboring Arab state, and their endeavor to fragment all the states of the region such as Iraq, Saudi Arabia, Egypt, and Sudan into paper statelets and through their disunion and weakness to guarantee Israel's survival and the continuation of the brutal crusade occupation of the Peninsula.

All these crimes and sins committed by the Americans are a clear declaration of war on Allah, his messenger, and Muslims. And ulema [Muslim scholars] have throughout Islamic history unanimously agreed that the jihad is an individual duty if the enemy destroys the Muslim countries. This was revealed by Imam Bin-Qadamah in "Al-Mughni," Imam al-Kisa'i in "Al-Bada'i," al-Qurtubi in his interpretation, and the shaykh of al-Islam in his books, where he said: "As for the fighting to repulse [an enemy], it is aimed at defending sanctity and religion, and it is a duty as agreed [by the ulema]. Nothing is more sacred than belief except repulsing an enemy who is attacking religion and life."

On that basis, and in compliance with Allah's order, we issue the following fatwa to all Muslims:

The ruling to kill the Americans and their allies—civilians and military—is an individual duty for every Muslim who can do it in any country in which it is possible to do it, in order to liberate the al-Aqsa Mosque and the holy mosque [Mecca] from their grip, and in order for their armies to move out of all the lands of Islam, defeated and unable to threaten any Muslim.

190

This is in accordance with the words of Almighty Allah, "and fight the pagans all together as they fight you all together," and "fight them until there is no more tumult or oppression, and there prevail justice and faith in Allah."

This is in addition to the words of Almighty Allah: "And why should ye not fight in the cause of Allah and of those who, being weak, are ill-treated (and oppressed)?—women and children, whose cry is: 'Our Lord, rescue us from this town, whose people are oppressors; and raise for us from thee one who will help!'"

We—with Allah's help—call on every Muslim who believes in Allah and wishes to be rewarded to comply with Allah's order to kill the Americans and plunder their money wherever and whenever they find it. We also call on Muslim ulema, leaders, youths, and soldiers to launch the raid on Satan's U.S. troops and the devil's supporters allying with them, and to displace those who are behind them so that they may learn a lesson.

Almighty Allah said: "O ye who believe, give your response to Allah and His Apostle, when He calleth you to that which will give you life. And know that Allah cometh between a man and his heart, and that it is He to whom ye shall all be gathered."

Almighty Allah also says: "O ye who believe, what is the matter with you, that when ye are asked to go forth in the cause of Allah, ye cling so heavily to the earth! Do ye prefer the life of this world to the hereafter? But little is the comfort of this life, as compared with the hereafter. Unless ye go forth, He will punish you with a grievous penalty, and put others in your place; but Him ye would not harm in the least. For Allah hath power over all things."

Almighty Allah also says: "So lose no heart, nor fall into despair. For ye must gain mastery if ye are true in faith."

Source

Bin Laden, Osama, and World Islamic Front. "Jihad against Jews and Crusaders," February 23, 1998. Retrieved from Federation of American Scientists website, http://www.fas.org/irp/world/para/docs/980223-fatwa.htm.

An al-Qaeda Manual Urges the Overthrow of "Apostate" Arab Rulers

The rapid growth of radical Islamic groups in the second half of the twentieth century stemmed in large part from popular discontent with the regimes of the Middle East. Corruption and repression were trademarks of many of these governments, as was secularism. Their rejection of Islamic law in the creation and operation of governmental laws and institutions deeply angered some fundamentalist Muslims. They insisted that if Arab peoples overthrew the "apostates"— Muslims who had turned their backs on their faith—and adopted sharia law, they would prosper and escape the evil influence of the United States and the West.

This message became a recurring theme in the recruiting and propaganda efforts of al-Qaeda and other Islamic terrorist organizations in the 1980s and 1990s, as the following excerpt from an al-Qaeda training manual shows. This booklet was discovered by police in Manchester, England, during a search of an al-Qaeda member's home computer. Originally written in Arabic, the manual—which also provides a glimpse into the ruthless military codes adopted by al-Qaeda— was later translated into English by investigators.

Introduction

Martyrs were killed, women were widowed, children were orphaned, men were handcuffed, chaste women's heads were shaved, harlots' heads were crowned, atrocities were inflicted on the innocent, gifts were given to the wicked, virgins were raped on the prostitution altar....

After expelling the colonialists, our Islamic nation was afflicted with apostate rulers who took over in the Moslem nation. These rulers turned out to be more infidel and criminal than the colonialists themselves. Moslems have endured all kinds of harm, oppression, and torture at their hands.

Those apostate rulers threw thousands of the Haraka Al-Islamyia (Islamic Movement) youth in gloomy jails and detention centers that were equipped with the most modern torture devices and [manned with] experts in oppression and torture.... But they [the rulers] did not stop there; they started to fragment the essence of the Islamic nation by trying to eradicate its Moslem identity. Thus, they started spreading godless and atheistic views among the youth. We found some that claimed that socialism was from Islam, democracy was the [religious] council, and the prophet—God bless and keep him—propagandized communism.

Colonialism and its followers, the apostate rulers, then started to openly erect crusader centers, societies, and organizations like Masonic Lodges, Lions and Rotary clubs, and foreign schools. They aimed at producing a wasted generation that pursued everything that is western and produced rulers, ministers, leaders, physicians, engineers, businessmen, politicians, journalists, and information specialists. [Koranic verse:] "And Allah's enemies plotted and planned, and Allah too planned, and the best of planners is Allah."

They [the rulers] tried, using every means and [kind of] seduction, to produce a generation of young men that did not know [anything] except what they [the rulers] want, did not say except what they [the rulers] think about, did not live except according to their [the rulers'] way, and did not dress except in their [the rulers'] clothes. However, majestic Allah turned their deception back on them, as a large group of those young men who were raised by them [the rulers] woke up from their sleep and returned to Allah, regretting and repenting.

The young men returning to Allah realized that Islam is not just performing rituals but a complete system: Religion and government, worship and Jihad [holy war], ethics and dealing with people, and the Koran and sword. The bitter situation that the nation has reached is a result of its divergence from Allah's course and his righteous law for all places and times. That [bitter situation] came about as a result of its children's love for the world, their loathing of death, and their abandonment of Jihad [holy war].

Unbelief is still the same.... It is the same unbelief that drove Sadat, Hosni Mubarak, Gadhafi, Hafez Assad, Saleh, Fahed—Allah's curse be upon the non-believing leaders—and all the apostate Arab rulers to torture, kill, imprison, and torment Moslems.

These young men realized that an Islamic government would never be established except by the bomb and rifle. Islam does not coincide or make a truce with unbelief, but rather confronts it.

The confrontation that Islam calls for with these godless and apostate regimes does not know Socratic debates, Platonic ideals nor Aristotelian diplomacy. But it knows the dialogue of bullets, the ideas of assassination, bombing, and destruction, and the diplomacy of the cannon and machine-gun.

The young came to prepare themselves for Jihad [holy war], commanded by the majestic Allah's order in the holy Koran. [Koranic verse:] "Against them make ready your strength to the utmost of your power, including steeds of war, to strike terror into (the hearts of) the enemies of Allah and your enemies, and others besides whom ye may not know, but whom Allah doth know."...

Principles of Military Organization:

Military Organization has three main principles without which it cannot be established.

1. Military Organization commander and advisory council
2. The soldiers (individual members)
3. A clearly defined strategy

Military Organization Requirements:

The Military Organization dictates a number of requirements to assist it in confrontation and endurance. These are:

1. Forged documents and counterfeit currency
2. Apartments and hiding places
3. Communication means
4. Transportation means
5. Information
6. Arms and ammunition
7. Transport

Missions Required of the Military Organization:

The main mission for which the Military Organization is responsible is:

The overthrow of the godless regimes and their replacement with an Islamic regime. Other missions consist of the following:

1. Gathering information about the enemy, the land, the installations, and the neighbors.
2. Kidnapping enemy personnel, documents, secrets, and arms.
3. Assassinating enemy personnel as well as foreign tourists.
4. Freeing the brothers who are captured by the enemy.
5. Spreading rumors and writing statements that instigate people against the enemy.

6. Blasting and destroying the places of amusement, immorality, and sin; not a vital target.

7. Blasting and destroying the embassies and attacking vital economic centers.

8. Blasting and destroying bridges leading into and out of the cities....

Source

The *al Qaeda* Manual. Retrieved from United States Air Force Air University website, http://www.au.af .mil/au/awc/awcgate/terrorism/alqaida_manual/manualpart1_1.pdf.

The CIA Warns of al-Qaeda Attacks on American Soil

During the spring and summer of 2001, U.S. counterterrorism officials expressed growing anxiety about the danger posed by Osama bin Laden and his Al-Qaeda network. Specifically, they worried that bin Laden was plotting a major terrorist attack on American soil. These fears were passed along to top national security officials in the Bush administration as well as the president himself. On August 6, 2001, for example, President Bush received a presidential daily briefing (PDB) from the CIA titled "Bin Laden Determined to Strike in US." The full text of this memo is reprinted below.

Bush officials later tried to discount the importance of this memo. They said that it only contained vague warnings and historical material about the al-Qaeda threat. But critics insisted that this memo should have prompted stronger anti-terrorism measures by the Bush White House, especially after CIA officials made a special trip in mid-August to Texas, where the president was vacationing, to personally brief him on the PDB's contents.

Bin Ladin Determined to Strike in US

Clandestine, foreign government, and media reports indicate Bin Ladin since 1997 has wanted to conduct terrorist attacks in the US. Bin Ladin implied in US television interviews in 1997 and 1998 that his followers would follow the example of World Trade Center bomber Ramzi Yousef and "bring the fighting to America."

After US missile strikes on his base in Afghanistan in 1998, Bin Ladin told followers he wanted to retaliate in Washington, according to a [—] service.

The millennium plotting in Canada in 1999 may have been part of Bin Ladin's first serious attempt to implement a terrorist strike in the US. Convicted plotter Ahmed Ressam has told the FBI that he conceived the idea to attack Los Angeles International Airport himself, but that Bin Ladin lieutenant Abu Zubaydah encouraged him and helped facilitate the operation. Ressam also said that in 1998 Abu Zubaydah was planning his own US attack.

Ressam says Bin Ladin was aware of the Los Angeles operation.

Although Bin Ladin has not succeeded, his attacks against the US Embassies in Kenya and Tanzania in 1998 demonstrate that he prepares operations years in advance and is not deterred by setbacks. Bin Ladin associates surveilled our Embassies in Nairobi and Dar es Salaam as early as 1993, and some members of the Nairobi cell planning the bombings were arrested and deported in 1997.

Al-Qa'ida members—including some who are US citizens—have resided in or traveled to the US for years, and the group apparently maintains a support structure that could aid attacks. Two al-Qua'da members found guilty in the conspiracy to bomb our embassies in East Africa were US citizens, and a senior EIJ member lived in California in the mid-1990s.

A clandestine source said in 1998 that a Bin Ladin cell in New York was recruiting Muslim-American youth for attacks.

We have not been able to corroborate some of the more sensational threat reporting, such as that from a [—] service in 1998 saying that Bin Ladin wanted to hijack a US aircraft to gain the release of "Blind Shaykh" 'Umar 'Abd al-Rahman and other US-held extremists.

Nevertheless, FBI information since that time indicates patterns of suspicious activity in this country consistent with preparations for hijackings or other types of attacks, including recent surveillance of federal buildings in New York.

The FBI is conducting approximately 70 full field investigations throughout the US that it considers Bin Ladin-related. CIA and the FBI are investigating a call to our Embassy in the UAE in May saying that a group of Bin Ladin supporters was in the US planning attacks with explosives.

Source

Central Intelligence Agency. "Bin Laden Determined to Strike in US." In *The 9/11 Commission Report: Final Report of the National Commission on Terrorist Attacks upon the United States.* By The National Commission on Terrorist Attacks Upon the United States [The 9/11 Commission]. Washington, DC: U.S. Government Printing Office, 2004, pp. 261-62. Retrieved from http://www.gpo.gov/fdsys/pkg/GPO-911REPORT/pdf/GPO-911REPORT.pdf.

A New York Police Officer Endures the Fall of the South Tower

On the morning of September 11, 2001, Lieutenant Terri Tobin was working for the New York City Police Department in the deputy commissioner's office of public information. She initially went down to the World Trade Center to work as a department spokesperson to news media covering the unfolding tragedy. Before that morning was over, however, Tobin helped rescue three people and evacuated dozens more out of a nearby building that was at risk of being crushed. She undertook these actions despite incurring serious injuries when the Twin Towers collapsed. In recognition of her heroism, the New York City Police Department gave her its prestigious Medal of Valor.

From 2001 to 2011 Tobin underwent surgery every year to deal with injuries suffered on September 11. She also had to have two-thirds of her teeth replaced. But she counts herself lucky to be alive, and she remains a proud member of the city's police department (by 2011 she had risen to the position of deputy inspector). In the following excerpt, Tobin recalls her harrowing experiences in downtown Manhattan in the minutes and hours after the terrorists struck the World Trade Center.

Just after we got started working on the morning of September 11, a sergeant came running in and said, "A plane just hit the World Trade Center! I'm heading over." Two seconds later the phone rang, and it was Chief Fahey. He said, "I want a lieutenant there. Send Terri." So I grabbed a sergeant and we headed over....

Obviously, I knew it was a big event, but the whole time I was going over there, I was thinking that it was this little Cessna from New Jersey. I was thinking that some guy had a heart attack and clipped the World Trade Center by accident. I was expecting to see half a plane sticking out of the Tower, never thinking that it was a commercial airliner.

We got there at 8:54 A.M. I remember the time, because my text pager had gone off, and it said that the highest level of mobilization had been called for the World Trade Center at Church and Vesey streets. I parked my car on the east side of West Street, and the mobilization was diagonal to where I parked. The World Trade Center covers 16 acres, so it was a mile walk.

The North Tower had been hit first. The streets were already closed down because of glass and debris. We had to kind of scoot around the outskirts, and as we were doing that, the second plane hit just after 9 o'clock.

Credit: From *Women at Ground Zero: Stories of Courage and Compassion* by Susan Hagen and Mary Carouba. Copyright © 2002 by Susan Hagen and Mary Carouba. Reprinted by permission.

The television images don't give you the impression of how bad it was when the second plane hit. It wasn't like the plane hit and the glass fell. As the building was heating up, all the windows were popping out. You can imagine these huge windows breaking into shards and falling to the ground. I'd be walking along, and *crash!*—glass and debris falling everywhere.

Then we started to see people jumping. It was horrendous. At first I did a double take, because the buildings were 110 stories tall. I thought, *Oh man, something's coming down.* At first, it was like a little speck. Then I realized it was a human being. People jumped alone and in groups, and, at one point, they said twenty people held hands and jumped. I can't imagine what hell it must have been inside there, with jumping being their only alternative. I can't imagine the fierceness of that fire. I heard later that one guy e-mailed his mother and said, "Mom, I have to jump. I hope you understand." In some cases, the windows were gone and people were holding on to the edge. At a certain point, I think it just got too hot and they had to let go.

As we approached the mobilization area, I saw First Deputy Commissioner Joe Dunne. He said, "Terri, there's a report of a third plane in the area. Get a helmet on." There was an Emergency Services Unit truck parked there, so I jumped on the truck and grabbed two helmets—one for myself, and one for the sergeant who was with me. This helmet is made of Kevlar and it's real heavy. It's made specifically for combat situations, because it can take a bullet.

After I got the helmet on, I saw a Channel 7 news crew. My job was to corral all the press together and get information out to them as quickly as possible so we could start doing emergency broadcasts. We needed to let the public know what areas were in the frozen zone, which trains were stopped, where people were being directed to evacuate, and all the other mechanical pieces of a disaster.

I went into the North Tower, looking for press. It was amazing how calm people were. Everything was going very smoothly, because I think those people were familiar with the evacuation drill. Obviously, they knew that the building had rocked, and there was fear. At one point, I know, there was an hour-long back-up to the thirty-first floor, just because of the volume of people making it down the accessible stairways. But everything was going smoothly.

I'm telling you, everywhere you looked, there was a cop. For people coming out of the Towers, there was absolutely no thinking. They didn't come down and have to wonder, *Where do I go?* It wasn't mass confusion.

Every five feet there was a cop saying, very calmly, "Please exit to your left. Exit to your left." So there was this very obvious route. Just follow the blue. At the same time, firefighters were coming in and going up. The response by emergency personnel was just phenomenal.

Everything was under control in the North Tower, so I crossed over to the South Tower, and I saw a photographer. The last phase of descent onto the concourse level was an escalator, and there was a photographer at the bottom of it. He was clicking away and slowing people down. Also, he was in the frozen zone. We were working really hard to get people out, so the last thing we wanted were unauthorized people getting in the way.

But I also realized that he had a job to do, so I said, "You've got two shots left." Then I literally grabbed him by the collar and walked him out to Liberty Street. I handed him off to a uniformed cop and said, "You need to walk him as far away from the frozen zone as you can. I don't want to see him again."

I was thinking, *This is going to be a long day, and there's going to be a lot of running around, so I should put my sneakers on.* I was walking back to my car and I got close enough to pop the trunk with the remote, when I heard a loud rumbling sound. It sounded like a train. I turned around, left my trunk open, and started walking back toward the South Tower. I was thinking, *Where is this train coming from?* It just wasn't clicking with me that there was no elevated train. They're all underground. I guess it was almost like I couldn't see the forest for the trees. I mean, I was right there. If I'd looked up, I would have known that the building was starting to pancake down.

Then I saw people running toward me, and they were screaming, "Go! Go! It's coming down!" Just for a second, I looked up and saw it. I thought, *I'm not going to outrun this.* But then I thought, *Maybe I can make it back to my car and jump in the back seat.* Before I could make a move, the force of the explosion literally blew me out of my shoes. It lifted me up and propelled me out, over a concrete barrier, all the way to the other side of the street. I landed face-first on a grassy area outside the Financial Center, and after I landed there, I just got pelted with debris coming out of this big black cloud.

And then I felt it, but what sticks with me is hearing it: the *whomp* of my helmet when I got hit in the head. The helmet literally went *crack*, split in half, and fell off my head. I realized then that I'd taken a real big whack in the head. I felt blood going down the back of my neck, and when I was able to reach around, I felt this chunk of cement sticking out three or four inches from the back of my head. It was completely embedded in my skull.

Then it got pitch black, and I thought, *I must have been knocked unconscious, because it's totally black.* But then I thought, *I wouldn't be thinking about how black it is if I'm unconscious.* And it was really hard to breathe. All I heard were people screaming. Screaming bloody murder. All sorts of cries. At that moment, I thought, *This is it. We're all going to die on the street.*

All this stuff just kept coming down and was piling up on me. All of a sudden, I heard these huge explosions. *Boom! Boom!* And I thought, *Now they've started bombing.* I was lying there. I was still getting pelted with stuff, I had a headful of cement, and now if they were bombing us, there was going to be no way out.

I don't know how much time passed, but I knew my eyes were burning, I was coughing, and my nose was running. From underneath the rubble, a short distance from me, I saw the silhouette of a firefighter's helmet. He turned on his flashlight and shouted over, "Are you okay?" I said, "Yeah, I'm okay." He said, "Cover your mouth and nose with the front of your blouse."

I reached around and grabbed someone's hand. I couldn't see him, but at least I had a hold of his fingers. I said, "I'm with the NYPD and there's a firefighter on my right. Just stay down!" And then it started to clear. It went from total blackness to what seemed like white ash, but it was actually pulverized cement sweeping through the air.

I realized that I was buried under all this rubble. I was finally able to move the top part of my body out, but my legs were still buried. I said to this person whose hand I was holding, "I'm going to try and get up, but I won't let you go." I lifted the upper part of my body out and I pulled on him, but he came up too easily. I looked down and realized that I just had hold of a hand and an arm. No one was attached to it....

I was sort of kneeling in the rubble, still trying to get the rest of my legs out. Attached to the piece of cement that hit me were building cables—not like thin phone lines, but thick cables—and I was literally draped in them. I had to physically take them up and over me, and it took a while to get untangled and get up. The firefighter came over and asked me if I was all right. Then he yelled out, "EMS! She's got cement in her head!"

Two guys from EMS came over, and they wouldn't even attempt to pull the cement out. They just wrapped my head. My hair was singed, I was covered in this white stuff, and I could smell burning hair and burning flesh. The odors were really bad. All around me, I heard people throwing up. I could hear that choking sound of people just wanting to spit out all the blackness, to clear it out of their lungs.

I was trying to cough all that stuff out, too. I'd just inhaled two minutes' worth of this dark black smoke and all this white stuff, and I didn't even know what it was. I spit out a chunk of what I thought was cement, but that wasn't what it was. The force of being hit on the head had blown my wisdom tooth out, root and all.

So now there were four of us standing there, and it became eerily quiet. We didn't hear anything. I turned around to look for my car, and it was totally engulfed in flames. There was a fire truck on fire, and there was an ambulance on fire. It literally looked like a war zone. It didn't click until later on, but those were the *booms* I heard earlier. The force of the structure coming down and the heat from the fire caused the gas tanks to explode....

[Tobin, the firefighter, and the two emergency paramedics then began trying to rescue people trapped in the wreckage.]

The first guy we got out was a firefighter who had rolled under an ambulance that didn't explode. As the rubble came down, it just kept piling against it, and he was trapped underneath.

So now he joined us, and we were listening for voices. It was just overwhelming. Where were the people? I was thinking how lucky I was because I was conscious. If I'd been knocked unconscious, I wouldn't have been able to call for help and no one would have seen me because I was underneath the rubble. That's why, in my heart, I thought they were going to find people who were just knocked unconscious but who maybe had a breathing area through the rubble where they could get oxygen. Even much later in the day, and even the next day, I still thought they were going to find people.

We got maybe three people out, and all of a sudden, another whole group of people came running toward us saying, "The other Tower is coming down! Run!" I was in this mental zone, and I was just thinking, *Where am I going to go?* I'm very familiar with the area, so I thought, *I'll run to the water.* I felt very unprotected at this time. The ash was really thick and I was barefoot, and certain things, like the steel beams that had fallen from the first Tower, were really hot. It amazed me that the soles of my feet weren't absolutely ripped apart.

So I was saying to myself, *I'm going to run toward the water.* There's just a railing, and I thought I'd jump over that and go into the Hudson River. I know that where there's water, there's oxygen. And as the stuff was coming down, I was thinking, *At least the water will get the impact, not my body.* As I was running, I realized that my foot hurt, and then all of a sudden, I got whacked in the back. I went straight down to my knees. I felt that same rush again. That same cloud of swirling debris was coming at me.

I knew at this point that I was not going to make it to the water, and I saw a building off to my right that I thought I could make it into. So I got up and took my gun out. I figured that if the door was locked, at least I could blow out the lock.

But the door opened and I went in. I was thinking at first that the building was under construction, because all I saw were white lights in yellow cages. It never dawned on me that they had lost their electricity. So I followed these lights and I got to the elevator bank, and all the elevators were stopped on the first floor. I figured, *Okay, everyone's gone.*

I'll tell you the truth, I just wanted to get away from the blast. There were these huge windows in the front of the building, and I was thinking, *Something's going to go right through those.* So I opened the door to the stairwell and looked up, and it was lined with residents of this apartment building. People had just come out of the shower, and there were little babies— probably a hundred people.

I told them we had to get out, because I thought everything was going to come down. I'm sure I didn't look credible. I was wearing torn pantyhose, my head was bandaged, and I was covered in dust. But everyone got out of the stairwell, and I told them to go into the lobby but to stay away from the windows. At least there would be a way out of the building if it started to come down.

I went to the front door, and outside it had turned to that white ash. It was exactly the same scenario as before. I saw two guys from our Technical Assistance Response Unit, and on the backs of their shirts was "TARU" in big white letters. I opened up the door and shouted, "TARU!" They turned immediately, and one of the guys knew me. I said, "Listen, we've got to get these people out."

He told me that they were evacuating people by boat to Jersey, so I said, "All right, let's get these people down there." He kind of turned white and said, "Well, we'll get *you* down there. We'll carry you." And I said, "I'm all right, I can walk." Then he said, "Terri, there's this windowpane stuck through your back, between your shoulder blades. It's sticking out of your blouse."

Obviously, I'd felt it and I knew that something was there, but I didn't know it was glass. All I could think of was what I'd learned in training, that if you go to a stabbing, you just wrap the knife to stabilize it, because the last thing you want to do is pull it out and cause more damage. So I said, "Just leave it. I'm okay." …

I really didn't feel like my medical condition was anything pressing. I think that the hand I pulled out of the rubble put that in perspective for me.…

Source

"Lieutenant Special Assignment Terri Tobin." In *Women at Ground Zero: Stories of Courage and Compassion.* Edited by Susan Hagen and Mary Carouba. Indianapolis: Alpha, 2002, pp. 88-96.

A North Tower Survivor Remembers His Narrow Escape

On September 11, 2001, Richard Moller was an employee at Marsh & McLennan, a business consulting and insurance brokerage company that occupied offices on eight floors of the North Tower of the World Trade Center. All eight floors—93 to 100—were located above the so-called "impact zone," where the hijacked American Airlines Flight 11 hit the building at 8:46 A.M.

Marsh & McLennan lost 295 employees and another 63 contract workers on 9/11. No one who had reached their desks for the day when AA 11 crashed was able to get out of the building alive. In the following account, Moller acknowledges that he was usually at his desk by 8:46 as well. But on the night of September 10, 2001, he forgot to grind coffee beans and set the automatic timer on his coffee machine for the next morning. As a result, he spent an extra five minutes on the morning of September 11 making coffee. Moller believes that this five-minute delay saved him from becoming one of the casualties of 9/11.

I just forgot. I can't really say why. But when my alarm went off at seven A.M. there was no coffee in the pot. The night before I had been watching *Band of Brothers* on HBO. There were really heavy war scenes and I was thinking, I can't imagine what it was like to go through something like that. Twelve hours later, I would know.

I have an apartment in Hoboken, New Jersey. Every morning I walk to the ferry. It takes about twenty minutes. The ferry then takes me across the Hudson River and docks at the World Financial Center. I walk from there to the World Trade Center, take an express elevator to the 78th floor, where I catch a local elevator to the 100th floor. That morning, I was getting off the elevator at the 78th floor when a Boeing 767 hit the building. The whole tower shook, the walls blew out and flames came shooting out of the elevator shafts. I was thrown to the floor and was covered in dust from the gypsum board and Sheetrock. If I had gotten an elevator just a few minutes earlier, I would be dead. That is how close I cut it. It was 90 seconds from the 78th floor to my desk on the 100th.

You can't get that close to dying without wondering how you managed to escape death. When I tried to reconstruct my morning, I realized any number of things, had they been different, could have put me on the 100th floor at

Credit: From *September 11: An Oral History* by Dean E. Murphy. Copyright © 2002 by Dean E. Murphy. Used by permission of Doubleday, a division of Random House, Inc.

8:46 [when the plane hit the tower]. It all started with the coffeemaker, but there was more. On Monday we had had a seminar for some clients outside the office and I had brought home my laptop and a thick stack of handouts to bring back to work on Tuesday. The stuff weighed a ton. I usually go to the gym after work, so I had my gym bag with me too. I was so loaded down that my 20-minute walk to the ferry probably took 22 or 23 minutes.

When I got to the boat ramp, the gate to the ferry was just starting to close. Any other morning, I might have made a mad dash for it. Not that morning. I had too much stuff. I can get a seat on the next one, I said to myself. The next ferry was already there, so I went and took a seat. That decision meant a delay of another eight minutes or so getting to Manhattan. Normally, I would never have thought of those eight minutes again, but then my life never depended on them. When the boat docked at the World Financial Center, I walked to the World Trade Center, dipped my ID card on the turnstile and took the elevator to the 78th floor. Why that particular elevator and not the one before it? Again, time was on my side that morning.

After the plane hit, I gathered up myself and my bags and headed for the nearest stairwell. There were three to choose from, I took the one on the west side of the building. But when I got down just two flights, to the 76th floor, there was a door that seemed to be locked. Several of us tried to get it open, but it wouldn't budge. We kicked it and threw our shoulders against it. We tried everything. After a couple of minutes, we gave up and turned around, going back to the 78th floor. There was a Port Authority official there who invited us all to go into an office. "You'll be safe in there," he announced. As I walked into the office, I noticed one of the big elevators from the ground floor was sitting there, doors open. Someone ran to go inside. I just grabbed him by the collar. "You can't go in there!" I told him. I am a risk management consultant, and one of the things I work on is fire prevention. You don't take elevators in an emergency like this.

When I got in the Port Authority office, I looked out the window, toward the Empire State Building, and all I could see was flaming pieces falling past me. Now I was getting scared. I picked up a phone and I decided to call my father, who lives on the Jersey shore. I hit 9, and got a dial tone, then punched in my father's number. He answered.

"Dad, something just happened here at work, I don't know what it is, some explosion or something, but I'm okay," I said.

He turned on the TV. "It looks like the top twenty floors are on fire," he said. "They are saying a plane hit the World Trade Center."

"Okay, Dad, I'm out of here," I said. "I'll talk to you when I'm out."

The man from the Port Authority said there was another way out and he pointed to a back door and a hallway. I had never seen that hallway before. I had to play hopscotch to get by. The ceiling panels had fallen. There was stuff coming out of the ductwork overhead. Someone was shooting a hose up at the ceiling. I got to the stairwell and there was a line of people going down. Somewhere on our way down, I don't remember when, a plane hit the other tower. But except for some smoke, the descent to the ground floor was not too difficult.

At the ground floor, I looked out the windows at the plaza. It was a horrible disaster scene. Fires. Flaming debris. Bodies and body parts. Right outside the window there was a person strapped to an airplane seat. There was still so much stuff falling from the sky that they told us we could not go outside. We were directed to a stairwell that led down to the mall [at the base of the tower]. A line of firemen told us where to go. I passed the Banana Republic, got to the Warner Bros. store and started walking up the escalator when the building began shaking up and down. A fireman at the top of the escalator started shouting, "Hit the deck!" I dropped my bags and went down on the stairs. The ceiling came down, ductwork, pipes and lights. I got hit all over. I was buried in a foot or two of debris. When it stopped, I pushed my way up out of it. Now it was absolute bedlam. I cannot tell you if the person right behind me lived or died.

I couldn't see and I was having trouble breathing. There was a fireman with a flashlight. I left my bags on the escalator and crawled toward him. I could hear people screaming. It was pandemonium. We got into Borders Books, feeling our way along. The fireman smashed a window to Church Street with his flashlight. I knocked out the bottom with my foot and we jumped outside. I ran as best I could. It looked like a blizzard. I could only see a few feet in front of me. At Vesey Street, it was easier to see. After a few blocks, some guys in an ambulance stopped me and took me to St. Vincent's [hospital]. They gave me oxygen and took X-rays and gave me a tetanus shot. I was sitting there in a wheelchair and I asked to use a phone. I called my parents. My father answered. I could hear my mother wailing in the background. They had seen the towers collapse on television. I then called my company's offices in Midtown to tell them I was all right. I was one of the first people they were able to account for. They asked me if I had seen anybody else. I couldn't say I had.

We had 22 people in our risk control department at Marsh. We lost 10 of the 22, including my boss. Throughout the company, 300 people died. We had a survivors' meeting a few days later, and I found out that nobody above the 92nd floor made it out alive. One of my coworkers, Keither Meerholz, who was also on the 78th floor sky lobby when the plane hit, and I were the highest in the building that made it out from Marsh.

Sometime later I got a letter from the New York Police Department. They had found some of my property. I went to the station and filled out some paperwork. They told me my stuff was in a warehouse in Queens. On my lunch hour, I took the subway to get it. It was my canvas bag with about 20 pounds of papers inside. The police had put the stuff in thick plastic bags. I didn't open them. They stunk like the Trade Center. As I was lugging the bag back on the subway, I realized that it was really heavy and it was just half of what I was carrying that morning. I thought about the ferry, and how I had just missed it. Thanks to the coffee and those extra bags, I was alive. A few more seconds here or there, and I would have been done. A lot of people ask me, "What are you going to do with your second chance on life?" I don't look at it that way. I am still working on my first chance.

Source

"Richard Moller: Cutting It as Close as a Cup of Coffee." In *September 11: An Oral History*. Compiled by Dean E. Murphy. New York: Doubleday, 2002, pp. 193-96.

A Survivor Recalls the Attack on the Pentagon

On the morning of September 11, 2001, Tracy Webb was a civilian employee of the Army, working at the Pentagon as a personnel administrator. Her department's offices were hit hard when hijackers crashed American Airlines Flight 77 into the Pentagon at 9:37 A.M. In the following oral history, Webb recalls her narrow escape from the flames and smoke that enveloped her office space after the attack.

Tuesdays are like Mondays to me because I don't work on Mondays. That means they get busy fast because people come to me about things that happened the day before. That Tuesday was no different. I got to work just before nine o'clock. Before I could even put my stuff down, people were coming to my desk. I was trying to break away to make a quick run to the cafeteria with two of my coworkers to get some coffee and something to eat. But it just wasn't happening. Specialist Michael Petrovich came by and told me about the World Trade Center. Then Dr. Betty Maxfield said she needed to speak to me for a few minutes about a program we were doing. I turned to my two friends and asked them to wait. "We'll go as soon as I'm finished," I promised. One of them, Dalisay Olaes, sat back down at her desk and called her husband about what was happening in New York. The other one, Odessa Morris, said she was going to the rest room, and went into the E ring through the door by my desk.

Looking back at that moment, I beat myself up about the cafeteria. Why didn't I just tell them to go ahead without me, that I would meet them there? Odessa would be alive if I had said that. Instead she went into the E ring, which would be the worst-hit place in the Pentagon.

I had just finished talking to Dr. Maxfield. She stood up, saying, "I'll talk to you later, Tracy," when we heard a big BOOM! It sounded like an earthquake. The whole place shook. I immediately jumped up from my desk and screamed at Dalisay. "Day!" I shouted, which is her nickname. "Tracy!" she hollered back. I looked toward the nearest exit, that same door to the E-ring that Odessa had used, and there was fire coming through it. Within five seconds, the room was completely filled with thick black smoke. The ceiling panels started falling down on top of us. The floor beneath us buckled up. I

Credit: From *September 11: An Oral History* by Dean E. Murphy. Copyright © 2002 by Dean E. Murphy. Used by permission of Doubleday, a division of Random House, Inc.

looked up and saw fireballs flying through the air. Then my computer burst into flames. Something hit me on my forehead and knocked out one of my contact lenses. I felt my head and it was on fire. Thank God I had braids, because they did not burn easily. But I also had a hairpiece in my hair, and it just burned up like paper. It also felt like little glass pieces were hitting me all over my body. I was later told it was glass from the airplane.

Some coworkers started running out of a conference room that was right near my cubicle. People were hollering all over the place. I'll never forget the agonizing screams, "Help me! Help me!" I couldn't see anything or anybody. Just the voices. The only light was the fireballs in the air. Someone coming out of the conference room yelled, "Get down! Get below the smoke!" I remember thinking, "If I am going to get out of here, I am going to need my keys," so I grabbed my pocketbook and got down. I started crawling in the opposite direction of the E ring, following Dalisay and one other person, who I thought was Specialist Petrovich. But after a short distance, I got separated from them. I still couldn't see a thing. I had lost my shoes. There was stuff all over the place and I got confused and disoriented. My hair must have been on fire again, because when the sprinklers suddenly came on, I felt instant relief on my head. It was weird, but I was oblivious to the pain.

There was nothing left to do but listen. I recognized the voice of one of the officers, Lt. Col. Robert Grunewald, coaching another colleague, Martha Carden. "Hang on there, Martha," he said. "Come on there with me. Come on, Martha." I followed the voice and ended up all the way near a door into the 4th corridor. I held my breath as much as I could so I wouldn't breathe all the smoke. I could smell flesh burning. But then, after what seemed like an eternity I heard Lt. Col. Grunewald say that we couldn't get out that way. After he said that, everything went strangely silent. I couldn't hear a thing. No more screaming, nothing. I crawled a little bit, but I had no idea where I was or where to go. There were holes everywhere. I got the awful idea that I was the only one left. I am not going to get out of here, I said to myself. I totally panicked and stood up. It was the wrong thing to do. I lost all my breath and I had sharp pains in my chest. I just knew I was going to die. I said, "Lord, give my mother the strength to take care of my kids." I dropped back down to the floor on my hands and knees, continuing to pray the whole time. I thought it was over.

All of a sudden, I heard someone in the distance yelling, "Over here! Over here!" I was overwhelmed; it was like the Lord had answered my prayers, right then and there. I started moving toward the voice when I felt someone tugging on my dress, I didn't know it, but it was Major Regina Grant, who had been one of the people in the conference room. My boss had been in there too, but they found his body later in the hallway. It seems Major Grant was with me the whole time. We couldn't see each other because the smoke was so thick. She had given up too, but she just happened to open her eyes when I was standing up. For some reason I didn't hear her, but when I fell back down, it gave her enough energy to shout for help one last time. Sgt. Major Tony Rose heard her and started yelling back. It was his voice that I was listening to and was following.

As we got closer to the voice, I could see some light in the smoke. We got to a door that Sgt. Major Rose was holding open and we crawled into the corridor. We were safe at last. Major Grant and I hugged but it was a short embrace and no time for tears. We had to keep moving. Col. Karl Knoblauch was holding the firewall open for us, as we slipped through the opening and made our way to the center courtyard. I later found out that we were lucky in that regard. Most of my colleagues who escaped our office had to jump out of the second-floor windows. I can't imagine myself doing that.

When we got to the center courtyard. I was throwing up black stuff and it was also coming out of my nose. I saw a coworker of mine there. He was burned really bad. He looked at me, "Are you all right, Tracy?" he asked. I was thinking, I should be asking you the same question. But I didn't say anything. I was overwhelmed. I couldn't breathe at all. I had to have oxygen. Then the pain just came rushing into my head, my back and my knees. My knees were torn up from crawling, and there was blood everywhere. People rushed to me with ice packs, but I couldn't have been there five minutes when people started yelling for us to get out of the center courtyard. They said another attack was coming.

I was terrified. We all started running to get outside the building to the north parking lot by the Potomac River. I had no shoes. I still can't believe it. I just ran as fast as I could. Major Denise McCann helped me. At that point, I still did not know what had happened. I believed it was a terrorist bomb. But when I got to the river, someone told me it had been a plane—and that they were afraid more planes were on the way. We were out there for about 30 minutes before an ambulance came and took me to a hospital. There were no more hijacked planes, but when the Air Force jets from Langley Air Force Base started flying around, it just scared me to death. I got down on the ground and waited for them to pass. It was there at the river that I finally let go. Everything caught up with me. I started shaking all over. I just couldn't stop shaking.

At Arlington Urgent Care, I was treated for second-degree burns on my head and my back. I also had cuts on my knees and smoke inhalation. My dress had not caught fire, but the intense heat caused the burns on my back. At the hospital, I tried to get in touch with my three children, but none of the calls went through. I kept getting a recording from Verizon saying all the lines were busy. That was a big mess. My kids were frantic. My oldest daughter, Ebony, who is seventeen, had helped me move to my new office in June so when she turned on the TV, she knew I had been where the plane hit. She kept calling me from school and home, but couldn't get through. I finally got in touch with a friend of mine and she went over to the house and told Ebony, Echoe, and Reginald that I was okay. But by then it was already five o'clock. They let me go home from the hospital that night, so that made things better for everyone.

When I think about that day, I know what happened to me was a miracle. When I see pictures of what was going on, it is amazing anyone got out. The only thing I can conclude is the Lord was not ready for me or I wasn't ready. How else to explain it? Major Grant could see me standing there when I couldn't even see the hand in front of me. It was just not my turn. Still, I beat myself up about some things, especially when I think of Odessa Morris. She was going to work only a half day that Tuesday. It was her 25th wedding anniversary and her husband was taking her to dinner. Just before she left for the rest room, I had been playing with her about it. "Oh, so what are you all going to do?" I teased. Now she has passed.

I am back at work. At first, I was located in another building, but we moved back to the Pentagon about a week and a half ago. It feels real eerie. Everybody is fighting over space while they work fast to put the place back together. When it is finished, they say they are going to put us back in the same area, but I have mixed feelings about that. Within our agency, about thirty people didn't make it. In my immediate office, three of eleven died. That was very, very emotional. People now say the Pentagon is the safest place to be. I thought that before this happened.

Source

"Tracy Webb: Her Hair Burning, She Follows a Voice to Safety." In *September 11: An Oral History*. Compiled by Dean E. Murphy. New York: Doubleday, 2002, pp. 211-15.

Mourning Lost Firefighters and Police Officers in New York

Maureen Brown was a twenty-six-year-old New York City police officer on September 11, 2001. By the end of that nightmarish day, Brown had been reassigned to work at the city morgue, where the bodies and possessions of firefighters, police officers, and civilians lost in the 9/11 attacks were being taken. As she admits in the following interview, her work at the morgue pushed her to her emotional limits. But Brown found strength in the knowledge that she was fulfilling an important and solemn duty in returning the bodies and valuables of 9/11 victims to their grieving families.

I've been a cop for four years. I was working patrol in the 48th Precinct in the South Bronx, and I was arresting someone, rolling around with a prisoner, when he resisted violently and I got hurt. A couple of other cops got hurt, too. I tore the cartilage off my shoulder and had to have surgery to put it back, but it didn't take. I'm doing physical therapy three times a week and I'll need to have surgery again.

After I got hurt on the job, I was put on restricted duty and transferred over to the Property Clerks Division in Queens, where we take in the property of deceased people, prisoners, and anything else that is found or seized. Any kind of property that ends up coming into the hands of the police, including drugs, money, guns, and narcotics, is vouchered and stored here for safekeeping.

After the first plane hit on the morning of September 11, we were watching it on TV at work, and it was a crazy madhouse. Everybody was in a state of shock, and we all felt helpless because we couldn't leave, and there was nothing we could do to help. We have all the drugs and guns at the Property Division, and we were on high security alert. The Property Division is a huge warehouse where we've stored everything that's been taken off the street for years and years, so we have thousands and thousands and thousands of guns. Anybody could come in here and try to take over.

I'm not really supposed to be in uniform or out on the street because of my shoulder, but that day, we all put our uniforms on and were ready to take action. People didn't know what to do, and all the phone lines were ringing.

Credit: From *Women at Ground Zero: Stories of Courage and Compassion* by Susan Hagen and Mary Carouba. Copyright © 2002 by Susan Hagen and Mary Carouba. Reprinted by permission.

Then all of a sudden, the phones got shut down. None of the phones were working in the whole area, because the Tower with the big antennae on it had just gone down. We stayed there that night until very late, and then we were told, "All right, you guys have to go down to work at the morgue tomorrow at 6 o'clock in the morning." … I didn't know that when there's a major incident, the people in the Property Clerks Division go down there to voucher everything and take control of all the property.

I thought, *Okay, we're going down to the morgue, and that's our job for the day.* I didn't realize how bad it was going to be. When we got down there, the whole street was blocked off, and huge refrigerated trucks, like meat trucks, were parked on the side street. I didn't get it at first that the reason those meat trucks were there was for the bodies. They were expecting all these bodies to come in, and they had to store them, obviously, in a freezer, or something along those lines, where it's cool, so the bodies wouldn't get bad.

We saw one of the guys from Property who'd worked there that night, and when he came out, he was crying. You know, he's a grown man, and he's crying. It was so moving for me to see a guy cry, a police officer. He said, "I'm telling you right now, you need to brace yourself. You're going to see a lot of dead firefighters, and you're going to see a lot of dead cops."

At that point, they were mostly finding the bodies of firefighters, because they were farther out in their trucks when the buildings came down. Not only that, but they were the only ones who could really be identified, because of the fireproof jackets with their names on the back. Identifying civilians was a lot harder, because their bodies were decapitated or burned or destroyed, and there was no way to tell who they were. On the news, they would give a body count of how many people they had found, and it was mostly firefighters. Firefighter after firefighter.

One of my brothers and my two brothers-in-law are firefighters, and my father was a fire captain who died in the line of duty. One of my sisters is a police lieutenant, and my other brother is an Amtrak police sergeant, so we knew a lot of people who were missing. Everybody knew I was at the morgue, and they'd call me up and say, "This person's missing and that person's missing. Let me know if something comes in." So every time I came in, I'd look at the paperwork from the night before to see if they'd found that person.

One of the first people who died was Father [Mychal] Judge, the fire department chaplain, who was close to my family. He'd been hit by debris while he was giving last rites to one of the firefighters who died when someone jumped out of the building and landed on him. Father Judge married my sister and brother-in-law, and he'd known my brother-in-law's family for years. One of my brothers talked to him almost on a daily basis. When I got to the morgue, they'd just removed his body, thank God, because I don't know if I could have handled that. His death was devastating for my family.

The morgue was at Bellevue Hospital, and it was somewhat of an assembly line because of the number of bodies and body parts coming in. A small truck would come through the barriers, and you'd know that these were new bodies coming. During the first few days, the bodies were coming in very quickly. They were finding 600 body parts a day—arms, legs, scalps. It was just horrendous stuff to see.…

One firefighter they brought in was so badly burned that his helmet was caved into his skull. It was a terrible thing for me to see. My dad was a firefighter, and he died in the line of duty in 1982, so it brought back a lot of feelings for me. It was the last place in the world I wanted to be. Seeing all these dead firefighters being brought in was just so sad. Last Father's Day, there was a big fire in Astoria and three firefighters were lost. It's very hard for the city to bury one or two firefighters a year, let alone 343. More firefighters were lost on September 11 than have been lost in the whole history of the fire department.

My heart really goes out to all the firefighters who lost members of their companies. I can't even imagine how they can still go to work. The firehouse around the block from my house lost nineteen people, and now they have all these wives and children sitting there, waiting there, day after day in the firehouse, waiting and waiting. Every time the firefighters came into the morgue to take another body out, they'd be crying.

One of the things the rescuers found was an arm with a tattoo that said "FDNY," so we knew it was a firefighter. They also found a stewardess's torso and hands, and the hands were tied together, like they'd been tied behind her back. No one is ready to see something like that.…

Everybody was silent down at the morgue. It was totally dead silence. People were like zombies. We were working fourteen hours a day, we'd go home, we'd watch the Towers coming down over and over again on TV, and we didn't sleep for weeks. Every now and then, someone would break down hysterical crying. Guys were crying, girls, everybody. I didn't really cry until two days into it, because I was in such a state of shock. But to see guys cry, and cops and firefighters, people crying all over the place, all these higher-up captains and stuff, it made me think, *What did they do to us? What did they do to our city?*

They were rolling in one body after another, and somebody working there would suddenly say, "I know this person. I went to school with this person." We didn't know who they were going to bring in next. I remember one girl who was down there when they brought in somebody she knew and how bad that was for her. We all knew people who worked in Lower Manhattan or who responded to the World Trade Center, and at some point we were all going to see someone we knew. We were going to voucher someone's driver's license, someone's wedding band, someone's jewelry, and it would hit us hard.…

It was so bad down there that every now and again, someone would just break down and have to leave. I'd have to try to compose myself, because I had to be professional about it in order to get the job done. I'd go home and talk to my sister, and I'd cry to her and say, "This is so horrible. I don't know if I can do this every day." Then I'd talk to my brother, who is thirty-something years old, and he'd be crying to me because he lost all his friends. He'd say, "No, Maureen, you have to do this job. You have to be the one who's down there doing this. You have to do it, because you'll do it the right way."

I understood what he meant by that, because not everybody could do this job. My brother knows I care. He knows this hit home for me and my family, and he knows I'm going to make sure that this person's property gets vouchered the right way. This wife is going to get her husband's wallet and that husband is going to get his wife's wedding ring, because that's closure for the family, and that's important to me. That will help people in the long run. I said to my brother, "You're right. You're right. I'll do it the right way, and I'll do it respectfully for the families who have lost these loved ones." That kept me going.

Source

"Maureen Brown." In *Women at Ground Zero: Stories of Courage and Compassion.* Edited by Susan Hagen and Mary Carouba. Indianapolis: Alpha, 2002, pp. 168-77.

President Bush Addresses the Nation after the 9/11 Attacks

At 8:30 P.M. Eastern time on the evening of September 11, President George W. Bush delivered a seven-minute televised address to the American people about the terrorist attacks that had claimed the lives of 3,000 airplane passengers, office workers, soldiers, firefighters, police officers, and paramedics earlier that day in New York, Virginia, and Pennsylvania. In this address, reprinted here, Bush sought to comfort grieving Americans—and to assure them that the United States would find the architects of the 9/11 attacks and bring them to justice.

Good evening. Today, our fellow citizens, our way of life, our very freedom came under attack in a series of deliberate and deadly terrorist acts. The victims were in airplanes, or in their offices; secretaries, businessmen and women, military and federal workers; moms and dads, friends and neighbors. Thousands of lives were suddenly ended by evil, despicable acts of terror.

The pictures of airplanes flying into buildings, fires burning, huge structures collapsing, have filled us with disbelief, terrible sadness, and a quiet, unyielding anger. These acts of mass murder were intended to frighten our nation into chaos and retreat. But they have failed; our country is strong.

A great people has been moved to defend a great nation. Terrorist attacks can shake the foundations of our biggest buildings, but they cannot touch the foundation of America. These acts shattered steel, but they cannot dent the steel of American resolve.

America was targeted for attack because we're the brightest beacon for freedom and opportunity in the world. And no one will keep that light from shining.

Today, our nation saw evil, the very worst of human nature. And we responded with the best of America—with the daring of our rescue workers, with the caring for strangers and neighbors who came to give blood and help in any way they could.

Immediately following the first attack, I implemented our government's emergency response plans. Our military is powerful, and it's prepared. Our emergency teams are working in New York City and Washington, D.C. to help with local rescue efforts.

Our first priority is to get help to those who have been injured, and to take every precaution to protect our citizens at home and around the world from further attacks.

The functions of our government continue without interruption. Federal agencies in Washington which had to be evacuated today are reopening for essential personnel tonight, and will be open for business tomorrow. Our financial institutions remain strong, and the American economy will be open for business, as well.

The search is underway for those who are behind these evil acts. I've directed the full resources of our intelligence and law enforcement communities to find those responsible and to bring them to justice. We will make no distinction between the terrorists who committed these acts and those who harbor them.

I appreciate so very much the members of Congress who have joined me in strongly condemning these attacks. And on behalf of the American people, I thank the many world leaders who have called to offer their condolences and assistance.

America and our friends and allies join with all those who want peace and security in the world, and we stand together to win the war against terrorism. Tonight, I ask for your prayers for all those who grieve, for the children whose worlds have been shattered, for all whose sense of safety and security has been threatened. And I pray they will be comforted by a power greater than any of us, spoken through the ages in Psalm 23: "Even though I walk through the valley of the shadow of death, I fear no evil, for You are with me."

This is a day when all Americans from every walk of life unite in our resolve for justice and peace. America has stood down enemies before, and we will do so this time. None of us will ever forget this day. Yet, we go forward to defend freedom and all that is good and just in our world.

Thank you. Good night, and God bless America.

Source

Bush, George W. Address to the Nation on the Terrorist Attacks, September 11, 2001. Retrieved from John T. Woolley and Gerhard Peters, The American Presidency Project, http://www.presidency.ucsb.edu/ws/index.php?pid=58057&st=&st1=#axzz1QmDKqBkP.

Osama bin Laden Taunts America after September 11

Less than a month after the September 11 attacks on the United States, the Arabic television station Al Jazeera broadcast a video message from al-Qaeda leader Osama bin Laden. In this videotape, first broadcast on October 7, bin Laden did not claim direct responsibility for the attacks. But he expressed clear satisfaction that the attacks had been so successful in taking American lives and bringing down the World Trade Center towers. In addition, he warned of future attacks unless the United States removed its "infidel armies" from the Middle East and Israeli territory was returned to the Palestinians.

Praise be to God and we beseech Him for help and forgiveness.

We seek refuge with the Lord of our bad and evildoing. He whom God guides is rightly guided but he whom God leaves to stray, for him wilt thou find no protector to lead him to the right way. I witness that there is no God but God and Mohammed is His slave and Prophet.

God Almighty hit the United States at its most vulnerable spot. He destroyed its greatest buildings. Praise be to God.

Here is the United States. It was filled with terror from its north to its south and from its east to its west. Praise be to God.

What the United States tastes today is a very small thing compared to what we have tasted for tens of years. Our nation has been tasting this humiliation and contempt for more than 80 years. Its sons are being killed, its blood is being shed, its holy places are being attacked, and it is not being ruled according to what God has decreed. Despite this, nobody cares.

When Almighty God rendered successful a convoy of Muslims, the vanguards of Islam, He allowed them to destroy the United States.

I ask God Almighty to elevate their status and grant them Paradise. He is the one who is capable to do so.

When these defended their oppressed sons, brothers, and sisters in Palestine and in many Islamic countries, the world at large shouted. The infidels shouted, followed by the hypocrites.

One million Iraqi children have thus far died in Iraq although they did not do anything wrong. Despite this, we heard no denunciation by anyone in the world or a fatwa by the rulers' ulema [body of Muslim scholars].

Israeli tanks and tracked vehicles also enter to wreak havoc in Palestine, in Jenin, Ramallah, Rafah, Beit Jala, and other Islamic areas and we hear no voices raised or moves made.

But if the sword falls on the United States after 80 years, hypocrisy raises its head lamenting the deaths of these killers who tampered with the blood, honour, and holy places of the Muslims.

The least that one can describe these people is that they are morally depraved. They champion falsehood, support the butcher against the victim, the oppressor against the innocent child. May God mete them the punishment they deserve.

I say that the matter is clear and explicit. In the aftermath of this event and now that senior US officials have spoken, beginning with Bush, the head of the world's infidels, and whoever supports him, every Muslim should rush to defend his religion.

They came out in arrogance with their men and horses and instigated even those countries that belong to Islam against us. They came out to fight this group of people who declared their faith in God and refused to abandon their religion. They came out to fight Islam in the name of terrorism.

Hundreds of thousands of people, young and old, were killed in the farthest point on earth in Japan [when the United States dropped atomic bombs on Hiroshima and Nagasaki at the end of World War II]. [For them] this is not a crime, but rather a debatable issue. They bombed Iraq and considered that a debatable issue. But when a dozen people of them were killed in Nairobi and Dar es Salaam, Afghanistan and Iraq were bombed and all hypocrite ones stood behind the head of the world's infidelity—behind the Hubal [an idol worshipped by pagans before the advent of Islam] of the age—namely, America and its supporters.

These incidents divided the entire world into two regions—one of faith where there is no hypocrisy and another of infidelity, from which we hope God will protect us. The winds of faith and change have blown to remove falsehood from the [Arabian] peninsula of Prophet Mohammed, may God's prayers be upon him.

As for the United States, I tell it and its people these few words: I swear by Almighty God who raised the heavens without pillars that neither the United States nor he who lives in the United States will enjoy security before we can see it as a reality in Palestine and before all the infidel armies leave the land of Mohammed, may God's peace and blessing be upon him.

God is great and glory to Islam.

May God's peace, mercy, and blessings be upon you.

Source

Bin Laden, Osama. "Bin Laden's Warning: Full Text." October 7, 2001. Retrieved from British Broadcasting Corporation (BBC) website, http://news.bbc.co.uk/2/hi/south_asia/1585636.stm.

Condoleezza Rice Defends the Bush Administration's Record on Terrorism

In 2004 the ongoing investigation of the 9/11 Commission and criticisms leveled by former counterterrorism czar Richard A. Clarke placed the performance of the Bush White House in the months leading up to September 11 under greater scrutiny than ever before. In response, administration officials strongly defended their pre-9/11 counterterrorism policies. They also rejected accusations that Bush and his inner circle did not view Osama bin Laden or al-Qaeda as serious threats. One of the point persons in this effort to limit the impact of the politically damaging charges was Condoleezza Rice, who was Bush's national security advisor on September 11. The following is an editorial written by Rice that appeared in the Washington Post on March 22, 2004.

The al Qaeda terrorist network posed a threat to the United States for almost a decade before the attacks of Sept. 11, 2001. Throughout that period—during the eight years of the Clinton administration and the first eight months of the Bush administration prior to Sept. 11—the U.S. government worked hard to counter the al Qaeda threat.

During the transition, President-elect Bush's national security team was briefed on the Clinton administration's efforts to deal with al Qaeda. The seriousness of the threat was well understood by the president and his national security principals. In response to my request for a presidential initiative, the counterterrorism team, which we had held over from the Clinton administration, suggested several ideas, some of which had been around since 1998 but had not been adopted. No al Qaeda plan was turned over to the new administration.

We adopted several of these ideas. We committed more funding to counterterrorism and intelligence efforts. We increased efforts to go after al Qaeda's finances. We increased American support for anti-terror activities in Uzbekistan.

We pushed hard to arm the Predator unmanned aerial vehicle so we could target terrorists with greater precision. But the Predator was designed to conduct surveillance, not carry weapons. Arming it presented many technical challenges and required extensive testing. Military and intelligence officials agreed that the armed Predator was simply not ready for deployment before the fall of 2001. In any case, the Predator was not a silver bullet that could have destroyed al Qaeda or stopped Sept. 11.

We also considered a modest spring 2001 increase in funding for the Northern Alliance. At that time, the Northern Alliance was clearly not going to sweep across Afghanistan and dispose of al Qaeda. It had been battered by defeat and held less than 10 percent of the country. Only the addition of American air power, with U.S. special forces and intelligence officers on the ground, allowed the Northern Alliance its historic military advances in late 2001. We folded this idea into our broader strategy of arming tribes throughout Afghanistan to defeat the Taliban.

Let us be clear. Even their most ardent advocates did not contend that these ideas, even taken together, would have destroyed al Qaeda. We judged that the collection of ideas presented to us were insufficient for the strategy President Bush sought. The president wanted more than a laundry list of ideas simply to contain al Qaeda or "roll back" the threat. Once in office, we quickly began crafting a comprehensive new strategy to "eliminate" the al Qaeda network. The president wanted more than occasional, retaliatory cruise missile strikes. He told me he was "tired of swatting flies."

Through the spring and summer of 2001, the national security team developed a strategy to eliminate al Qaeda—which was expected to take years. Our strategy marshaled all elements of national power to take down the network, not just respond to individual attacks with law enforcement measures. Our plan called for military options to attack al Qaeda and Taliban leadership, ground forces and other targets—taking the fight to the enemy where he lived. It focused on the crucial link between al Qaeda and the Taliban. We would attempt to compel the Taliban to stop giving al Qaeda sanctuary—and if it refused, we would have sufficient military options to remove the Taliban regime. The strategy focused on the key role of Pakistan in this effort and the need to get Pakistan to drop its support of the Taliban. This became the first major foreign-policy strategy document of the Bush administration — not Iraq, not the ABM Treaty, but eliminating al Qaeda.

Before Sept. 11, we closely monitored threats to our nation. President Bush revived the practice of meeting with the director of the CIA every day— meetings that I attended. And I personally met with George Tenet regularly and frequently reviewed aspects of the counterterror effort.

Through the summer increasing intelligence "chatter" focused almost exclusively on potential attacks overseas. Nonetheless, we asked for any indication of domestic threats and directed our counterterrorism team to coordinate with domestic agencies to adopt protective measures. The FBI and the Federal Aviation Administration alerted airlines, airports and local authorities, warning of potential attacks on Americans.

Despite what some have suggested, we received no intelligence that terrorists were preparing to attack the homeland using airplanes as missiles, though some analysts speculated that terrorists might hijack airplanes to try to free U.S.-held terrorists. The FAA even issued a warning to airlines and aviation security personnel that "the potential for a terrorist operation, such as an airline hijacking to free terrorists incarcerated in the United States, remains a concern."

We now know that the real threat had been in the United States since at least 1999. The plot to attack New York and Washington had been hatching for nearly two years. According to the FBI, by June 2001 16 of the 19 hijackers were already here. Even if we had known exactly where Osama bin Laden was, and the armed Predator had been available to strike him, the Sept. 11 hijackers almost certainly would have carried out their plan. So, too, if the Northern Alliance had somehow managed to topple the Taliban, the Sept. 11 hijackers were here in America—not in Afghanistan.

President Bush has acted swiftly to unify and streamline our efforts to secure the American homeland. He has transformed the FBI into an agency dedicated to catching terrorists and preventing future attacks. The president and Congress, through the USA Patriot Act, have broken down the legal and bureaucratic walls that prior to Sept. 11 hampered intelligence and law enforcement agencies from collecting and sharing vital threat information. Those who now argue for rolling back the Patriot Act's changes invite us to forget the important lesson we learned on Sept. 11.

In the immediate aftermath of the attacks, the president, like all Americans, wanted to know who was responsible. It would have been irresponsible not to ask a question about all possible links, including to Iraq—a nation that had supported terrorism and had tried to kill a former president. Once advised that there was no evidence that Iraq was responsible for Sept. 11, the president told his National Security Council on Sept. 17 that Iraq was not on the agenda and that the initial U.S. response to Sept. 11 would be to target al Qaeda and the Taliban in Afghanistan.

Because of President Bush's vision and leadership, our nation is safer. We have won battles in the war on terror, but the war is far from over. However long it takes, this great nation will prevail.

Source

Rice, Condoleezza. "9/11: For the Record," *Washington Post,* March 22, 2004, p.A21. Retrieved from http://www.washingtonpost.com/ac2/wp-dyn?pagename=article&contentId=A13881-2004Mar21.

Richard Clarke's Explosive Testimony before the 9/11 Commission

Beginning in 2003, former Bush administration official Richard Clarke repeatedly denounced President George W. Bush and his top aides for not doing more to prevent the terrorist attacks of September 11, 2001, from occurring. Since Clarke had been the top counterterrorism official in both the Clinton and Bush administrations, his charges received huge amounts of media attention. Clarke leveled his accusations through a wide range of media, from television interviews to a bestselling book called Against All Enemies. *But his best-known critique of Bush and his national security team came on March 24, 2004, when he testified under oath at a Washington, D.C., hearing of the 9/11 Commission. In the following excerpts from his dramatic testimony, Clarke answers questions from three commission members: Democrats Timothy J. Roemer and Richard Ben-Veniste and Republican James R. Thompson.*

ROEMER: You coordinated counterterrorism policy in both the Clinton and the Bush administrations. I want to know, first of all: Was fighting Al Qaida a top priority for the Clinton administration from 1998 to the year 2001? How high a priority was it in that Clinton administration during that time period?

CLARKE: My impression was that fighting terrorism, in general, and fighting Al Qaida, in particular, were an extraordinarily high priority in the Clinton administration—certainly no higher priority. There were priorities probably of equal importance such as the Middle East peace process, but I certainly don't know of one that was any higher in the priority of that administration.

ROEMER: With respect to the Bush administration, from the time they took office until September 11th, 2001, you had much to deal with: Russia, China, G-8, Middle East. How high a priority was fighting Al Qaida in the Bush administration?

CLARKE: I believe the Bush administration in the first eight months considered terrorism an important issue, but not an urgent issue.

Well, President Bush himself says as much in his interview with Bob Woodward in the book "Bush at War." He said, "I didn't feel a sense of urgency."

George Tenet and I tried very hard to create a sense of urgency by seeing to it that intelligence reports on the Al Qaida threat were frequently given to the president and other high-level officials. And there was a process under way to address Al Qaida. But although I continued to say it was an urgent problem, I don't think it was ever treated that way.

ROEMER: You have said in many ways—and you've issued some blistering attacks on the Bush administration. But you've not held those criticisms from the Clinton administration, either. We heard from Mr. [Sandy] Berger earlier that you were critical of the Clinton administration on two areas: not providing aid to the Northern Alliance, and not going after the human conveyor belts of jihadists coming out of the sanctuaries in Afghanistan.

Are there more in the Clinton administration years—the USS *Cole,* the response there?

CLARKE: Well, I think first of all, Mr. Berger is right to say that almost everything I ever asked for in the way of support from him or from President Clinton, I got. We did enormously increase the counterterrorism budget of the federal government, initiated many programs, including one that is now called Homeland Security.

Mr. Berger is also right to note that I wanted a covert action program to aid Afghan factions to fight the Taliban, and that was not accomplished. He's also right to note that on several occasions, including after the attack on the *Cole,* I suggested that we bomb all of the Taliban and Al Qaida infrastructure, whether or not it would succeed in killing bin Laden. I thought that was the wrong way of looking at the problem....

ROEMER: On January 25th, we've seen a memo that you've written to Dr. Rice urgently asking for a principals' review of Al Qaida. You include helping the Northern Alliance, covert aid, significant new '02 budget authority to help fight Al Qaida and a response to the USS *Cole.* You attach to this document both the Delenda Plan of 1998 and a strategy paper from December 2000.

Do you get a response to this urgent request for a principals' meeting on these? And how does this affect your time frame for dealing with these important issues?

CLARKE: I did get a response, and the response was that in the Bush administration I should, and my committee, counterterrorism security group, should report to the deputies committee, which is a sub-Cabinet level committee, and not to the principals and that, therefore, it was inappropriate for me to be asking for a principals' meeting. Instead, there would be a deputies' meeting.

ROEMER: So does this slow the process down to go to the deputies rather than to the principals or a small group as you had previously done?

CLARKE: It slowed it down enormously, by months. First of all, the deputies committee didn't meet urgently in January or February.

Then when the deputies committee did meet, it took the issue of Al Qaida as part of a cluster of policy issues, including nuclear proliferation in South Asia, democratization in Pakistan, how to treat the various problems, including narcotics and other problems in Afghanistan, and launched on a series of deputies' meetings extending over several months to address Al Qaida in the context of all of those inter-related issues.

That process probably ended, I think in July of 2001. So we were ready for a principals' meeting in July. But the principals calendar was full and then they went on vacation, many of them in August, so we couldn't meet in August, and therefore the principals met in September.

ROEMER: So as the Bush administration is carefully considering from bottom up a full review of fighting terrorism, what happens to these individual items like a response to the USS *Cole,* flying the Predator? Why aren't these decided in a shorter time frame as they're also going through a larger policy review of how this policy affects Pakistan and other countries—important considerations, but why can't you do both?

CLARKE: The deputies committee, its chairman, Mr. Hadley, and others thought that all these issues were sufficiently inter-related, that they should be taken up as a set of issues, and pieces of them should not be broken off.

ROEMER: Did you agree with that?

CLARKE: No, I didn't agree with much of that.

ROEMER: Were you frustrated by this process?

CLARKE: I was sufficiently frustrated that I asked to be reassigned....

My view was that this administration, while it listened to me, didn't either believe me that there was an urgent problem or was unprepared to act as though there were an urgent problem.

And I thought, if the administration doesn't believe its national coordinator for counterterrorism when he says there's an urgent problem and if it's unprepared to act as though there's an urgent problem, then probably I should get another job....

ROEMER: You then wrote a memo on September 4th to Dr. Rice expressing some of these frustrations several months later, if you say the time frame is May or June when you decided to resign. A memo comes out that we have seen on September the 4th. You are blunt in blasting DOD [Department of Defense] for not willingly using the force and the power. You blast the CIA for blocking Predator. You urge policy-makers to imagine a day after hundreds of Americans lay dead at home or abroad after a terrorist attack and ask themselves what else they could have done. You write this on September the 4th, seven days before September 11th.

CLARKE: That's right.

ROEMER: What else could have been done, Mr. Clarke?

CLARKE: Well, all of the things that we recommended in the [Delenda] plan or strategy—there's a lot of debate about whether it's a plan or a strategy or a series of options.

But all of the things we recommended back in January were those things on the table in September. They were done. They were done after September 11th. They were all done. I didn't really understand why they couldn't have been done in February....

* * * *

BEN-VENISTE: Good afternoon, Mr. Clarke. I want to focus on the role of the national security adviser and your relationship with the national security adviser in the Clinton administration as compared with the Bush administration. Can you point to any similarities or differences?

CLARKE: Well, I think the similarity is that under all four national security advisers for whom I worked, I was told by each of the four, beginning with Brent Scowcroft, that if I ever had any—I hate to use the word, Senator, "actionable intelligence," the phrase—if I ever had reason to believe that there was something urgent that they could act on that I could interrupt anything that they were doing, that I have an open door any time I needed it day or night if there was something about to happen.

I think the difference between the two national security advisers in the Clinton administration and the national security adviser in the Bush administration is that on policy development, I dealt directly with the national security advisers in the Clinton administration. But policy development on counterterrorism I was told would be best done with the deputy national security adviser. So I spent less time talking about the problems of terrorism with the national security adviser in this administration....

BEN-VENISTE: With respect to the level of threat and the intelligence information that you were receiving, is it fair to say that in the summer of 2001, the threat level either approached or exceeded anything that you had previously been receiving?

CLARKE: I think it exceeded anything that George Tenet or I had ever seen.

BEN-VENISTE: And I think the phrase which has received some currency in our hearings of someone's hair being on fire originated with you, saying that basically you knew that something drastic was about to happen and that the indicators were all consistent in that regard.

CLARKE: That's right.

BEN-VENISTE: Did you make a determination that the threat was going to come from abroad, as an exclusive proposition? Or did you understand that given the fact that we had been attacked before and that the plans had been interrupted to attack us before that the potential existed for Al Qaida to strike at us on our homeland?

CLARKE: The CIA said in their assessments that the attack would most likely occur overseas, most probably in Saudi Arabia, possibly in Israel. I thought, however, that it might well take place in the United States based on what we had learned in December '99, when we rolled up operations in Washington state, in Brooklyn, in Boston.

The fact that we didn't have intelligence that we could point to that said it would take place in the United States wasn't significant in my view, because, frankly, sir—I know how this is going to sound but I have to say it—I didn't think the FBI would know whether or not there was anything going on in the United States by Al Qaida....

BEN-VENISTE: Did you know that the two individuals who had been identified as Al Qaida had entered the United States and were presently thought to be in the country?

CLARKE: I was not informed of that, nor were senior levels of the FBI.

BEN-VENISTE: Had you known that these individuals were in the country, what steps, with the benefit of hindsight, but informed hindsight, would you have taken, given the level of threat?

CLARKE: To put the answer in context, I had been saying to the FBI and to the other federal law enforcement agencies and to the CIA that because of this intelligence that something was about to happen that they should lower their threshold of reporting, that they should tell us anything that looked the slightest bit unusual.

In retrospect, having said that over and over again to them, for them to have had this information somewhere in the FBI and not told to me, I still find absolutely incomprehensible....

* * * *

THOMPSON: Mr. Clarke, as we sit here this afternoon, we have your book and we have your press briefing of August 2002. Which is true?

CLARKE: Well, I think the question is a little misleading.

The press briefing you're referring to comes in the following context: *Time* magazine had published a cover story article highlighting what your staff briefing talks about. They had learned that, as your staff briefing notes, that there was a strategy or a plan and a series of additional options that were presented to the national security adviser and the new Bush team when they came into office.

Time magazine ran a somewhat sensational story that implied that the Bush administration hadn't worked on that plan. And this, of course, coming after 9/11 caused the Bush White House a great deal of concern.

So I was asked by several people in senior levels of the Bush White House to do a press backgrounder to try to explain that set of facts in a way that minimized criticism of the administration. And so I did.

Now, we can get into semantic games of whether it was a strategy, or whether it was a plan, or whether it was a series of options to be decided upon. I think the facts are as they were outlined in your staff briefing.

THOMPSON: Well, let's take a look, then, at your press briefing, because I don't want to engage in semantic games. You said, the Bush administration decided, then, you know, mid-January—that's mid-January, 2001—to do two things: one, vigorously pursue the existing policy—that would be the Clinton policy—including all of the lethal covert action findings which we've now made public to some extent. Is that so? Did they decide in January of 2001 to vigorously pursue the existing Clinton policy?

CLARKE: They decided that the existing covert action findings would remain in effect.

THOMPSON: OK. The second thing the administration decided to do is to initiate a process to look at those issues which had been on the table for a couple of years and get them decided. Now, that seems to indicate to me that proposals had been sitting on the table in the Clinton administration for a couple of years, but that the Bush administration was going to get them done. Is that a correct assumption?

CLARKE: Well, that was my hope at the time. It turned out not to be the case.

THOMPSON: Well, then why in August of 2002, over a year later, did you say that it was the case?

CLARKE: I was asked to make that case to the press. I was a special assistant to the president, and I made the case I was asked to make.

THOMPSON: Are you saying to me you were asked to make an untrue case to the press and the public, and that you went ahead and did it?

CLARKE: No, sir. Not untrue. Not an untrue case. I was asked to highlight the positive aspects of what the administration had done and to minimize the negative aspects of what the administration had done. And as a special assistant to the president, one is frequently asked to do that kind of thing. I've done it for several presidents....

Source

Testimony of Richard A. Clarke before the 9/11 Commission. In "Transcript: Wednesday's 9/11 Commission Hearings." *Washington Post*, March 24, 2004. Retrieved from http://www.washington post.com/wp-dyn/articles/A20349-2004Mar24.html.

The 9/11 Commission Issues Its Final Report

On July 22, 2004, the National Commission on Terrorist Attacks Upon the United States—better known as the 9/11 Commission—released its long-awaited report. The 567-page report became a national bestseller, and the commission itself received generally good reviews for its examination of the attacks and the security holes that allowed them to happen. Following is an excerpt from the 9/11 Commission's executive summary of its findings.

GENERAL FINDINGS

Since the plotters were flexible and resourceful, we cannot know whether any single step or series of steps would have defeated them. What we can say with confidence is that none of the measures adopted by the U.S. government from 1998 to 2001 disturbed or even delayed the progress of the al Qaeda plot. Across the government, there were failures of imagination, policy, capabilities, and management.

Imagination

The most important failure was one of imagination. We do not believe leaders understood the gravity of the threat. The terrorist danger from Bin Ladin and al Qaeda was not a major topic for policy debate among the public, the media, or in the Congress. Indeed, it barely came up during the 2000 presidential campaign.

Al Qaeda's new brand of terrorism presented challenges to U.S. governmental institutions that they were not well-designed to meet. Though top officials all told us that they understood the danger, we believe there was uncertainty among them as to whether this was just a new and especially venomous version of the ordinary terrorist threat the United States had lived with for decades, or it was indeed radically new, posing a threat beyond any yet experienced.

As late as September 4, 2001, Richard Clarke, the White House staffer long responsible for counterterrorism policy coordination, asserted that the government had not yet made up its mind how to answer the question: "Is al Qida a big deal?"

A week later came the answer.

Policy

Terrorism was not the overriding national security concern for the U.S. government under either the Clinton or the pre-9/11 Bush administration.

The policy challenges were linked to this failure of imagination. Officials in both the Clinton and Bush administrations regarded a full U.S. invasion of Afghanistan as practically inconceivable before 9/11.

Capabilities

Before 9/11, the United States tried to solve the al Qaeda problem with the capabilities it had used in the last stages of the Cold War and its immediate aftermath. These capabilities were insufficient. Little was done to expand or reform them.

The CIA had minimal capacity to conduct paramilitary operations with its own personnel, and it did not seek a large-scale expansion of these capabilities before 9/11. The CIA also needed to improve its capability to collect intelligence from human agents.

At no point before 9/11 was the Department of Defense fully engaged in the mission of countering al Qaeda, even though this was perhaps the most dangerous foreign enemy threatening the United States.

America's homeland defenders faced outward. NORAD itself was barely able to retain any alert bases at all. Its planning scenarios occasionally considered the danger of hijacked aircraft being guided to American targets, but only aircraft that were coming from overseas.

The most serious weaknesses in agency capabilities were in the domestic arena. The FBI did not have the capability to link the collective knowledge of agents in the field to national priorities. Other domestic agencies deferred to the FBI.

FAA capabilities were weak. Any serious examination of the possibility of a suicide hijacking could have suggested changes to fix glaring vulnerabilities—expanding no-fly lists, searching passengers identified by the CAPPS screening system, deploying federal air marshals domestically, hardening cockpit doors, alerting air crews to a different kind of hijacking possibility than they had been trained to expect. Yet the FAA did not adjust either its own training or training with NORAD to take account of threats other than those experienced in the past.

Management

The missed opportunities to thwart the 9/11 plot were also symptoms of a broader inability to adapt the way government manages problems to the new challenges of the twenty-first century. Action officers should have been able to draw on all available knowledge about al Qaeda in the government. Management should have ensured that information was shared and duties were clearly assigned across agencies, and across the foreign-domestic divide.

There were also broader management issues with respect to how top leaders set priorities and allocated resources. For instance, on December 4, 1998, DCI [Director of Central Intelligence] Tenet issued a directive to several CIA officials and the DDCI [Deputy Director of Central Intelligence] for Community Management, stating: "We are at war. I want no resources or people spared in this effort, either inside CIA or the Community." The memorandum had little overall effect on mobilizing the CIA or the intelligence community. This episode indicates the limitations of the DCI's authority over the direction of the intelligence community, including agencies within the Department of Defense.

The U.S. government did not find a way of pooling intelligence and using it to guide the planning and assignment of responsibilities for joint operations involving entities as disparate as the CIA, the FBI, the State Department, the military, and the agencies involved in homeland security....

Are We Safer?

Since 9/11, the United States and its allies have killed or captured a majority of al Qaeda's leadership; toppled the Taliban, which gave al Qaeda sanctuary in Afghanistan; and severely damaged the organization. Yet terrorist attacks continue. Even as we have thwarted attacks, nearly everyone expects they will come. How can this be?

The problem is that al Qaeda represents an ideological movement, not a finite group of people. It initiates and inspires, even if it no longer directs. In this way it has transformed itself into a decentralized force. Bin Ladin may be limited in his ability to organize major attacks from his hideouts. Yet killing or capturing him, while extremely important, would not end terror. His message of inspiration to a new generation of terrorists would continue.

Because of offensive actions against al Qaeda since 9/11, and defensive actions to improve homeland security, we believe we are safer today. But we are not safe.

Source

The National Commission on Terrorist Attacks Upon the United States [The 9/11 Commission]. *The 9/11 Commission Report: Final Report of the National Commission on Terrorist Attacks Upon the United States—Executive Summary.* Washington, DC: U.S. Government Printing Office, 2004, pp. 9-11, 16. Retrieved from http://www.gpo.gov/fdsys/pkg/GPO-911REPORT/pdf/GPO-911REPORT-24.pdf.

President Obama Announces the Death of Osama bin Laden

On May 1, 2011, President Barack Obama made a dramatic nationally televised address to announce that U.S. Navy SEALs operating under his orders had killed Osama bin Laden in a daring helicopter raid in Abbottabad, Pakistan. Obama's announcement, which commenced at 11:35 P.M. Eastern Daylight time, triggered celebrations and expressions of relief all across the United States and in many other parts of the world. It had taken nearly ten years of relentless searching by U.S. military and intelligence resources to find bin Laden. But with the May 1 raid, said Obama, the man most responsible for the September 11 terrorist attacks had finally been brought to justice. Following is the full text of Obama's remarks.

Good evening. Tonight, I can report to the American people and to the world that the United States has conducted an operation that killed Osama bin Laden, the leader of al Qaeda, and a terrorist who's responsible for the murder of thousands of innocent men, women, and children.

It was nearly 10 years ago that a bright September day was darkened by the worst attack on the American people in our history. The images of 9/11 are seared into our national memory—hijacked planes cutting through a cloudless September sky; the Twin Towers collapsing to the ground; black smoke billowing up from the Pentagon; the wreckage of Flight 93 in Shanksville, Pennsylvania, where the actions of heroic citizens saved even more heartbreak and destruction.

And yet we know that the worst images are those that were unseen to the world. The empty seat at the dinner table. Children who were forced to grow up without their mother or their father. Parents who would never know the feeling of their child's embrace. Nearly 3,000 citizens taken from us, leaving a gaping hole in our hearts.

On September 11, 2001, in our time of grief, the American people came together. We offered our neighbors a hand, and we offered the wounded our blood. We reaffirmed our ties to each other, and our love of community and country. On that day, no matter where we came from, what God we prayed to, or what race or ethnicity we were, we were united as one American family.

We were also united in our resolve to protect our nation and to bring those who committed this vicious attack to justice. We quickly learned that the 9/11 attacks were carried out by al Qaeda—an organization headed by Osama bin Laden, which had openly declared war on the United States and was committed to killing innocents in our country and around the globe. And so we went to war against al Qaeda to protect our citizens, our friends, and our allies.

Over the last 10 years, thanks to the tireless and heroic work of our military and our counterterrorism professionals, we've made great strides in that effort. We've disrupted terrorist attacks and strengthened our homeland defense. In Afghanistan, we removed the Taliban government, which had given bin Laden and al Qaeda safe haven and support. And around the globe, we worked with our friends and allies to capture or kill scores of al Qaeda terrorists, including several who were a part of the 9/11 plot.

Yet Osama bin Laden avoided capture and escaped across the Afghan border into Pakistan. Meanwhile, al Qaeda continued to operate from along that border and operate through its affiliates across the world.

And so shortly after taking office, I directed Leon Panetta, the director of the CIA, to make the killing or capture of bin Laden the top priority of our war against al Qaeda, even as we continued our broader efforts to disrupt, dismantle, and defeat his network.

Then, last August, after years of painstaking work by our intelligence community, I was briefed on a possible lead to bin Laden. It was far from certain, and it took many months to run this thread to ground. I met repeatedly with my national security team as we developed more information about the possibility that we had located bin Laden hiding within a compound deep inside of Pakistan. And finally, last week, I determined that we had enough intelligence to take action, and authorized an operation to get Osama bin Laden and bring him to justice.

Today, at my direction, the United States launched a targeted operation against that compound in Abbottabad, Pakistan. A small team of Americans carried out the operation with extraordinary courage and capability. No Americans were harmed. They took care to avoid civilian casualties. After a firefight, they killed Osama bin Laden and took custody of his body.

For over two decades, bin Laden has been al Qaeda's leader and symbol, and has continued to plot attacks against our country and our friends and allies. The death of bin Laden marks the most significant achievement to date in our nation's effort to defeat al Qaeda.

Yet his death does not mark the end of our effort. There's no doubt that al Qaeda will continue to pursue attacks against us. We must—and we will—remain vigilant at home and abroad.

As we do, we must also reaffirm that the United States is not—and never will be—at war with Islam. I've made clear, just as President Bush did shortly after 9/11, that our war is not against Islam. Bin Laden was not a Muslim leader; he was a mass murderer of Muslims. Indeed, al Qaeda has slaughtered scores of Muslims in many countries, including our own. So his demise should be welcomed by all who believe in peace and human dignity.

Over the years, I've repeatedly made clear that we would take action within Pakistan if we knew where bin Laden was. That is what we've done. But it's important to note that our counterterrorism cooperation with Pakistan helped lead us to bin Laden and the compound where he was hiding. Indeed, bin Laden had declared war against Pakistan as well, and ordered attacks against the Pakistani people.

Tonight, I called President Zardari, and my team has also spoken with their Pakistani counterparts. They agree that this is a good and historic day for both of our nations. And going forward, it is essential that Pakistan continue to join us in the fight against al Qaeda and its affiliates.

The American people did not choose this fight. It came to our shores, and started with the senseless slaughter of our citizens. After nearly 10 years of service, struggle, and sacrifice, we know well the costs of war. These efforts weigh on me every time I, as Commander-in-Chief, have to sign a letter to a family that has lost a loved one, or look into the eyes of a service member who's been gravely wounded.

So Americans understand the costs of war. Yet as a country, we will never tolerate our security being threatened, nor stand idly by when our people have been killed. We will be relentless in defense of our citizens and our friends and allies. We will be true to the values that make us who we are. And on nights like this one, we can say to those families who have lost loved ones to al Qaeda's terror: Justice has been done.

Tonight, we give thanks to the countless intelligence and counterterrorism professionals who've worked tirelessly to achieve this outcome. The American people do not see their work, nor know their names. But tonight, they feel the satisfaction of their work and the result of their pursuit of justice.

We give thanks for the men who carried out this operation, for they exemplify the professionalism, patriotism, and unparalleled courage of those who serve our country. And they are part of a generation that has borne the heaviest share of the burden since that September day.

Finally, let me say to the families who lost loved ones on 9/11 that we have never forgotten your loss, nor wavered in our commitment to see that we do whatever it takes to prevent another attack on our shores.

And tonight, let us think back to the sense of unity that prevailed on 9/11. I know that it has, at times, frayed. Yet today's achievement is a testament to the greatness of our country and the determination of the American people.

The cause of securing our country is not complete. But tonight, we are once again reminded that America can do whatever we set our mind to. That is the story of our history, whether it's the pursuit of prosperity for our people, or the struggle for equality for all our citizens; our commitment to stand up for our values abroad, and our sacrifices to make the world a safer place.

Let us remember that we can do these things not just because of wealth or power, but because of who we are: one nation, under God, indivisible, with liberty and justice for all.

Thank you. May God bless you. And may God bless the United States of America.

Source

Obama, Barack. Remarks on the Death of Al Qaida Terrorist Organization Leader Usama bin Laden, May 1, 2011. Retrieved from John T. Woolley and Gerhard Peters, The American Presidency Project, http://www.presidency.ucsb .edu/ws/index.php?pid=90315&st=&st1=#axzz1Zv5ajtEW.

IMPORTANT PEOPLE, PLACES, AND TERMS

Actionable intelligence
Information gleaned from spying and other intelligence work that is sufficiently strong for officials to make decisions and approve courses of action.

al-Qaeda
Radical Islamic terrorist organization founded by Osama bin Laden that carried out the September 11 attacks on the United States.

Alec Station
A special CIA department that was solely focused on Osama bin Laden and al-Qaeda.

Arab
Member of an ethnically distinct people historically concentrated in the Middle East and North Africa, where the Arabic language and Islamic faith are dominant.

Arab world
Arabic-speaking countries, usually understood to encompass the Middle East as well as parts of northern Africa and central Asia.

Atta, Mohamed (1968-2001)
Egyptian-born al-Qaeda member who led the hijacking crews on September 11; Atta flew American Airlines Flight 11 into the North Tower of the World Trade Center.

Bin Laden, Osama (1957-2011)
A native of Saudi Arabia, bin Laden was the founder and leader of al-Qaeda, the terrorist organization responsible for the September 11 terrorist attacks in the United States.

Bush, George W. (1946-)
The forty-third president of the United States (2001-2009), Bush had been president for eight months when 9/11 occurred.

Cell
A small local terrorist outfit that is part of a much larger group.

Clarke, Richard A. (1951-)
A top counterterrorism official in the Clinton and Bush administrations, Clarke emerged in 2004 as a fierce critic of the Bush White House's performance on terrorism issues.

Cleric
Minister or religious leader.

Cold War
A period of intense political and military rivalry between the United States and the Soviet Union that began in the aftermath of World War II and lasted until the breakup of the Soviet Union in 1991.

Colonialism
A situation in which one nation claims ownership over another territory or region and establishes control over its political, cultural, and economic affairs.

Fatwa
A ruling, calling, or judgment by an Islamic religious authority, leader, or scholar. In the context of the 9/11 attacks, Osama bin Laden issued two fatwas in the late 1990s that were essentially calls for Muslims to wage "holy war" against America.

FDNY
Fire Department of New York.

First responders
People whose jobs entail taking responsibility for the protection and preservation of the health and well-being of people in cases of medical emergencies and disasters. Prominent examples of first responders include firefighters, police officers, and emergency medical technicians (paramedics).

Hazmi, Nawaf al- (1976-2001)

The Saudi-born Hazmi was one of two al-Qaeda members (along with Khalid al-Mihdhar) who were detected in America in early 2000 by the CIA, which failed to alert any other agencies to their presence. Hazmi was one of the five men who hijacked American Airlines Flight 77, which crashed into the Pentagon as part of the September 11 attacks.

Hussein, Saddam (1937-2006)

Iraqi dictator whose regime became a major focus of post-9/11 U.S. antiterrorism policies.

Intelligence

Collection of information of military or political value.

Islam

Religion of the Muslims, a monotheistic faith based on the teachings of the Koran and the Prophet Muhammed.

Islamic Group

Fundamentalist Islamic movement in Egypt led by Sheikh Omar Abdel Rahman that became devoted to the overthrow of Egypt's secular government; responsible for the 1997 Luxor Massacre in Egypt.

Islamism

An extremist and often violent ideology far different than the common Muslim's faith in and practice of Islam.

Israel

Jewish state with a democratic form of government that is located in the Middle East, on the eastern shore of the Mediterranean Sea.

Jihad

Important religious duty of people of the Islamic faith.

Madrassa

Islamic religious school.

Middle East

A geographic area usually understood to include northern Africa and southwest Asia.

Mihdhar, Khalid al- (1975-2001)

The Saudi-born Mihdhar was one of two al-Qaeda members (along with Nawaf al-Hazmi) who were detected in America in early 2000 by the CIA. The agency failed to alert any other agencies to their presence, and Mihdhar participated in the hijacking of American Airlines Flight 77, which crashed into the Pentagon as part of the September 11 attacks.

Mohammed, Khaled Sheikh (1964?-)

Kuwaiti-born al-Qaeda operative and chief architect of the September 11 terrorist attacks.

Moussaoui, Zacarias (1968-)

Islamic terrorist sometimes referred to as the twentieth hijacker (though he did not actually participate in the hijackings) who is serving a life sentence in the U.S. prison system for conspiring to kill American citizens on September 11.

Mubarak, Hosni (1928-)

Egyptian military leader and politician who ruled Egypt from 1981 to 2011, when he was overthrown in a popular revolt.

Mujahideen

Holy warriors, usually associated with Islamic fighters in Afghanistan.

Muslim

Follower of the Islamic religious faith.

Muslim Brotherhood

Fundamentalist Islamic organization founded in the late 1920s that supports establishing the Koran as the supreme law in Arab states. Well-known for its charitable works, the Brotherhood's official rejection of violence has produced breakaway groups that do employ terrorism as a way of achieving their goals.

Nasser, Gamal Abdel (1918-1970)

Prominent Arab leader who led Egypt from 1956 to 1970.

NYPD

New York Police Department.

Palestine

Historical region of the Middle East at the eastern end of the Mediterranean Sea. Long occupied by an Arabic people (the Palestinians), the region is now mostly contained within the borders of Israel. The term is also sometimes used in reference to a prospective Palestinian state that would encompass the Gaza Strip, the West Bank, and other land areas that are now part of Israel.

PAPD
Port Authority Police Department.

Pentagon
Headquarters of the U.S. Department of Defense, in Arlington County, Virginia. The term is also sometimes used to refer to the U.S. military leadership.

Port Authority
An agency formed and maintained to develop waterfront property for various economic, industrial, and recreational uses.

Qutb, Sayyid (1906-1966)
Egyptian scholar whose writings were enormously influential in shaping the beliefs of Osama bin Laden and other Islamic terrorists in the late twentieth century.

Rahman, Sheikh Omar Abdel (1938-)
Also known as the Blind Sheikh, Rahman is a radical Egyptian Muslim who has been linked to numerous terrorist attacks; in 1996 he was sentenced to life in prison in the United States for his involvement in the 1993 World Trade Center attack.

Rice, Condoleezza (1954-)
National Security Advisor (2001-2005) and Secretary of State (2005-2009) to President George W. Bush.

Sadat, Anwar (1918-1981)
Reform-minded president of Egypt from 1970 until his assassination in 1981.

Secular
Non-religious.

Sharia
Islamic legal codes based on teachings of the Koran and the Prophet Mohammed.

Takfir

A Muslim person who is said to have abandoned his or her Islamic faith.

Taliban

A violent, fundamentalist Islamic movement with a profoundly anti-woman orientation that ruled Afghanistan from 1996 to 2001—and which continues to fight for political control of the country.

Tenet, George (1953-)

Director of the Central Intelligence Agency (CIA) from 1997 to 2004

United Nations (UN)

Global organization of nations that was created in 1945 to foster international cooperation in various economic, political, social, and military matters.

Wahhabism

Strict form of Islam that is practiced in Saudi Arabia and other parts of the Middle East.

West

A term sometimes used to denote the United States and other modern, industrialized countries with representative forms of government, especially in Europe.

Yousef, Ramzi (1967-)

Kuwaiti-born terrorist who masterminded the 1993 World Trade Center bombing in New York City.

Zawahiri, Ayman al- (1951-)

Egyptian-born leader of Al-Jihad and longtime advisor to Osama bin Laden; became the head of al-Qaeda after bin Laden's death in May 2011.

CHRONOLOGY

1922

Egypt receives its independence from England. *See p. 8.*

1928

The Muslim Brotherhood is founded in Egypt. *See p. 12.*

1948

The state of Israel is founded in the region of the Middle East historically known as Palestine at the conclusion of the Arab-Israeli War. *See p. 9.*

1954

Gamal Abdel Nasser becomes president of Egypt two years after leading a military coup that overthrew King Farouk. *See p. 12.*

1964

Sayyid Qutb smuggles his radical *Milestones* out of an Egyptian prison. *See p. 14.*

King Saud of Saudi Arabia is overthrown by his younger brother, Faisal. *See p. 19.*

1966

Sayyid Qutb is executed by Egyptian authorities on August 29. *See p. 15.*

1967

June 5-10 – The Six-Day War between Israel and Arab states ends in humiliating defeat for the latter countries. *See p. 15.*

1972

Palestinian terrorists murder eleven Israeli athletes and coaches at the Summer Olympic Games in Munich, West Germany. *See p. 18.*

1979

March 26 – Egyptian President Anwar Sadat and Israeli Prime Minister Menachem Begin sign the Egypt-Israel Peace Treaty in Washington, D.C. *See p. 21.*

November 20 – Islamic radicals seize the Grand Mosque of Mecca. *See p. 20.*

December – Soviet forces invade Afghanistan. *See p. 28.*

1981

October 6 – Egyptian President Anwar Sadat is assassinated by members of the terrorist group al-Jihad. *See p. 25.*

Ayman al-Zawahiri begins a three-year stay in the Egyptian prison system. *See p. 26.*

1984

Cleric Abdullah Azzam issues a fatwa for Muslims to go to Afghanistan and help drive the Soviets out. *See p. 28.*

1986

Osama bin Laden and Ayman al-Zawahiri meet in Pakistan and become allies. *See p. 30.*

1988

Bin Laden gives his evolving radical Islamic organization the name "al-Qaeda" and takes steps to make it more structured and permanent. *See p. 31.*

1989

Soviet forces withdraw from Afghanistan. *See p. 31.*

1991

U.S. military forces lead an international coalition that chases Iraq out of Kuwait. In the aftermath of the Persian Gulf War, large numbers of U.S. troops are stationed in Saudi Arabia and other Arab states. *See p. 32.*

1992

Bin Laden moves to Sudan. *See p. 34.*

1993

February 26 – An Islamic terrorist named Ramzi Yousef detonates a bomb underneath the World Trade Center in a failed attempt to bring down its twin towers. *See p. 36.*

October – The loss of eighteen U.S. troops in Somalia prompts President Bill Clinton to withdraw all American forces from the war-torn country. *See p. 37.*

1994

Saudi authorities revoke bin Laden's citizenship. *See p. 37.*

1995

June 26 – Members of the Islamic Group and al-Qaeda nearly succeed in assassinating Egyptian President Hosni Mubarak. *See p. 38.*

1996

Bin Laden leaves Sudan for Afghanistan, where he quickly establishes close ties with Taliban leaders who have seized control of the war-shattered country. *See p. 42.*

The CIA opens Alec Station to track the activities of Osama bin Laden and al-Qaeda. *See p. 126.*

June 25 – Islamic terrorists bomb Khobar Towers in Dhahran, Saudi Arabia, where U.S. forces are stationed. *See p. 46.*

August 23 – Bin Laden issues his first fatwa against the United States and Israel. *See p. 44.*

1997

November 17 – Islamic terrorists carry out the Luxor Massacre in Egypt. *See p. 46.*

1998

February 23 – Bin Laden issues his second fatwa against the United States and Israel. *See p. 48.*

August 7 – Al-Qaeda terrorists carry out suicide bombings of two American embassies in Africa. *See p. 49.*

August 20 – The United States carries out Operation Infinite Reach against al-Qaeda camps in Afghanistan. *See p. 50.*

1999

Bin Laden gives approval to Khaled Sheikh Mohammed's plan to hijack American airliners and fly them into the World Trade Center and other U.S. sites of symbolic and strategic importance. *See p. 57.*

2000

Al-Qaeda begins sending operatives to the United States to take flight lessons so that they can pilot hijacked airliners. *See p. 57.*

The CIA discovers that two known al-Qaeda operatives, Nawaf al-Hazmi and Khalid al-Mihdhar, are in the United States, but the agency does not share this information with other national security agencies or distribute it widely within its own departments. *See p. 127.*

October 12 – Al-Qaeda operatives attack the USS *Cole* using a small boat packed with explosives. *See p. 52.*

2001

January – The Hart-Rudman Report warns that the United States is extremely vulnerable to terrorist attacks on American soil. *See p. 106.*

June – The last of the 9/11 hijackers enter the United States. *See p. 59.*

June – Al-Qaeda and al-Jihad officially merge. *See p. 38.*

August 6 – President George W. Bush receives a CIA memo warning "Bin Ladin Determined to Strike in US." *See p. 133.*

September 11 – Al-Qaeda hijackers board four commercial airliners flying out of three airports on the eastern seaboard. *See p. 63.*

8:46 A.M. – Hijackers crash American Airlines Flight 11 into the North Tower of the World Trade Center. *See p. 63.*

9:03 A.M. – Hijackers crash United Airlines Flight 175 into the South Tower of the World Trade Center. *See p. 66.*

9:37 A.M. – Hijackers crash American Airlines Flight 77 into the Pentagon. *See p. 69.*

9:42 A.M. – The Federal Aviation Administration grounds all flights over or bound for the continental United States for the first time in the nation's history.

9:59 A.M. – The South Tower of the World Trade Center collapses. *See pp. 74 and 93.*

10:03 A.M. – United Airlines Flight 93 crashes outside of Shanksville, Pennsylvania, apparently as a result of a struggle for control of the plane between hijackers and passengers. *See p. 71.*

10:28 A.M. – The North Tower of the World Trade Center collapses. *See pp. 75 and 96.*

8:30 P.M. – President George W. Bush addresses the nation from the White House about the terrorist attacks. *See p. 80.*

October 7 – When the Taliban refuse to hand over bin Laden, the United States and its allies launch Operation Enduring Freedom military campaign. *See p. 138.*

November – The Taliban government in Kabul collapses. *See p. 138.*

2002

June 25 – Recovery and clean-up operations at Ground Zero conclude. In all, an estimated 1.8 million tons of debris are removed from the site and 19,435 body parts are recovered. *See p. 98.*

November 25 – The United States establishes a Department of Homeland Security.

November 27 – The National Commission on Terrorist Attacks Upon the United States, better known as the 9/11 Commission, is established. *See p. 107.*

2003

March 20 - American military forces go to war against Iraq. They succeed in invading Iraq, overthrowing Saddam Hussein's government, and setting up a military occupation of the country. *See p. 142.*

May 1 – President Bush announces an end to major combat operations in Iraq, but U.S. military involvement in Iraq continues to deepen. *See p. 142.*

December 13 – Saddam Hussein is captured by U.S. forces. *See p. 142.*

2004

March 24 – Former counterterrorism czar Richard Clarke appears before the 9/11 Commission and harshly criticizes the Bush administration's counterterrorism record. *See p. 114.*

April 8 – National Security Advisor Condoleezza Rice testifies before the 9/11 Commission and strongly defends the Bush administration's record on counterterrorism. *See p. 116.*

April 28 – Media reports reveal that U.S. personnel have tortured Arab prisoners at Abu Ghraib Prison in Iraq. *See p. 144.*

July 22 – The 9/11 Commission Report is released. *See p. 117.*

October - Hamid Karzai becomes the first democratically elected president of Afghanistan. *See p. 138.*

2006

June 7 – U.S. troops kill al-Qaeda member Abu Mousab al-Zarqawi, who led the terrorist network's activities in Iraq. *See p. 143*

December 30 – Saddam Hussein is executed in Iraq after being found guilty of war crimes. *See p. 142.*

2010

December 17 – A Tunisian peddler named Mohamed Bouazizi sets himself on fire to protest repressive government policies. His suicide becomes the trigger for the so-called Arab Spring, a popular reform movement that sweeps across the Arab World in 2011. *See p. 147.*

2011

May 1 – President Barack Obama announces that U.S. Special Forces have killed Osama bin Laden in Pakistan. *See p. 145.*

June 22 – President Obama announces the beginning of a long-awaited military withdrawal from Afghanistan. *See p. 139.*

September 11 – Americans across the country mark the tenth anniversary of the 9/11 attacks in private moments and public ceremonies. *See p. 152.*

SOURCES FOR FURTHER STUDY

Council on Foreign Relations. "U.S. War in Afghanistan." Retrieved from http://www.cfr .org/afghanistan/us-war-afghanistan/p20018. This resource provides an up-to-date account of the history of America's military involvement in Afghanistan. The offerings on this website, which is produced by one of the nation's most distinguished foreign policy organizations, range from a multimedia timeline of events to in-depth essays on various aspects of the U.S. experience fighting the Taliban, working to root out terrorist camps, and supporting the installation of a new government.

Hafiz, Dilara, Imran Hafiz, and Yasmine Hafiz. *The American Muslim Teenager's Handbook.* Gilbert, AZ: Acacia, 2007. A slim but informative work that uses a conversational tone to help readers understand what it is like to be a Muslim teenager in America. In the process, the authors—a Muslim mother and her two teenage children—puncture many myths and misunderstandings about the Islamic faith and those who follow it.

Internet Archive. "Understanding 9/11: A Television News Archive." Retrieved from http://www.archive.org/details/911. This valuable website provides more than 3,000 hours of footage of domestic and international news coverage of the September 11 terrorist attacks and their aftermath. The materials, arranged in user-friendly form, illustrate how Americans gradually came to understand—with dawning horror—that they were witnessing the worst terrorist attack in U.S. history as it unfolded.

Levitas, Mitchel, Nancy Lee, and Lonnie Schlein, eds. *A Nation Challenged: A Visual History of 9/11 and Its Aftermath: Young Reader's Edition.* New York: New York Times/ Callaway, 2002. After September 11 the *New York Times* newspaper company collected hundreds of photographs of the tragedy taken by its photographers and published them in this book. The unforgettable images are supplemented with essays and diagrams (such as one that shows the layout of an underground al-Qaeda bunker).

National Commission on Terrorist Attacks Upon the United States website. 2004. Retrieved from http://govinfo.library.unt.edu/911/report/index.htm. This website provides the complete text of the 9/11 Commission Report, broken down by section. It also provides the individual testimony of people who testified at the 9/11 hearings, press releases issued by the panel, and background information about the formation of the commission.

USAToday.com. "How 9/11 Changed America." Retrieved from http://www.usatoday.com /news/911/changed-america/index.html. This powerful interactive website uses an impressive array of archival materials and contemporary audio, video, photographic, and textual resources to mark the tenth anniversary of the September 11 attacks.

BIBLIOGRAPHY

Books

Anonymous [Scheuer, Michael]. *Through Our Enemies' Eyes: Osama bin Laden, Radical Islam, and the Future of America.* Washington, DC: Brassey's, 2002.

Bernstein, Richard. *Out of the Blue: The Story of September 11, 2001, from Jihad to Ground Zero.* New York: Times Books, 2002.

Breitweiser, Kristen. *Wake-Up Call: The Political Education of a 9/11 Widow.* New York: Warner Books, 2006.

Bush, George W. *Decision Points.* New York: Crown, 2010.

Calvert, John. *Sayyid Qutb and the Origins of Radical Islam.* New York: Columbia University Press, 2010.

Clarke, Richard A. *Against All Enemies: Inside America's War on Terror.* New York: Free Press, 2004.

Coll, Steve. *Ghost Wars: The Secret History of the CIA, Afghanistan, and bin Laden, from the Soviet Invasion to September 10, 2001.* New York: Penguin, 2004.

Der Spiegel Writers and Editors. *Inside 9-11: What Really Happened.* New York: St. Martin's Press, 2002.

Dwyer, Jim, and Kevin Flynn. *102 Minutes: The Untold Story of the Fight to Survive Inside the Twin Towers.* New York: Times Books, 2005.

Esposito, John. *Unholy War: Terror in the Name of Islam.* New York: Oxford University Press, 2002.

Fink, Mitchell, and Lois Mathias. *Never Forget: An Oral History of September 11, 2001.* New York: Regan Books, 2002.

Graham, Bob, with Jeff Nussbaum. *Intelligence Matters: The CIA, the FBI, Saudi Arabia, and the Failure of America's War on Terror.* New York: Random House, 2004.

Hagen, Susan, and Mary Carouba. *Women at Ground Zero: Stories of Courage and Compassion.* Indianapolis: Alpha, 2002.

Hoge, James F. Jr., and Gideon Rose. *How Did This Happen? Terrorism and the New War.* New York: Public Affairs, 2001.

Kean, Thomas H., and Lee H. Hamilton, with Benjamin Rhodes. *Without Precedent: The Inside Story of the 9/11 Commission.* New York: Knopf, 2006.

Kessler, Ronald. *The CIA at War: Inside the Secret Campaign against Terror.* New York: St. Martin's Griffin, 2003.

Lance, Peter. *Cover Up: What the Government Is Still Hiding About the War on Terror.* New York: Regan Books, 2004.

Long, David E., Bernard Reich, and Mark Gasiorowski, eds. *The Government and Politics of the Middle East and North Africa.* 5th ed. Boulder, CO: Westview Press, 2007.

Longman, Jere. *Among the Heroes: United Flight 93 and the Passengers and Crew Who Fought Back.* New York: HarperCollins, 2002.

Lundberg, Kirsten. *Piloting a Bipartisan Ship: Strategies and Tactics of the 9/11 Commission.* Cambridge, MA: Kennedy School of Government, 2005.

Mann, James. *Rise of the Vulcans: The History of Bush's War Cabinet.* New York: Viking, 2004.

Murphy, Dean E., Comp. *September 11: An Oral History.* New York: Doubleday, 2002.

National Commission on Terrorist Attacks Upon the United States [The 9/11 Commission]. *The 9/11 Commission Report.* New York: Norton, 2004.

Oren, Michael B. *Six Days of War: June 1967 and the Making of the Modern Middle East.* New York: Oxford University Press, 2002.

Rich, Frank. *The Greatest Story Ever Sold: The Decline and Fall of Truth, from 9/11 to Katrina.* New York: Penguin Press, 2006.

Rubin, Barry, and Judith Colp Rubin. *Anti-American Terrorism and the Middle East: A Documentary Reader.* Oxford: Oxford University Press, 2002.

Sammon, Bill. *Fighting Back: The War on Terrorism from Inside the Bush White House.* New York: Regnery, 2002.

Shenon, Philip. *The Commission: The Uncensored History of the 9/11 Investigation.* New York: Twelve, 2008.

Smith, Dennis. *A Decade of Hope: Stories of Grief and Endurance from 9/11 Families and Friends.* New York: Viking, 2011.

Suskind, Ron. *The One Percent Doctrine: Deep Inside America's Pursuit of Its Enemies Since 9/11.* New York: Simon & Schuster, 2006.

Tenet, George, with Bill Harlow. *At the Center of the Storm.* New York: HarperCollins, 2007.

U.S. Congress, House Permanent Select Committee on Intelligence and Senate Select Committee on Intelligence. *Joint Inquiry Report.* 107th Congress, 2nd Session. Washington, DC: Government Printing Office, 2002.

Waldman, Jackie, with Brenda Welchlin and Karen Frost. *America September 11: The Courage to Give: The Triumph of the Human Spirit.* Berkeley, CA: Conari Press, 2001.

Waterbury, John. *The Egypt of Nasser and Sadat: The Political Economy of Two Regimes.* Princeton, NJ: Princeton University Press, 1983.

Woodward, Bob. *Bush at War.* New York: Simon & Schuster, 2002.

Woodward, Bob. *State of Denial.* New York: Simon & Schuster, 2006.

Wright, Lawrence. *The Looming Tower: Al-Qaeda and the Road to 9/11.* New York: Vintage Books, 2006.

Zegart, Amy B. *Flying Blind: The CIA, the FBI, and the Origins of 9/11.* Princeton, NJ: Princeton University Press, 2007.

Periodicals

May, Ernest. "When Government Writes History," *New Republic*, May 23, 2005.

Mayer, Jane. "The House of bin Laden," *New Yorker*, November 12, 2001.

Padgett, Tim. "The Interrupted Reading: The Kids with George W. Bush on 9/11." *Time.com*, May 3, 2011. Retrieved from http://www.time.com/time/magazine/article/0,9171,206 9582,00.html.

Zeman, Ned, David Wise, David Rose, and Brian Burrough. "The Path to 9/11: Lost Warnings and Fatal Errors." *Vanity Fair*, November 2004.

Online Resources

Combating Terrorism Center at West Point. "Harmony Program." Retrieved from http://www.ctc.usma.edu/programs-resources/harmony-program.

Frontline (PBS). "Looking for Answers," 2001. Retrieved from http://www.pbs.org/wgbh/pages/frontline/shows/terrorism/

National Geographic Channel. "Inside 9/11." Retrieved from http://channel.nationalgeographic.com/series/inside-911#tab-Overview.

National September 11 Memorial & Museum website. Retrieved from http://www.911memorial.org/.

Washington Post. "Remembering 9/11: A Look Back at the September 11 Attacks," September 2011. Retrieved from http://www.washingtonpost.com/9-11.

PHOTO AND ILLUSTRATION CREDITS

INDEX